210 TRADITIONAL QUILT BLOCKS

EACH BLOCK IS EXPLAINED WITH STEP BY STEP PICTURES

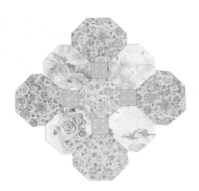
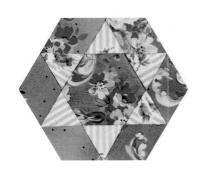

SUMMARY OF BLOCKS

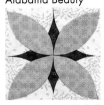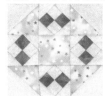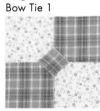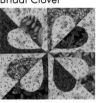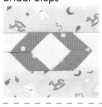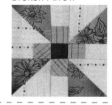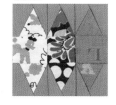

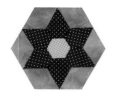

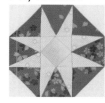

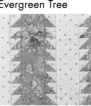

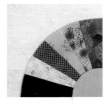

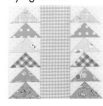
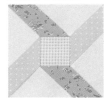

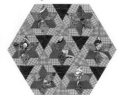

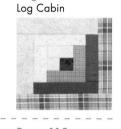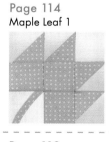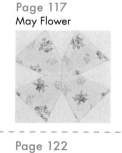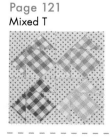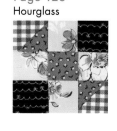

Page 131
Orange Peel

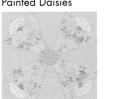

Page 132
Painted Daisies

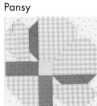

Page 133
Pansy

Page 134
Peeled Orange

Page 135
Peony

Page 136
Pete's Paintbox

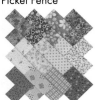

Page 137
Picket Fence

Page 138
Pin Cushion

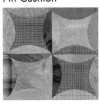

Page 139
Pine Tree

Page 140
Pineapple

Page 141
Pinwheel 1

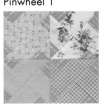

Page 142
Pinwheel 2

Page 143
Pinwheel 3

Page 144
Pinwheel 4

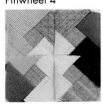

Page 145
Pinwheel 5

Page 145
Pinwheel 6

Page 146
Plane

Page 147
Pointed Star

Page 148
Polka Dot

Page 149
Pot

Page 150
Puzzle

Page 151
Rail Fence

Page 152
Railroad Crossing

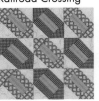

Page 152
Railroad Crossing

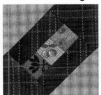

Page 153
Ribbon 1

Page 154
Ribbon 2

Page 155
Ribbon 3

Page 156
Ribbon Bow

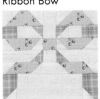

Page 157
Rock Garden

Page 158
Rolling Star

Page 159
Rolling Stone

Page 160
Rose

Page 161
Rose Dream

Page 162
Rose of Sharon

Page 163
Scrap Windmill

Page 164
Scrap Basket

Page 165
Season

Page 166
Sawtooth

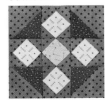

Page 167
Shoo Fly

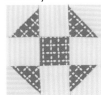

Page 167
Monkey Wrench

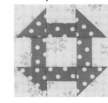

Page 168
Single Wedding Ring

Page 169
Snail's Trail

5

Page 170
Snow Ball 1

Page 171
Snow Ball 2

Page 172
Spinning Machine

Page 173
Spool 1

Page 174
Spool 2
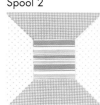

Page 174
Spool 3

Page 175
Spool 4

Page 176
Spring Beauty

Page 177
Stamp Basket

Page 178
Star Flower

Page 179
Stick Diamond

Page 180
Storm at Sea

Page 181
Strawberry Basket

Page 182
Strip Star

Page 183
Sunburst

Page 184
Sunflower 1

Page 185
Sunflower 2

Page 186
Sunrose

Page 187
Tennessee Circle

Page 188
Thirteen Squares

Page 189
Thousands Pyramids

Page 190
Three Stars

Page 191
Tile Puzzle

Page 192
Time and Energy

Page 193
Tree

Page 194
Triangles and Squares

Page 195
Tulip

Page 196
Tumbler

Page 197
Turkey Trucks

Page 198
Twinkling Star

Page 199
Twisted Log Cabin

Page 200
Twisting Spool

Page 201
Walking Triangles
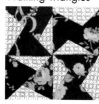

Page 202
Wheat
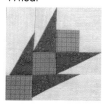

Page 203
Whirling Triangles
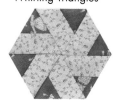

Page 204
Wild Goose Chase

Page 205
Wild Wave

Page 206
Windblown Square

Page 207
Winding Ways

Page 208
Window Fan

Page 209
Winter Dahlia

Page 210
Yacht

CREATING TEMPLATES AND BASIC ASSEMBLY

CREATING TEMPLATES

Use thick paper or thick tracing paper. A tracing-paper template is practical for use with patterned fabrics.

STRAIGHT EDGES

1 Copy the template diagram, englarging it as required. Place in on your chosen template paper. Make a hole at each corner using a pin.

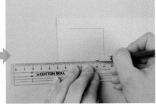

2 Remove the copied template. Join the holes using a ruler and pencil. Make other templates with straight edges in the same way.

CURVED EDGES

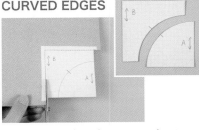

Copy the template diagram, englarging it as required. Glue the copy onto your chosen template paper, then cut out. It is possible to make templates with a combination of edges using this technique.

REINFORCING CORNERS

SQUARES AND RECTANGLES

Stick adhesive tape on the corners and fold it around the edges.

POINTED CORNERS

Stick adhesive tape on the tip and fold one end to the back of the template, then cut off the excess. Repeat with the other end.

Triangles

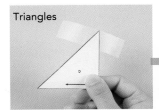

The tip of a curved edge

EXTREME POINTS

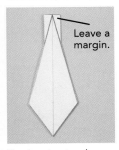

Leave a margin.

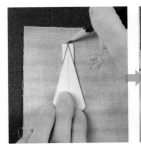

Don't cut out a sharp corner; leave a small margin around it to avoid warping

To transfer this type of template to fabric, mark the corner, then connect it to the other lines.

FABRIC GRAIN

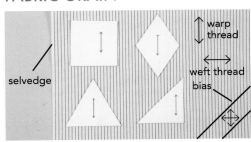

warp thread

weft thread

bias

selvedge

A fabric's grain runs lengthwise, with the warp threads parallel to the selvedge. Align straight edges or centre lines of templates to the warp or weft threads. The bias is cut at 45 ° to a straight edge.

TRANSFERRING TEMPLATES

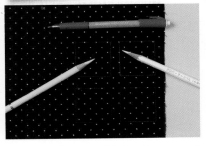

Trace template onto fabric using a pencil or crayon. Use light coloured leads to transfer a template to a dark coloured fabric, and a dark coloured lead on a light coloured fabric.

TECHNIQUE

wrong side of fabric

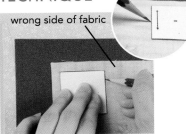

Place the fabric on a cutting mat, right side down, then place the template on top. Trace around it, adding a 7mm seam allowance all round, then cut out. Drawing around the template also transfers the seam lines to the fabric that you will follow when sewing.

It is possible to simply mark corners and then connect them using a ruler.

Turn a template over to create a symmetrical piece.

STARTING KNOT

Cut the end of the thread 3mm from the knot.

1 Thread the needle. Hold the end of the thread between the index finger and the tip of the needle.

2 Wrap the thread two to three times around the tip of the needle.

3 Using your index finger and thumb, draw the coiled thread down the needle and along the thread to form a knot.

FINISHING KNOT

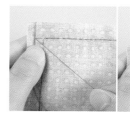

1 Place the needle at the end of your stitching (left). Wrap the thread two to three times around the needle (right).

2 Hold the coiled thread with your thumb, then draw out the needle to form a knot. Trim the excess thread.

PINNING

 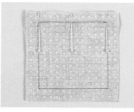

1 Bring two pieces of fabric right sides together. Insert a pin in the corner mark and take it through both layers so it emerges at the corresponding corner or mark.

2 Take up a few threads of fabric with the pin tip then take it out perpendicular to the edge of the fabric. Pin the ends, then the centre. With large pieces, pin at regular intervals.

JUNCTIONS IN SEAMS

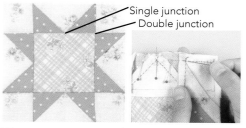
Single junction
Double junction

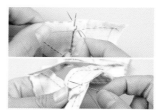

When sewing a seam, make an extra stitch at the junction point between several pieces (right) to reinforce that point and avoid a gap forming. There is no need to do this for a single junction.

Insert the needle perpendicular to the fabric and make one stitch. Sew through thick parts stitch by stitch.

STITCHING

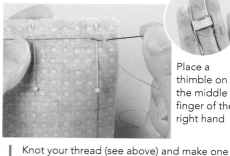
Place a thimble on the middle finger of the right hand

1 Knot your thread (see above) and make one stitch outside the drawn seam line. Going along the seam line, make an extra stitch to secure the thread at the beginning.

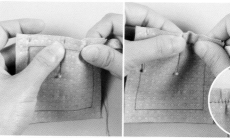

2 Hold the needle with the thumb and index finger of your right hand. Bend the middle finger so the thimble presses against the eye of the needle and use it to push the needle. Move the fabric with your left hand as you thread the needle through, taking small, even stitches.

3 Make a few stitches along the drawn seam line, then draw the needle through.

4 Stitch to just outside the seam line. Slide your fingers along the stitching to smooth out any puckering.

5 Make an extra stitch at the end and then finish off with a knot (see above).

6 Neatly trim the seam allowances to 6mm.

7 Fold the seam allowance, using your fingertips to press it in place; do not stretch the fabric.

Acorn

* *

One of the simplest blocks you can make, this consists of only four pieces, all with straight edges. With no corners to worry about, it's an idea block for a beginner. If you cut out large-sized pieces, make sure you mark the centre point of the edges to be joined to get a neat match.

Folding the seam allowances

Templates

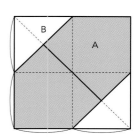

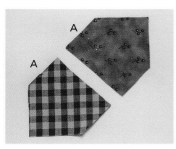

1 Prepare two pieces A

2 Pin the two pieces A right sides together as shown. Sew along the seam line, making an extra stitch at the start and end.

3 Trim the allowance to 6mm.

4 Fold the allowance towards the dark coloured piece (block 1 complete).

5 Prepare one block 1 and two pieces B. Mark the centre points of the long edges on each piece B.

6 Pin block 1 and piece B right sides together, matching the centre point on piece B to the seam on block 1. Sew along the seam line.

7 Trim the allowance to 6mm, then fold it towards block 1.

8 Join on the other piece B in the same way.

✳ Assembling Several Blocks

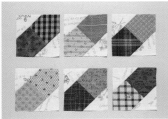

1 Make as many blocks as required and lay them out flat to check their positioning

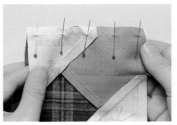

2 Bring two blocks right sides together and pin as shown. Sew along the seam line, making an extra stitch at the start and end.

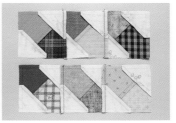

3 Join the blocks in horizontal strips. Fold the seam allowances in alternate directions between the strips.

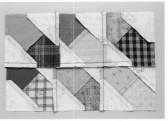

4 Sew the strips along the seam line. Fold the allowances to one side.

Alabama Beauty

Level ✿✿✾✾✾

❊·❊

Begin by joining pieces A, B, B 'and C to form four small blocks. Match up marks and pin closely together to avoid any discrepancy. Sew to the centre marks to fold the allowances into the shape. Choose a light colour for pieces B and B', and two contrasting colours for pieces A and C.

Folding the seam allowances

Templates

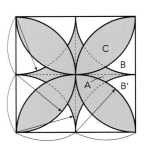

✳ Marking the templates

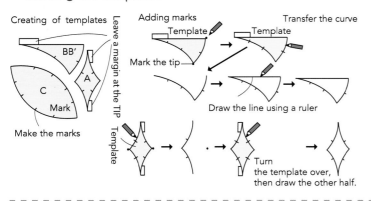

Creating of templates · Leave a margin at the TIP · Adding marks · Template · Transfer the curve · Mark the tip · Mark the tip · Draw the line using a ruler · Turn the template over, then draw the other half. · Template · BB' · A · C · Mark · Make the marks

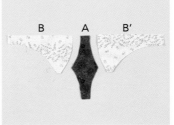

1 Prepare one piece A, one piece B and one piece B', marking as shown left. Lay them out flat to check their positioning.

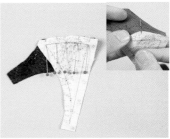

2 Bring pieces A and B right sides together, matching up the marks. Pin, postioning the pins close together.

3 Sew along the seam, making an extra stitch at the beginning and end. Fold the seam allowance towards piece B.

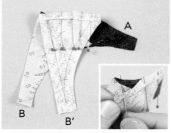

4 Join a piece B' to piece A in the same way, folding the seam allowance towards piece B' (block 1 complete). Make three more blocks 1.

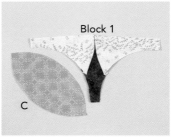

5 Prepare one block 1 and one piece C. Bring them right sides together, matching marks, and pin.

6 Sew along the seam, making an extra stitch at the beginning and end. Fold the allowances towards piece C (block 2 complete).

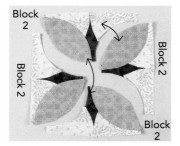

7 Make three more blocks 2.

8 Pin two blocks 2 right sides together. Sew from the start to the end of the seam line. Fold the allowances towards piece C (block 3 complete). Join the other two blocks 2 in the same way.

9 Pin the two blocks 3 right sides together. Sew along the seam. Make an extra stitch in the centre, without stitching through the allowances, to avoid the formation of a hole. Fold the seam allowances in a sprial.

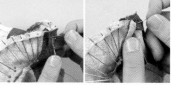

Alice's Patchwork

Use dark colours for pieces A and D to form this flower pattern. Mark the curved edges of pieces D and E. Make four small blocks, then join them together, making sure the junction points match up.

Folding the seam allowances

Templates

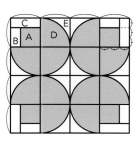

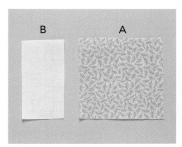

1 Prepare one piece A and one piece B.

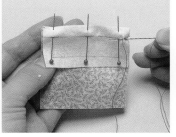

2 Pin pieces A and B right sides together as shown. Sew along the seam line, making an extra stitch at the start and end.

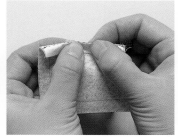

3 Trim the seam allowance to 6mm, then fold it towards piece A (block 1 complete).

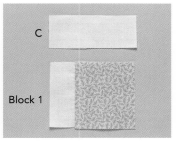

4 Lay block 1 and piece C out flat to check their positioning.

5 Pin block 1 and piece C right sides together; sew. Fold the seam allowance towards block 1 (block 2 complete).

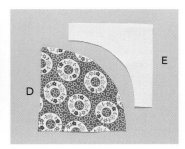

6 Mark the centre of the curve on pieces D and E.

7 Pin piece D to piece E, right sides together and matching the marked points. Sew along the seam.

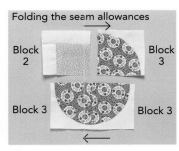

8 Fold the seam allowances towards piece D (block 3 complete). Prepare two more blocks 3.

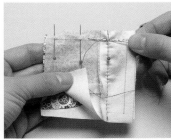

9 Pin block 2 and a block 3 right sides together and sew along the seam. Join two blocks 3 together.

10 Pin the two strips right sides together. Sew along the seam, making an extra stitch at the junction points (block 4 complete).

11 Prepare three more blocks 4. Join them in pairs, taking care to position the blocks as shown.

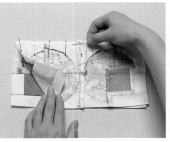

12 Pin the two pairs of blocks 4 right sides together. Sew along the seam, making an extra stitch at the junction points.

Anvil

Level ✿ ✾ ✾ ✾ ✾

✳ · ✳

Join pieces A and B to make strips; join pieces C and B to make other strips. When the strips are joined, add the triangular pieces D to form the corners of the block. Make extra stitches at seam junctions to avoid gaps. Choose strong colours for pieces A and C to contrast with the background.

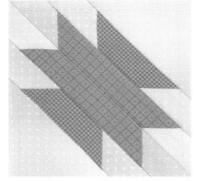

Folding the seam allowances

Templates

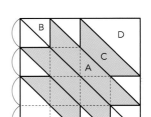

1   Draw round the templates on the wrong sides of the fabrics. Add 7mm seam allowances, then cut out.

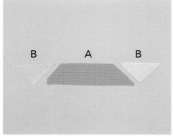

2   Prepare one piece A and two pieces B. Lay them out flat to check their positioning.

3   Bring pieces A and B right sides together and pin, being careful to keep seam lines matching.

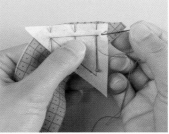

4   Sew along the seam line, making an extra stitch at the start and end

---

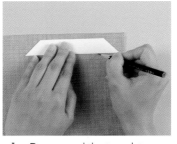

5   Trim the seam allowance to 6mm.

6   Fold the seam allowance towards piece A.

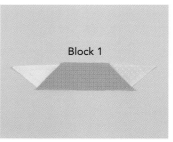

7   Pin piece A and the other piece B right sides together. Sew as in step 4. Fold the seam allowances towards piece A (block 1 complete).

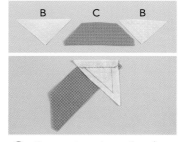

8   Prepare two pieces B and one piece C. Pin pieces B and C right sides together, then sew as in step 4.

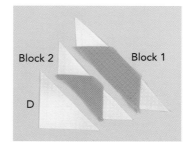

9   Join the other piece B and the C in the same way. Fold the seam allowances towards piece C (block 2 complete). Prepare one block 1, one block 2 and one piece D.

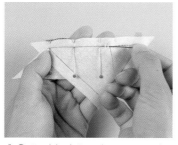

10   Pin block 2 and piece D right sides together. Sew as shown, making an extra stitch at the start and end. Fold the seam allowance towards block 2.

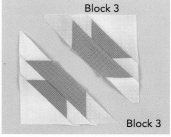

11   Join the block 1 to block 2 in the same way. Fold the seam allowances towards block 1 (block 3 complete). Make another block 3.

12   Pin the two blocks 3 right sides together. Sew, making extra stitches at the junctions. Fold the seam allowances to one side.

Apple Tree

* · *

This figurative block is composed of many pieces. The leaves of the apple tree are formed by pieces A and B; the pieces C represent the fruit so choose a pink or red for these. Join pieces into diagonal strips, then join these. Check the positioning and direction at each step.

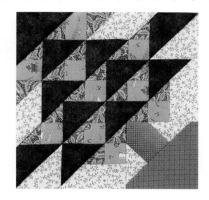

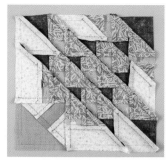
Folding the seam allowances

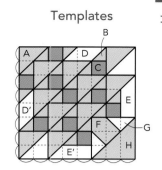
Templates

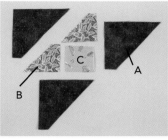

1 Prepare three pieces A, two pieces B and one piece C.

2 Pin one piece B and the piece C right sides together. Sew along the seam line. Fold the allowance towards piece C.

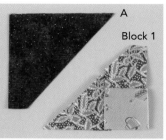

3 Join on the other piece B. Fold the allowance towards piece C (block 1 complete). Join block 1 and a piece A along their long edges. Fold the allowances towards piece A (block 2 complete).

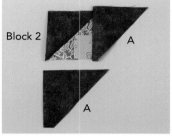

4 Pin block 2 and one piece A right sides together. Sew along the seam line. Fold the allowances towards piece A. Join on the other piece A (block 3 complete).

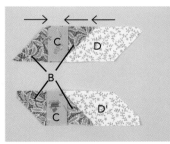

5 Join two pieces B, one piece C and one piece D as shown. Join two pieces B, one piece C and one piece D'. Fold the allowances in the direction of the arrows (blocks 4 and 4' complete).

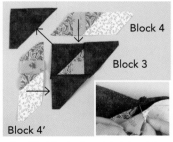

6 Pin blocks 3 and 4 right sides together, matching the seam junctions. Sew along the seam line. Join the block 4' in the same way.

7 Pin the block from step 6 and one piece A right sides together. Sew along the seam line, working stitch by stitch on the overlapping allowances (first strip complete).

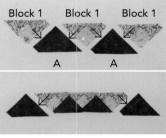

8 Join three blocks 1 and four pieces A to make the second strip. Fold the allowances towards the pieces A.

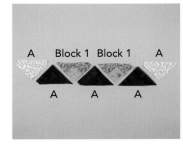

9 Join two blocks 1 and five pieces A as shown to make the third strip. Fold the allowances towards the pieces A.

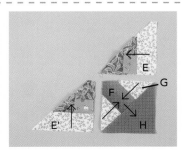

10 Join one block 1 and one piece E. Join one block 1 and one piece E'. Join one piece F, two pieces G and one piece H as as shown. Join all together to form the fourth strip. Fold the allowances in the direction of the arrows.

11 Lay out the four strips flat to check their positioning.

12 Pin two strips right sides together. Sew along the seam line. Make an extra stitch at the seam junctions.

13

Arabic Lattice

Level ✱✿✿✿✿

❋*❋

First assemble four pieces A, then add pieces B in a clockwise order. This block is made up of only eight pieces with a simple central block. Arab lattice is, therefore, accessible to beginners. Alternate fabric pieces in light and dark colours.

Folding the seam allowances

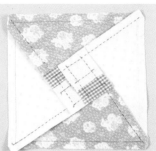

Templates

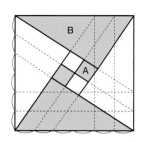

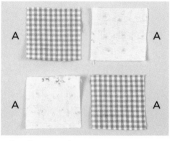

1 Prepare four pieces A. Lay them out flat to check their positioning.

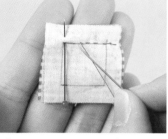

2 Pin two pieces A right sides together, then stitch along one seam line. Fold the allowances towards the darker fabric (block 1 complete).

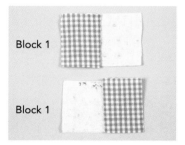

3 Make another block 1. Lay both blocks 1 out flat to check their positioning.

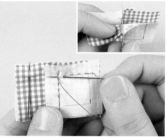

4 Bring the two blocks 1 right sides together, then pin the ends and the junction. Stitch together, making an extra stitch at the junction (block 2 complete).

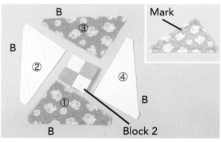

5 Prepare four pieces B and mark them as indicated. Lay them out around block 2 as shown; they will be assembled in numerical order.

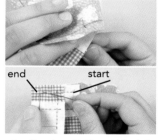

6 Pin piece B ① and block 2 right sides together, aligning the mark and the corner of block 2. Sew up to the mark.

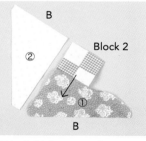

7 Fold the seam allowance towards piece B

8 Pin the block from step 7 and the piece B ② right sides together as shown and sew the seam.

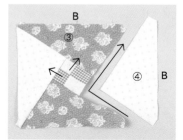

9 Join the block from step 8 and the piece B ③ in the same way.

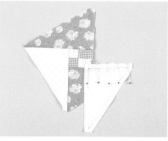

10 Pin the block from step 9 and the piece B ④, right sides together. Do not pierce the seam allowances of the pieces A.

11 Sew along the seam as shown. Make an extra stitch to secure the thread but do not cut it.

12 Pin along the second edge of piece B ④, then continue to sew to the end. Fasten off.

Arrow

Level ✿✿✾✾✾

* *

Use three different fabrics for the pieces B and C on one block; then, on the adjacent block, use the same fabric for C as used on one piece B on the previous block. Make the same fabrics match up to create an arrow shape. Combine fabrics and shapes in the same way to join blocks and create the design.

Folding the seam allowances

Templates

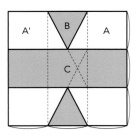

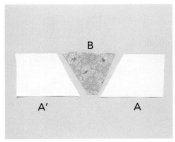

1 Prepare one piece A, one piece A' and one piece B.

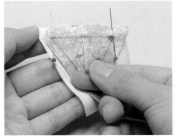

2 Bring the pieces A and B right sides together, then pin.

3 Sew along the seam line, making an extra stitch at the start and end.

4 Trim the allowance to 6mm, then fold it towards piece B. Join on piece A' in the same way (block 1 complete).

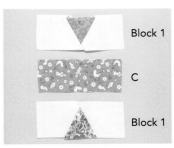

5 Prepare two blocks 1 and one piece C.

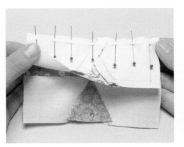

6 Bring block 1 and piece C right sides together, then pin at the ends, at the seam junction and in between.

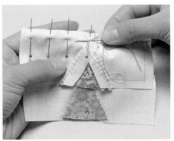

7 Sew along the seam line. Make an extra stitch at the start, end and seam junction. Fold the allowances towards piece C. Join on the other block 1 (block 2 complete).

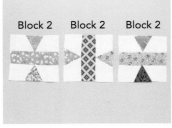

8 Prepare three blocks 2, using a fabric combination and arrangement as above.

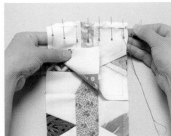

9 Pin two blocks 2 right sides together, matching up seam junctions. Sew along the seam line, making an extra stitch at seam junctions. Join on the other block 2.

10 Fold the allowances outwards. Make three strips, using a fabric combination and arrangement as above.

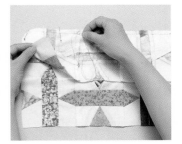

11 Pin two strips right sides together at the ends, the junctions and in between. Sew along the seam line. Make an extra stitch at the seam junctions.

* Tip

Because all the sides of the triangle piece B are the same, mark the bottom edge so you know which one it is.

Arrowhead

Level ✿✿✾✾✾

✳･✳

Start by joining four small pieces A to form the central block then add on B and B' pieces to make the central strip. Use more B and B' pieces with C pieces to make triangles that join to either side of the central strip.

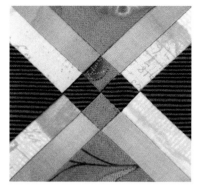

Folding the seam allowances

Templates

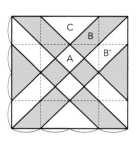

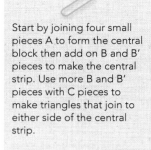

1 Prepare two pieces A.

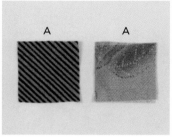

2 Pin the two blocks 1 right sides together as shown. Sew along the seam line, making an extra stitch at the start and end.

3 Trim the allowance to 6mm, then fold it towards the dark coloured piece (block 1 complete).

4 Make another block 1.

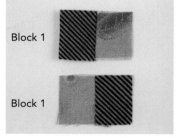

5 Pin the two blocks 1 right sides together. Sew along the seam line, making an extra stitch at the seam junction (block 2 complete).

6 Pin one piece B and one piece B' right sides together. Sew along the seam line (block 3 complete).

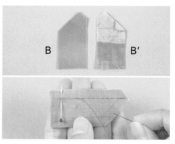

7 Prepare one block 2 and three blocks 3. Alternate the direction of fold for the allowances on adjacent blocks.

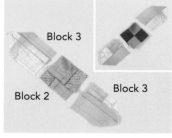

8 Pin a block 2 and 3 right sides together, matching the seam junctions. Sew along the seam line. Make an extra stitch at the seam junction (block 4 complete).

9 Pin one piece B and one piece C right sides together. Sew along the seam line. Fold the allowances towards piece C (block 5 complete). Join a piece B' and C (block 5' complete).

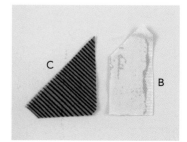

10 Pin the blocks 5 and 5' right sides together. Sew along the seam line. Fold the allowances towards block 5' (block 6 complete). Make two blocks 6.

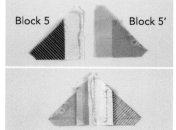

11 Prepare one block 4 and two blocks 6.

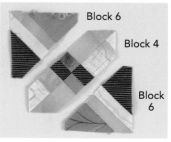

12 Pin a block 4 and 6 right sides together. Sew along the seam line. Make an extra stitch at seam junctions. Fold the allowances towards block 6. Join the other block 6 in the same way.

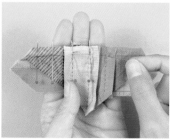

Aunt Vinah's Favourite

Level ✿✿✾✾✾

* *

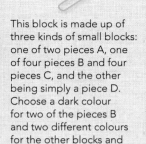

This block is made up of three kinds of small blocks: one of two pieces A, one of four pieces B and four pieces C, and the other being simply a piece D. Choose a dark colour for two of the pieces B and two different colours for the other blocks and background.

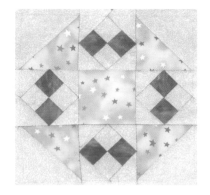

Folding the seam allowances

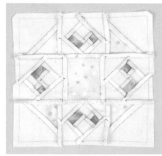

Templates

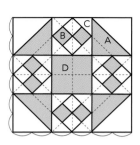

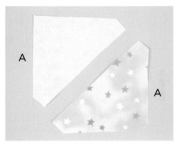

1 Prepare two pieces A.

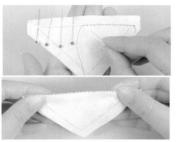

2 Pin the two pieces A right sides together as shown. Sew along the seam line. Trim the allowances, then fold them towards the dark coloured piece (block 1 complete).

Block 1

3 Make four blocks 1.

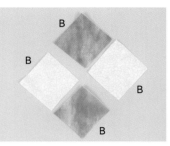

4 Prepare four pieces B.

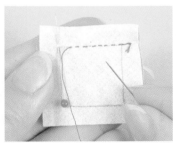

5 Pin two pieces B right sides together as shown. Sew along the seam line, making an extra stitch at the start and end. Join the other two pieces B.

6 Fold the allowances towards the dark coloured pieces. Pin the two blocks right sides together.

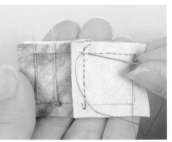

7 Sew along the seam line, making an extra stitch at the seam junctions. Fold the allowances to one side (block 2 complete).

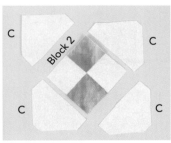

Block 2

8 Prepare one blocks 2 and four pieces C.

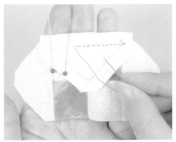

9 Pin two pieces C right sides together. Sew along the seam line. Fold the allowances towards block 2.

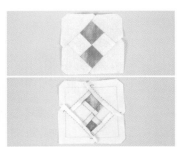

10 Assemble the other three blocks C in the same way (block 3 complete). Make three more blocks 3.

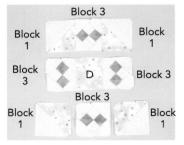

Block 3

11 Lay out four blocks 1, four blocks 3 and one piece D as shown to check their positioning. Join them in threes to get thee strips.

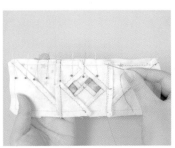

12 Pin two strips right sides together, then pin the ends, the junctions and between the pins. Sew along the seam line. Join on the third strip.

Baby Blocks

Level ★★☆☆☆

This block is made up of diamond-shaped pieces, all the same size. By combining three shades of one colour – light, medium and dark – you can create a pattern of interlocking cubes. When folding seam allowances where several meet, fold them down in a spiral.

Folding the seam allowances

Templates

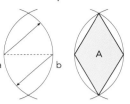

Draw a line (a–b) whose length corresponds to one side of a diamond. Draw two intersecting curves with a radius this length. Connect the intersections of the curves and points a and b to obtain the diamonds A.

1 Prepare three pieces A; one dark coloured, one medium coloured and one light coloured piece.

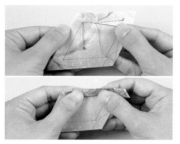

2 Pin the dark and medium coloured pieces right sides together. Sew along the seam line. Fold the allowances towards the medium coloured piece.

3 Lay out the block just made and the light coloured piece A to check their positioning.

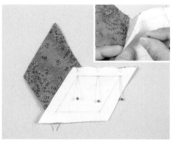

4 Pin the light coloured piece and the medium coloured piece right sides together without piercing allowances.

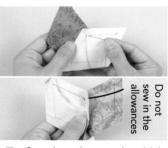

Do not sew in the allowances

5 Sew along the seam line. Make an extra stitch at the corner without sewing through the allowances.

6 Pin the next edge of the light coloured piece to the dark one. Take the needle through the corner and continue to sew. Make an extra stitch at the end.

7 Trim allowances if necessary. Fold down the allowances at the centre in a spiral (block 1 complete).

Block 1   Block 1

8 Prepare two blocks 1 and pin them right sides together with the medium and dark coloured pieces matching. Sew without piercing the allowances.

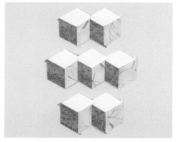

9 Join blocks 1 in the same way as in step 8 to form strips.

10 Pin two strips right sides together, matching a light coloured edge to a medium coloured one. Sew, making an extra stitch at the corner.

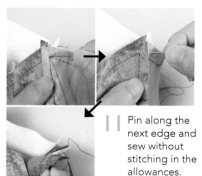

11 Pin along the next edge and sew without stitching in the allowances.

12 Continue to sew the other edges in the same way.

Basket

The 'basket' part of this design is made up of triangular and square pieces; the 'handle' is a bias strip that is then appliquéd in place. Choose two different fabrics for the basket and handle, with a different one for the background.

Folding the seam allowances

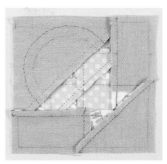

Templates

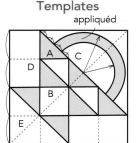

For the handle, cut a bias strip twice the width of the handle template.

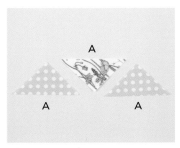

1 Prepare three pieces A.

2 Pin two pieces A right sides together. Sew along the seam line.

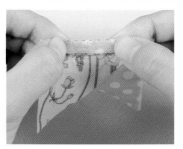

3 Fold the allowance towards the piece that will be in the centre. Join on the other piece A (block 1 complete).

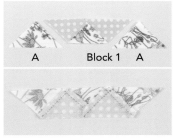

4 Join two other pieces to block 1 in the same way. Fold the allowances as shown (block 2 complete).

5 Prepare two pieces A and one piece B. Join them as in steps 2 and 3 (block 3 complete).

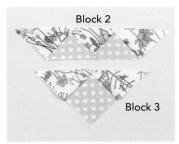

6 Prepare one block 2 and one blocks 3.

7 Pin blocks 2 and 3 right sides together. Sew along the seam line. Fold the allowances towards block 3 (block 4 complete).

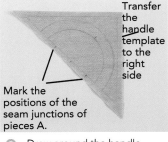

8 Draw around the handle template on the right side of piece C. Along the long edge, mark the positions of the seam junctions on the long edge of block 4.

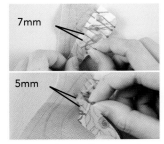

9 Pin the handle strip and piece C right sides together so that one edge of the strip overlaps the inner line of the drawn handle by 5mm. Pin at 7mm intervals.

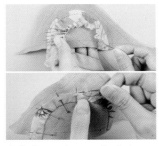

10 Sew using small stitches. Fold the strip over to the right side. Turning the edge under as you go, slip stitch the edge in place.

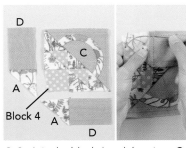

11 Join the block 4 and the piece C. Fold the allowances towards block 4. Join two pieces A and two pieces D as shown, then join them to either side of block 4.

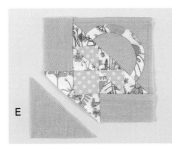

12 Join one piece E to the block made in step 11. Fold the allowances towards the basket motif.

Bear's Paw

This block represents bear's paws; complete with strong coloured fabrics for pieces A and C so the paw motif stands out. All the different pieces used to assemble this block have straight edges so it is not too difficult to achieve.

Folding the seam allowances

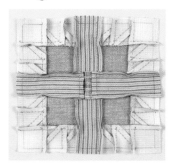

Templates

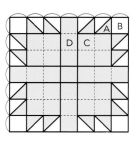

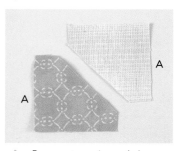

1 Prepare two pieces A. Lay them out flat to check their positioning.

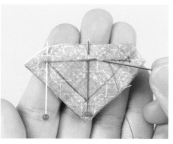

2 Bring two pieces A right sides together, then pin along the seam as shown. Sew, making an extra stitch at the start and end of the seam.

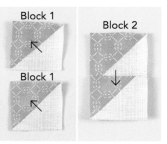

3 Fold the seam allowance towards the dark coloured piece (block 1 complete). Make another block 1. Pin two blocks 1 right sides together, then sew (block 2 complete).

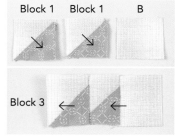

4 Join two blocks 1 and one piece B (block 3 complete).

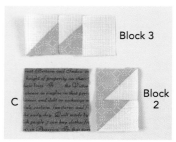

5 Prepare one block 2, one block 3 and one piece C.

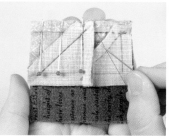

6 Pin the piece C and block 2 right sides together; sew. Fold the seam allowance towards piece C

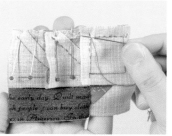

7 Pin block 3 and the block in step 6 right sides together, as shown; sew (block 4 complete). Make four blocks 4.

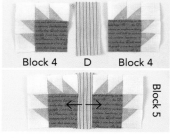

8 Sew one piece D between two blocks 4. Fold the seam allowances towards blocks 4 (block 5 complete). Make another block 5.

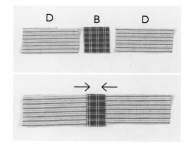

9 Join one piece B and two pieces D to form a strip. Fold the seam allowances towards piece B.

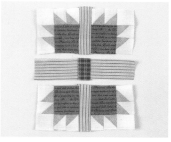

10 Lay out the strip and two blocks 5 flat to check their positioning.

11 Pin the strip and a block 5 right sides together, making sure the seam junctions match up.

12 Sew, making extra stitches at the seam junctions. Join the other block 5 to the other side of the strp Fold the seam allowances towards the strips.

Bethlehem Star

Level ✿✿✺✺✺

✱ ✴ ✱

Small triangular blocks are joined to a central hexagon and then diamond-shaped pieces are added to make a large hexagonal block. Make sure corners match up to get a neat finish and make extra stitches at seam junctions to avoid gaps forming at these points. Choose two contrasting fabrics.

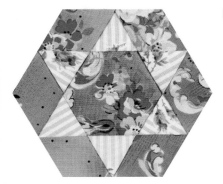

Folding the seam allowances

Templates

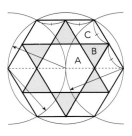

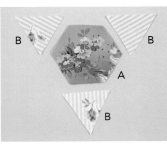

1 Prepare one piece A and three pieces B

2 Pin pieces A and B right sides together as shown. Sew along the seam line, making an extra stitch at the start and end.

3 Trim the allowance to 6mm, then fold it towards piece B. Join on the other pieces B in the same way (block 1 complete).

4 Prepare one piece B and two pieces C

5 Pin the pieces B and C right sides together. Sew along the seam line. Fold the allowances towards piece B.

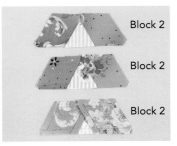

6 Join the other piece C in the same way (block 2 complete). Make three blocks 2.

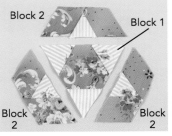

7 Prepare one block 1 and three blocks 2.

8 Pin blocks 1 and 2 right sides together, then sew along the seam line. Fold the allowances towards block 2. Join the other two blocks 2 in the same way.

✳ Assembling Several Blocks

1 Join the blocks to form strips, matching up seam junctions; you will need to make half blocks for every other strip. Fold the allowances to one side.

2 Pin two strips right sides together along the first edge. Sew, without piercing the allowances. Make an extra stitch. Pin the second edge, then sew to the next corner.

3 Make an extra stitch, then pin the third edge. Sew to the next corner. Continue to join the strips in the same way.

B

21

Bird of Paradise

Level ★★☆☆☆

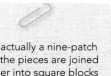

This is actually a nine-patch block; the pieces are joined together into square blocks and then these are joined in threes to make strips. Make sure corners match up to get a well-defined motif at the centre of the block. Use different fabrics for the 'arms' of the star-like shape.

Folding the seam allowances

Templates

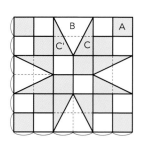

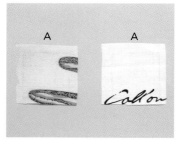

1 Prepare two pieces A.

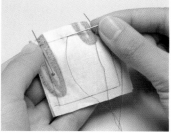

2 Pin pieces A and B right sides together as shown. Sew along the seam line, making an extra stitch at the start and end.

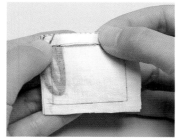

3 Trim the allowance to 6mm, then fold it towards the dark coloured piece (block 1 complete).

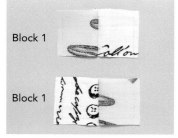

4 Make two blocks 1.

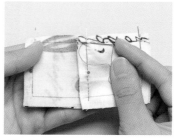

5 Pin the two blocks 1 right sides together. Sew along the seam line, making an extra stitch at the seam junctions (block 2 complete).

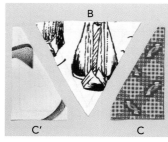

6 Prepare one piece B, one piece C and one piece C'.

7 Pin pieces B and C right sides together. Sew along the seam line. Join on piece C'. Fold the allowances towards pieces C and C' (block 3 complete).

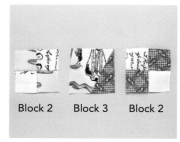

8 Prepare two blocks 2 and one block 3. Lay them out flat to check their positioning.

9 Pin the blocks shown in step 8 right sides together and sew along the seam lines. Fold the allowances outward.

10 Prepare one block 2 and two blocks 3, then join as in step 9. Fold the allowances towards the centre.

11 Prepare another strip as in steps 8 and 9. Lay out the three strips flat to check their positioning.

12 Pin two strips right sides together. Sew along the seam line, making extra stitches at the seam junctions. Join on the third strip in the same way.

B
Bird of Paradise

Bird in the Air

Level ✿ ✿ ✿ ✿ ✿

❋·❋

This block consists of small triangles and one large one; the smaller triangles are said to represent flying birds. Join pieces A into small blocks, then assemble these into a large triangle. Join this to the piece B triangle. Choose two bold and contrasting colours for this block.

Folding the seam allowances

Templates

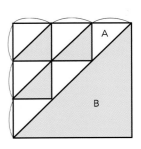

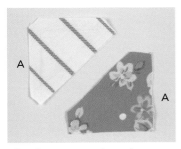

1 Prepare two pieces A.

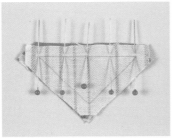

2 Bring the two pieces A right sides together along the long edges, then pin as shown.

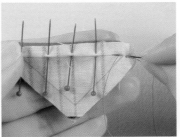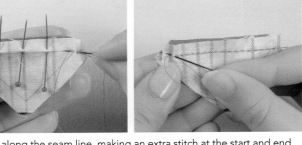

3 Sew along the seam line, making an extra stitch at the start and end.

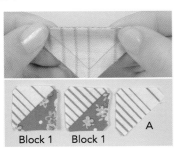

4 Fold the allowance towards the dark coloured piece (block 1 complete). Prepare two blocks 1 and one piece A.

5 Pin one block 1 and the piece A right sides together, then sew along the seam line. Fold the allowances towards the dark coloured piece.

6 Join on another block 1 to make the top strip shown. Join a block 1 and a piece A to make a second strip. Prepare another piece A.

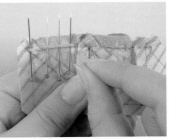

7 Bring the two strips right sides together and pin along the seam.

8 Sew along the seam line, making an extra stitch at the start and end, and at the seam junctions.

9 Join the piece A to the block made in step 8 (block 2 complete). Prepare one piece B.

10 Pin block 2 and piece B right sides together along the long edges. Sew along the seam line.

* Tip

You can fold the allowances where six pieces meet on block 2 in a spiral shape. If you do this, make sure you do not stitch in the allowances.

23

Blazing Star

The diamond-shaped pieces A are joined together four at a time to form eight diamond-shaped blocks. These are then joined to form the central star motif. Pieces B, C and D form the background. Use a dark fabric for the tips and centre of the star so it stands out against the background fabrics.

Folding the seam allowances

Templates

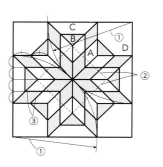

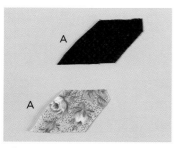

1 Prepare two pieces A

2 Pin the pieces A right sides together as shown. Sew along the seam line, making an extra stitch at the start and end.

3 Trim the allowance to 6mm, then fold it towards the dark coloured piece (block 1 complete).

4 Prepare two blocks 1.

5 Pin the two blocks 1 right sides right sides together as shown. Sew along the seam line, making an extra stitch at the seam junction (block 2 complete).

6 Make eight blocks 2. Join them in pairs. Fold the allowances in one direction (four blocks 3 complete). Join the blocks 3 in pairs (two blocks 4 complete)

7 Pin the two blocks 4 right sides right sides together as shown. Sew along the seam line, making an extra stitch at the seam junctions (block 5 complete).

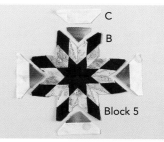

8 Prepare one blocks 5, four pieces B and four pieces C.

9 Pin pieces B and C right sides together, then sew along the seam line. Fold the allowances towards the dark piece B (block 6 complete). Make three more blocks 6.

10 Pin blocks 5 and 6 right sides together along the first edge without piercing the allowance of piece A. Sew, making an extra stitch; do not cut the thread.

11 Pin the second edge, then sew to the end. Join the three other blocks 6 to block 5 in the same way.

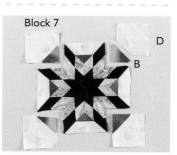

12 Join one piece B and one piece D. Fold the allowances towards the dark piece B (block 7 complete). Make four blocks 7. Join them to the centre block as described in steps 10 and 11.

Bow Tie 1

This block represents a bow tie. If you choose a checked or striped fabric for the bow tie motif, make sure you cut out the A and B pieces following the direction of the pattern. When the A piece is placed between the B pieces, it is positioned at an angle so the pattern runs in that directions too.

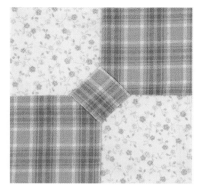

Folding the seam allowances

Templates

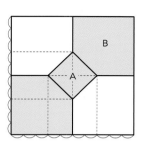

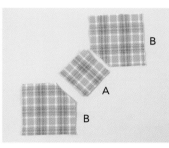

1 Prepare one piece A and two pieces B.

2 Bring the pieces A and B right sides together and pin.

3 Sew along the seam line, making an extra stitch at the start and end.

4 Trim the allowance to 6mm, then fold it towards piece A Join on the other piece B in the same way (block 1 complete).

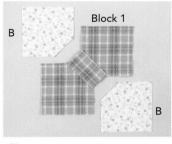

5 Prepare one block 1 and two pieces B.

6 Bring block 1 and a piece B right sides together, then pin along the first edge. Do not pierce the allowances at the corners.

7 Sew along the seam line to the corner. Make an extra stitch; do not cut the thread.

8 Pin the second edge, matching the next corner to the next corner on the A piece.

9 Continue sewing without stitching into the corner allowances.

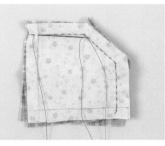

10 Pin and sew the third edge in the same way. Fold back the allowances towards block 1. Join on the other piece B in the same way.

Bow Tie 2

Level ★★✿✿✿

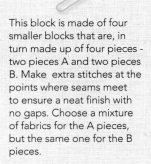

This block is made of four smaller blocks that are, in turn made up of four pieces - two pieces A and two pieces B. Make extra stitches at the points where seams meet to ensure a neat finish with no gaps. Choose a mixture of fabrics for the A pieces, but the same one for the B pieces.

Folding the seam allowances

Templates

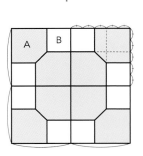

1 Prepare two pieces A.

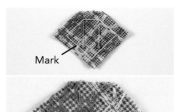

2 Pin pieces A and B right sides together as shown. Sew along the seam line, making an extra stitch at the start and end.

3 Trim the allowance to 6mm, then fold it to one side (block 1 complete).

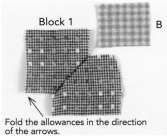

4 Prepare one block 1 and one pieces B.

5 Bring block 1 and the piece B right sides together, then pin the first edge without piercing the allowances of piece A.

6 Sew up to the corner. Make an extra stitch; do not cut the thread.

7 Pin along the second edge, then sew to the end, making an extra stitch at the end of the seam.

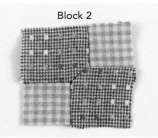

8 Join on another piece B in the same way. Fold the allowances towards block 1 (block 2 complete). Make four blocks 2.

9 Bring two blocks 2 right sides together and pin, matching up the seam junctions.

10 Sew along the seam line, making extra stitches at the seam junctions. Sew stitch by stitch through overlapping allowances.

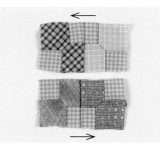

11 Assemble the other two blocks 2 in the same way. Fold the allowances in the direction of the arrows.

12 Pin the two strips right sides together. Sew along the seam line, making extra stitches at the seam junctions. Fold the allowances to one side.

Brickroad

Level ★★☆☆☆

This block represents a crossroads. Choose a strong coloured fabric for the pieces C that form the cross motif. Join pieces A, B and C to make two triangular blocks. Bring them together with a central strip. The straight-edged pieces make this block a good one for beginners.

Folding the seam allowances

Templates

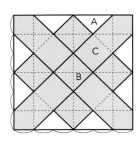

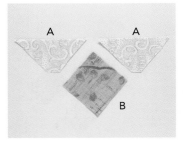

1 Prepare two pieces A and one piece B.

2 Pin pieces A and B right sides together as shown. Sew along the seam line, making an extra stitch at the start and end.

3 Trim the allowance to 6mm, then fold it towards piece B Join on the other piece A in the same way (block 1 complete).

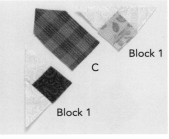

4 Prepare two blocks 1 and one piece C.

5 Pin block 1 and piece C right sides together. Sew along the seam line. Fold the allowance towards piece C. Join on the other block 1 in the same way (block 2 complete).

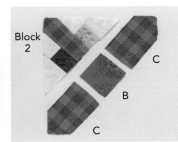

6 Prepare one piece B and two pieces C.

7 Pin the pieces B and C right sides together. Sew along the seam line. Fold the allowances towards the piece B. Join on the other piece C (block 3 complete).

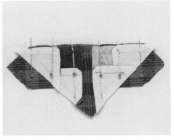

8 Bring blocks 2 and 3 right sides together and pin.

9 Sew along the seam line, making an extra stitch at the start and end.

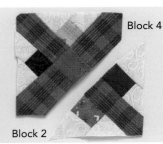

10 Fold the allowances towards block 3 (block 4 complete). Prepare another block 2.

11 Pin blocks 2 and 4 right sides together, then then sew as in steps 8 and 9.

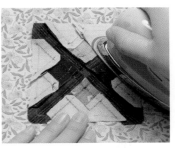

12 Fold the allowances towards block 4; press.

Brickwork

Level ★★☆☆☆

This block is made up of square, rectangular and triangular pieces. Although there are quite a few pieces they are all joined along straight edges, making this an easy block. Form a central diagonal strip then join triangles to either side. Make extra stitches at seam junctions to avoid mismatch.

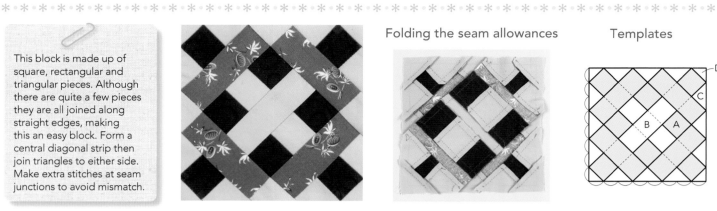

Folding the seam allowances

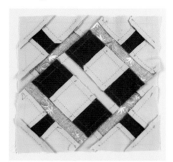

Templates

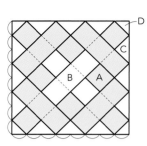

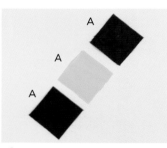

1 Prepare three pieces A.

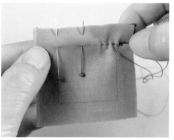

2 Pin two pieces A right sides together. Sew along the seam line, making an extra stitch at the start and end.

3 Trim the allowance to 6mm, then fold it to the outer piece A. Join on the other piece A in the same way (block 1 complete).

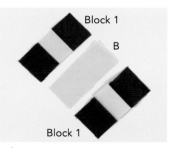

4 Prepare two blocks 1 and one piece B.

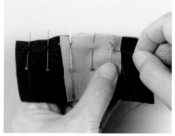

5 Pin a block 1 and piece B right sides together. Sew along the seam line. Fold the allowances towards the piece B (block 2 complete).

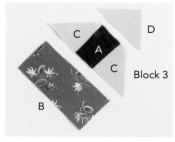

6 Join one piece A and two pieces C. Fold the allowances towards piece A (block 3 complete). Prepare one piece B and one piece D.

7 Pin block 3 and piece D right sides together. Sew along the seam line. Fold the allowances towards block 3. Join on the piece B (block 4 complete).

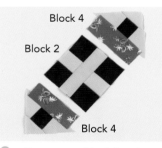

8 Prepare one block 2 and two blocks 4. Join them, sewing along the seam lines. Fold the allowances outwards (block 5 complete).

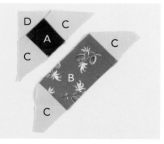

9 Join one piece A, two pieces C and one piece D. Join one piece B and two pieces C. Fold the allowances towards pieces A and B.

10 Pin the two blocks from step 9 right sides together. Sew along the seam line. Fold the allowances towards the piece B (block 6 complete).

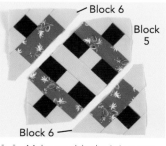

11 Make two blocks 6. Lay out one block 5 and two blocks 6 flat to check their positioning.

12 Pin a block 5 and 6 right sides together. Sew along the seam line. Make an extra stitch at the seam junctions. Join on the other block 6.

Bridal Bouquet

Level ★★★☆☆

This block represents a bouquet of flowers. It is assembled in two parts, divided diagonally across the block. Make sure corners and seam junctions match up – especially at the centre point – and make extra stitches at seam junctions to avoid gapping.

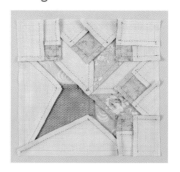

Folding the seam allowances

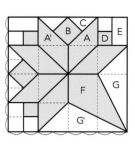

Templates

B

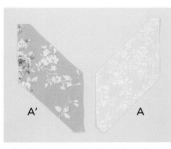

1 Prepare one piece A and one piece A'. Mark with seam lines.

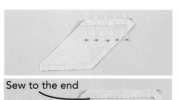

Sew to the end

2 Pin the pieces A and A' right sides together. Sew along the seam line. Fold the allowances towards piece A (block 1 complete).

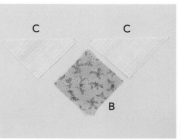

3 Prepare one piece B and two pieces C. Join them, sewing along the seam line. Fold the allowances towards piece B (block 2 complete).

Block 2

Block 1

4 Bring blocks 1 and 2 right sides together and pin the first edge without piercing the allowance. Sew along the seam line, make an extra stitch, then pin the second edge; sew to the end. Fold the allowances towards block 1 (block 3 complete).

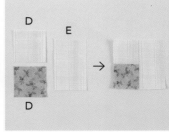

5 Prepare two pieces D and one piece E. Sew the two pieces D along the seam line. Then join these two pieces and E. Fold the allowances towards the dark piece D (block 4 complete).

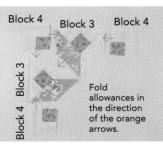

Block 4 Block 3 Block 4

Block 3

Block 4

Fold allowances in the direction of the orange arrows.

6 Prepare two blocks 3 and three blocks 4. Lay them flat to check their positioning.

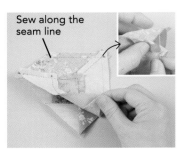

Sew along the seam line

7 Pin and sew the two blocks 3 right sides together as shown. Join on the blocks 4 as described in step 4 (block 5 complete).

8 Join one piece F, G and G'. Fold the allowances towards piece F. Join on one piece A and one piece A' as described in step 4. Fold the allowances towards pieces A and A' (block 6 complete).

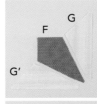
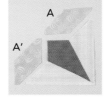

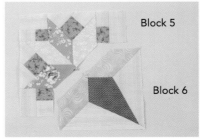

Block 5

Block 6

9 Pin blocks 5 and 6 right sides together. Join as described in step 4, sewing stitch by stitch on overlapping allowances.

Bridal Clover

Level ★ ★ ✿ ✿ ✿

✳ ✳

This block is made up of eight triangular shapes, joined together in pairs to form four squares; a heart shape sits at the centre of each square. It is important to match up curved edges. Snipping into the curved the allowances makes it easier to sew and fold them.

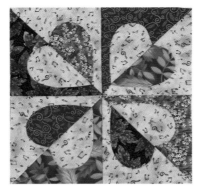

Folding the seam allowances

Templates

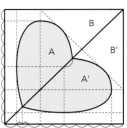

Draw the curve freehand

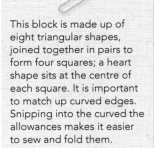

1 Prepare one piece A and one piece B. Mark the the curved edges as shown.

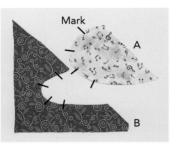

2 Snip into the curved allowance on piece B up to 3mm from the seam line.

3 Bring piece B and piece A right sides together, then pin to the first mark. Sew up to the mark; do not cut the thread.

4 Pin between the next set of marks, then continue sewing to the next one. Make extra stitches at the marks to prevent gaps forming.

5 Continue to pin and sew in the same way to the end of the seam. Make one extra stitch at the end.

6 Fold the allowances towards the dark piece B (block 1 complete).

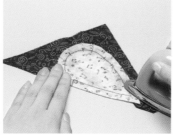

7 Join one piece A' and one piece B' in the same way as in steps 2 to 6. Fold the allowances towards piece A' (block 1' complete).

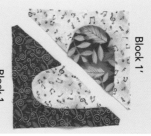

Block 1

Block 1'

8 Bring blocks 1 and 1' right sides together and pin.

9 Sew along the seam line, making an extra stitch at the seam junctions.

10 Trim the allowance if necessary.

11 Fold the allowance towards block 1' (block 3 complete). Make three more blocks 3.

12 Join the blocks 3 in pairs to make two strips, then join these.

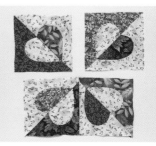

Bridal Steps

Make small blocks with pieces A, A' and B, then join them with a piece C to form a central strip. Two pieces D form the outer strips of this block. Choose brightly coloured for pieces A and A' so the motif stands out.

Folding the seam allowances

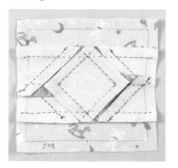

Templates

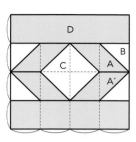

1 Prepare one piece A and one piece B.

2 Pin pieces A and B right sides together as shown. Sew along the seam line, making an extra stitch at the start and end.

3 Trim the allowance to 6mm, then fold it towards piece A (block 1 complete). Join another piece A and B the same way.

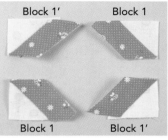

4 Join two pieces A and pieces B' in the same way to make two blocks 1'. Lay out flat the two blocks 1 and 1' to check their positioning.

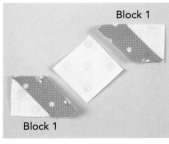

5 Prepare two blocks 1 and one piece C.

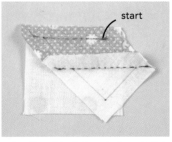

6 Pin a block 1 and piece C right sides together as shown. Sew along the seam line, making an extra stitch at the start and end.

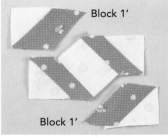

7 Lay out two blocks 1' and the block made in step 6 flat to check their positioning.

8 Bring two blocks right sides together and pin the first edge. Sew along the seam line without piercing the allowance of piece A.

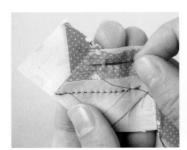

9 Make one extra stitch; do not cut the thread.

10 Pin the second edge and sew along the seam line. Join the other block in the same way.

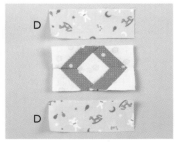

11 Prepare two pieces D and the block from step 10.

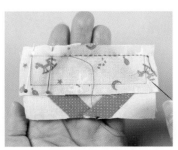

12 Pin a piece D and the block right sides together. Sew along the seam line. Join on the other piece D. Fold the allowances towards pieces D.

Broken Arrow

* *

This is a relatively easy block to put together, with all the component pieces having straight edges. Make extra stitches at the corners and junctions of seams to avoid gapping. Choose three shades of fabric colour, placing the darkest at the centre.

Folding the seam allowances

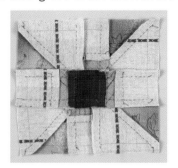

Templates

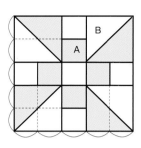

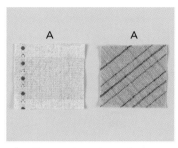

1   Prepare two pieces A.

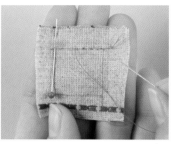

2   Pin the two pieces A right sides together as shown. Sew along the seam line, making an extra stitch at the start and end of the seam.

3   Trim the allowance to 6mm, then fold it towards the dark coloured piece (block 1 complete).

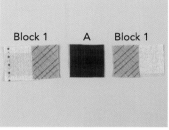

4   Prepare one block A and two blocks 1. Bring one block 1 and piece A right sides together, and pin.

5   Sew along the seam line, making an extra stitch at the start and end of the seam. Fold the allowance towards block 1. Join on the other block 1 in the same way (block 2 complete).

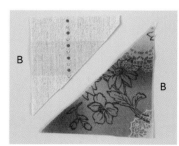

6   Prepare two pieces B. Pin them right sides together along the long edges.

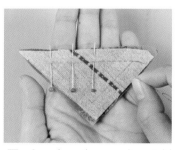

7   Sew along the seam line. Fold the allowance towards the dark coloured piece (block 3 complete).

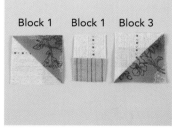

8   Prepare one block 1 and two blocks 3.

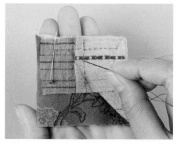

9   Pin a block 1 and 3 right sides together; sew. Join on the other block 3. Fold the allowances to one side (block 4 complete).

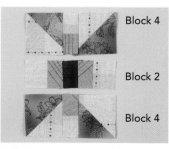

10   Prepare a second block 4. Lay out a block 2 and two blocks 4 flat to check their positioning.

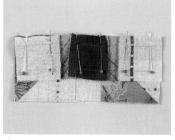

11   Pin a block 4 to block 2, matching up seam lines and seam junctions.

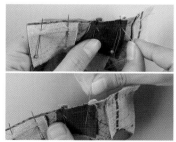

12   Sew, working stitch by stitch on overlapping allowances. Join on the other block 4. Fold the allowances towards the blocks 4.

Butterfly at the Crossroad

* *

This block is made up of three simple shapes, pieces A, B and C. Begin by constructing a nine-square block at the centre and then make strips from the other pieces to go around that. Use two colours for the nine squares and match the triangles to one of the colour to create a star-like effect at the corners.

Folding the seam allowances

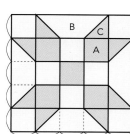

Templates

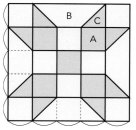

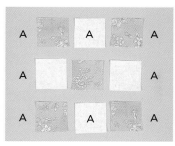

1 Prepare nine pieces A

2 Pin two pieces A right sides together as shown. Sew, making an extra stitch at the start and end of the seam.

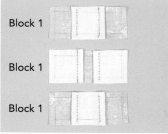

3 Join more pieces A to form three strips. Fold the allowances towards the darker coloured (three blocks 1 complete).

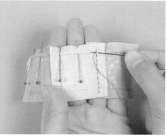

4 Pin two blocks 1 right sides together; sew. Fold the allowances towards the upper and lower blocks (block 2 complete).

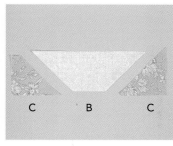

5 Prepare one piece B and two pieces C. Pin a piece C to the piece B right sides together.

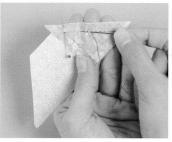

6 Sew along the seam line, making an extra stitch at the start and end of the seam. Join on the other piece C in the same way (block 3 complete).

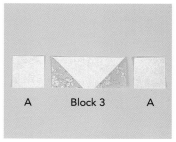

7 Fold the seam allowances of block 3 towards pieces C. Prepare two pieces A.

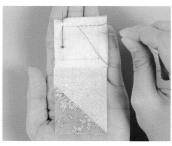

8 Pin block 3 and a piece A right sides together as shown; sew. Join on the other piece A (block 4 complete). Make a second block 4.

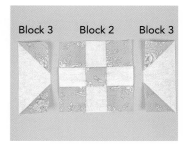

9 Prepare one block 2 and two blocks 3.

10 Pin a block 2 and 3 right sides together, matching seam lines. Sew along the seam line. Fold the allowances towards the centre (blocks 5 complete).

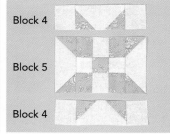

11 Lay out the two blocks 4 and the block 5 to check their positioning.

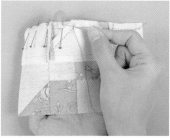

12 Pin a block 4 and 5 right sides together as shown; sew. Join on the other block 4 on the opposite side. Fold the allowances towards block 5.

Cactus Flower

Level ★★✿✿✿

* *

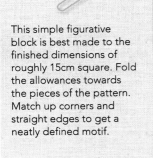

This simple figurative block is best made to the finished dimensions of roughly 15cm square. Fold the allowances towards the pieces of the pattern. Match up corners and straight edges to get a neatly defined motif.

Folding the seam allowances

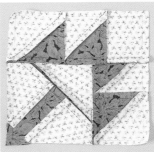

Templates

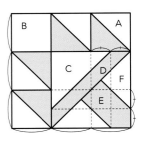

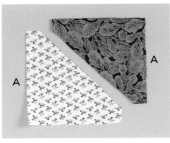

1 Prepare two pieces A.

2 Pin the two pieces A right sides together as shown. Sew, making an extra stitch at the start and end of the seam.

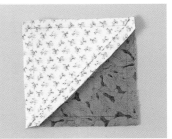

3 Trim the allowance to 6mm, then fold it towards the dark coloured piece (block 1 complete).

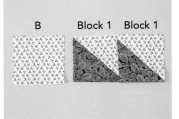

4 Make four blocks 1. Lay out flat two blocks 1 and one piece B to check their positioning.

5 Pin the two blocks 1 right sides together and sew, making an extra stitch at the start and end of the seam (block 2 complete).

6 Pin block 2 and piece B right sides together and sew. Fold the allowances to one side.

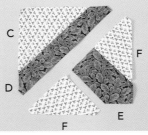

7 Prepare one piece C, D, E and two pieces F.

8 Pin the pieces C and D right sides together as shown and sew. Fold the allowances towards piece D.

9 Pin a piece E and F right sides together as shown. Sew along the seam line. Fold the allowance towards piece E. Join on the other piece F.

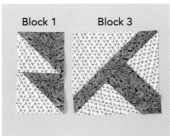

10 Join the blocks made in steps 8 and 9 (block 3 complete). Join two blocks 1, then join them to block 3 (block 4 complete).

11 Bring the strip made in step 6 and block 4 right sides together. Pin, making sure seams match up.

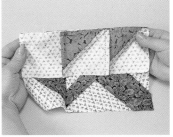

12 Sew along the seam line, making an extra stitch at the start and end, and at the seam junctions.

Cake Stand

* · *

Use a combination of dark and light coloured fabrics to make this design stand out. Make strips and join them to a central block composed of two pieces B. Assemble one piece E at the end of the work. Keep corners sharp and matching up for a neat finish.

Folding the seam allowances

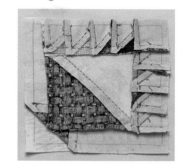

Templates

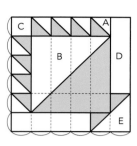

C

Cake Stand

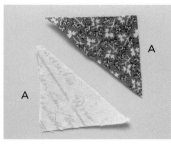

1 Prepare two pieces A. Mark with the seam lines.

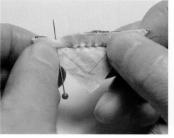

2 Pin the two pieces A right sides together along the longest edge. Sew, making an extra stitch at the start and end of the seam.

3 Trim the seam allowance to 6mm, then fold it towards the darker coloured piece (block 1 complete).

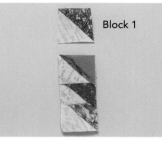

4 Make four blocks 1. Lay them out flat to check their positioning.

5 Pin two blocks 1 right sides together and sew. Join together four blocks 1 (block 2 complete).

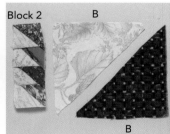

6 Prepare one block 2 and two pieces B. Join the two pieces B right sides together. Fold the allowances towards the dark coloured piece (block 3 complete).

7 Pin blocks 2 and 3 right sides together as shown; sew. Fold the allowances towards piece B (block 4 complete).

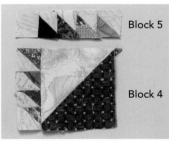

8 Join four blocks 1 and one piece C (block 5 complete). Pin blocks 4 and 5 right sides together; sew. Fold the allowances towards the pieces B (block 6 complete).

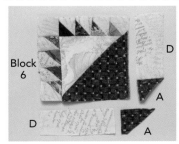

9 Prepare two pieces A and two pieces D. Join the pieces A and D right sides together, folding the allowances towards piece A.

10 Pin block 6 and the blocks made in step 9, right sides together as shown; sew. Fold the allowances towards block A + D.

11 Prepare one piece E.

12 Pin the block made in step 10 and piece E right sides together as shown Sew along the seam line and fold the allowances towards piece E.

California

Level ★ ★ ☆ ☆ ☆

* *

Join together three pieces A, then two pieces B to form a central diagonal strip. Then join A, B and C pieces to form outer diagonal strips. Use darker colours for the pieces A and C to form a cross shape on a lighter background.

Folding the seam allowances

Templates

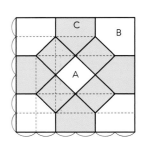

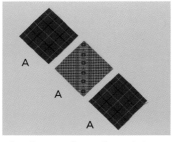

1 Prepare three pieces A. Lay them out flat to check their positioning.

2 Pin two pieces A right sides together. Sew along the seam, making an extra stitch at the start and end.

3 Trim the seam allowance to 6mm, then fold it towards the darker coloured piece.

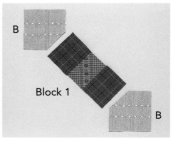

4 Join on the other piece A (block 1 complete). Prepare two pieces B.

5 Pin block 1 and one piece B right sides together as shown. Sew from the start to end. Fold the seam allowance towards block 1. Join on the other piece B (block 2 complete).

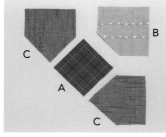

6 Prepare one piece A, one piece B and two pieces C. Lay them out flat to check their positioning.

7 Pin the pieces A and C right sides together as shown; sew. Fold the seam allowances towards piece A. Join on the other piece C (block 3 complete).

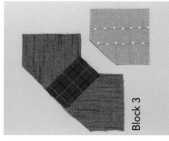

8 Prepare a block 3 and piece B.

9 Pin block 3 and the first edge of piece B right sides together. Sew along the seam line then make an extra stitch. Do not cut the thread.

10 Pin and sew along the second and third edges of piece B. Fold the seam allowances towards block 3 (block 4 complete).

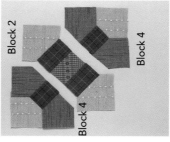

11 Make another block 4.

12 Pin block 2 and a block 4, right sides together. Sew as in steps 9 and 10. Fold the seam allowances towards block 2. Join on the other block 4.

Card Trick

* *

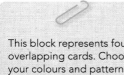

This block represents four overlapping cards. Choose your colours and patterns so each 'card' stands out. Four triangular pieces are assembled to create squares. The key thing when assembling the pieces is to match up the colours correctly.

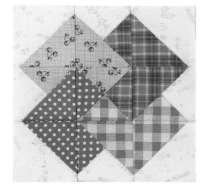

Folding the seam allowances

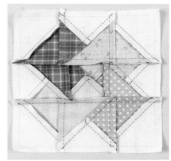

Templates

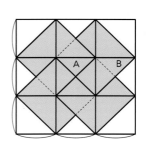

C

Card Trick

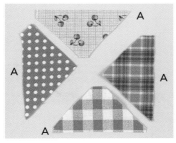

1 Prepare the four pieces A in each of four colours for the 'cards'.

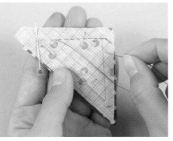

2 Bring two pieces A right sides together, and pin along one seam line. Sew, making an extra stitch at the start and end (block 1 complete).

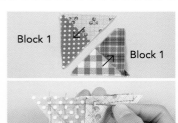

3 Make another block 1 with the two other pieces A. Fold back the seam allowances in alternate directions. Pin the two blocks 1 right sides together along the long edge, then sew (block 2 complete).

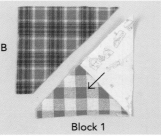

4 Join one block 1 and one piece B. Pin them right sides together along the long edges. Sew, then fold the seam allowances towards piece B (block 3 complete).

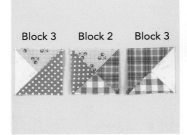

5 Prepare one block 2 and two blocks 3 for the central strip, making sure to match up colours correctly.

6 Pin the blocks right sides together and sew the seams. Sew stitch by stitch through overlapping seam allowances. Fold the seam allowances towards block 2.

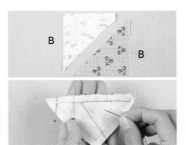

7 Pin two pieces B right sides together along the long edges. Sew the seam (block 4 complete).

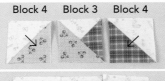
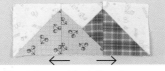

8 Join one block 3 and two blocks 4 to make a strip. Fold the seam allowances towards blocks 4. Make another strip using the appropriate colours.

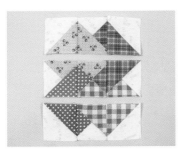

9 Three strips are complete. Lay them out flat to check their positioning.

10 Bring two strips right sides together, then pin, making sure to match up the junction points.

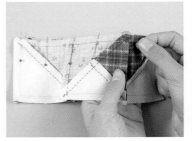

11 Sew along the seam, making extra stitches at the junction points. Sew stitch by stitch through overlapping seam allowances. Fold the allowances towards the centre.

Cat

Level ★★☆☆☆

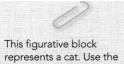

This figurative block represents a cat. Use the same colour fabric for the head, body and legs, and a different fabric in the same colour shade, for the ears and tail. You can use buttons to suggest the cat's eyes, or embroider them on.

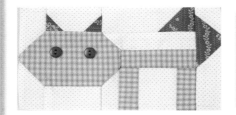

Folding the seam allowances

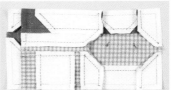

Templates

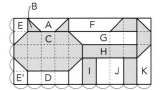

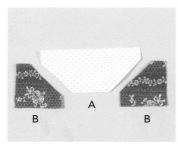

1 Prepare one piece A and two pieces B.

2 Pin the pieces A and B right sides together as shown. Sew along the seam line. Join on the other piece B. Fold the allowances towards pieces B (block 1 complete).

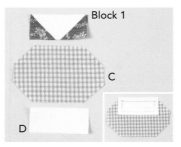

3 Join one block 1, one piece C and one piece D, sewing along the seam lines. Make a extra stitch at the start and end of the seam. Fold the allowances towards piece C (block 2 complete).

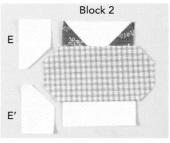

4 Prepare one block 2, one piece E and one piece E'.

5 Bring block 2 and piece E right sides together and pin the first edge. Sew along the seam line, making an extra stitch at the end; do not cut the thread.

6 Pin the second edge. Sew, without stitching into the allowances of piece B. Fold the allowances towards block 2. Join on one piece E'. (block 3 complete).

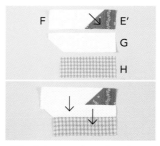

7 Join one piece F and one piece E', then join on one piece G and one piece H. Fold the allowances in the direction of the arrows (block 4 complete).

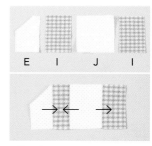

8 Join one piece E, two pieces I and one piece J as shown. Fold the allowances towards piece I (block 5 complete).

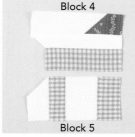

9 Join blocks 4 and 5, sewing along the seam line. Fold the allowances towards block 4 (block 6 complete).

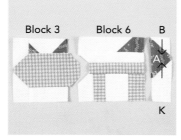

10 Join pieces A, B and K as shown to make the tail section. Lay out the blocks flat to check their positioning.

11 Bring block 6 and block 3 right sides together and pin along the first edge. Sew along the seam line without piercing the allowances.

12 Pin and sew the second edge. Join the other edges in the same way. Join on the tail section.

38

Centenary Festival

✳ · ✳

Join pieces A, B, C and D to make small triangular blocks and join pieces A, B, C and E to form a strip. Join the triangular blocks to either side of the strip to complete this block. Align seam junctions to get a good finish. Sew stitch by stitch through any layers.

Folding the seam allowances

Templates

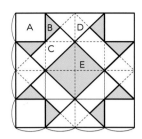

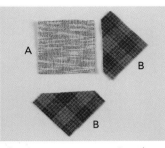

1 Prepare one piece A and two pieces B.

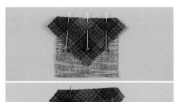

2 Pin pieces A and B right sides together as shown. Sew along the seam line, making an extra stitch at the start and end.

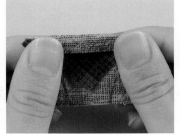

3 Trim the allowance to 6mm, then fold it towards piece B

4 Join on the other piece B in the same way (block 1 complete). Make four blocks 1. Prepare one piece C.

5 Pin one block 1 and piece C right sides together. Sew along the seam line. Fold the allowances towards piece C (block 2 complete).

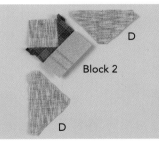

6 Prepare one block 2 and two pieces D.

7 Pin block 2 and one piece D right sides together. Sew along the seam line, working stitch by stitch on overlapping allowances.

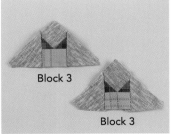

8 Join on the other piece D in the same way (block 3 complete). Fold the allowances towards block 2. Make two blocks 3.

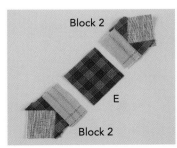

9 Prepare two blocks 2 and one piece E.

10 Join the two blocks 2 and piece E. Fold the allowances towards pieces C (block 4 complete).

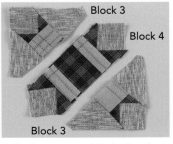

11 Prepare two blocks 3 and one block 4.

12 Pin blocks 3 and 4 right sides together. Sew along the seam line, making an extra stitch at the seam junctions. Fold the allowances towards block 4.

Chevron

Level  ★★★☆☆

This block is made up of several rectangles, all the same size, that are arranged at angles to each other to form a chevron pattern similar to floor tiles. Choose two fabrics for one row of rectangles and a different two fabrics for the second to emphasise the zigzag pattern.

Folding the seam allowances

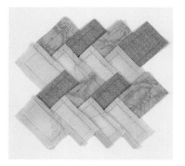

Templates

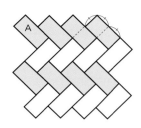

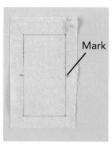

Mark

1 Prepare two pieces A. Mark the centre point of the seam line on both long edges.

Align this corner with the centre mark on othe piece

Sew along short edge

2 Pin two pieces A right sides together as shown, aligning the end of the short edge on one piece with the centre mark on the long side of the other. Sew along the short-edge seam line, making an extra stitch at the start and end.

3 Fold the allowance towards the dark coloured piece (block 1 complete).

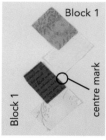

Block 1

Block 1

centre mark

4 Make two blocks 1.

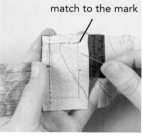

match to the mark

5 Pin the two blocks 1 right sides together as shown, matching the end of the short seam to the centre mark as in step 2; sew.

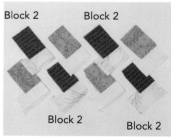

Block 2   Block 2

Block 2   Block 2

6 Fold the allowances towards the upper block (block 2 complete). Make four blocks 2.

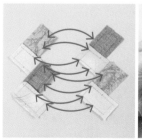

7 Bring two blocks 2 right sides together, then pin along the first edge without piercing the allowances at the corner.

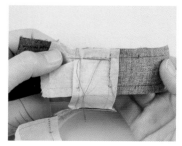

8 Sew along the first edge seam line. Make an extra stitch; do not cut the thread.

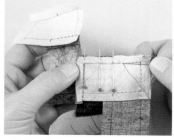

9 Pin the second edge, then sew along the seam line without stitching in the allowances. Make an extra stitch; do not cut the thread.

10 Pin the third edge without piercing the corner allowances. Take out the needle through the corner of the third edge.

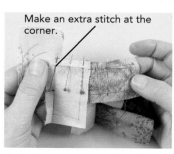

Make an extra stitch at the corner.

11 Continue to sew the edges in the same way. Join the remaining blocks together in the same way.

Cool Fan

Level ★★★☆☆

This block looks similar to the Fan but here that section features triangular pieces A, B and C. The A and B pieces are joined together to form the fan and then the quarter-circle D and outer section E are joined. If you use a light fabric for the B and C pieces the design will stand out.

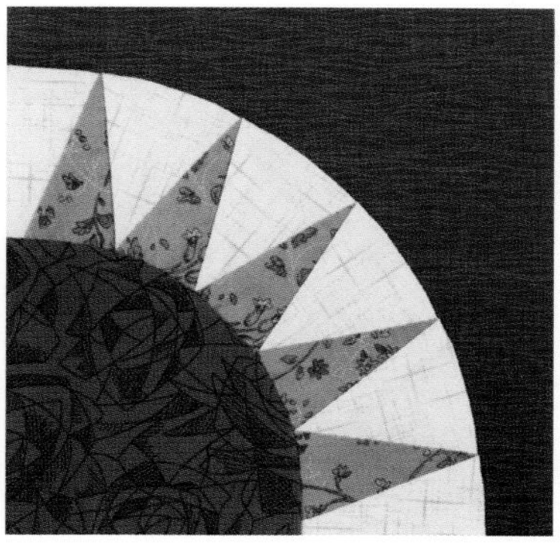

Folding the seam allowances

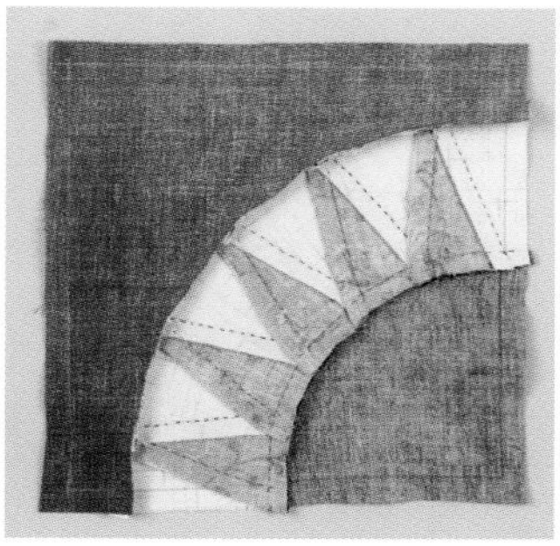

Templates

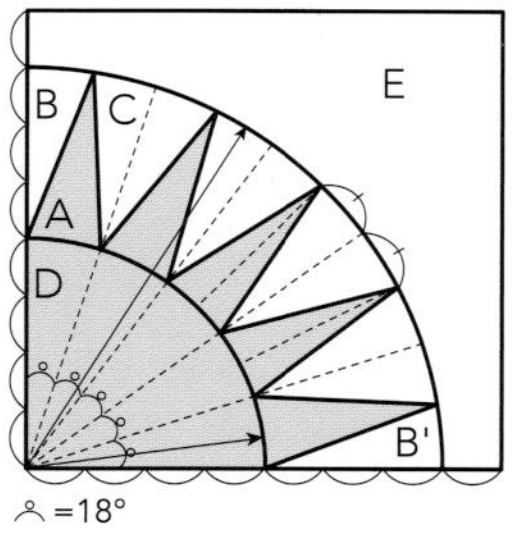

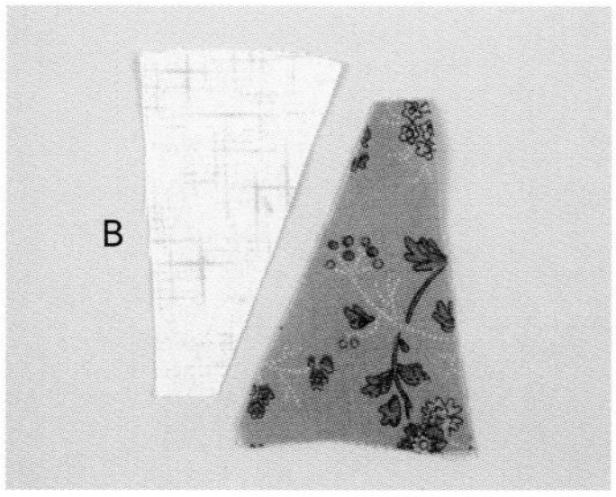

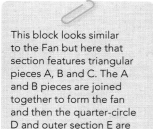

1 Prepare one piece A and one piece B.

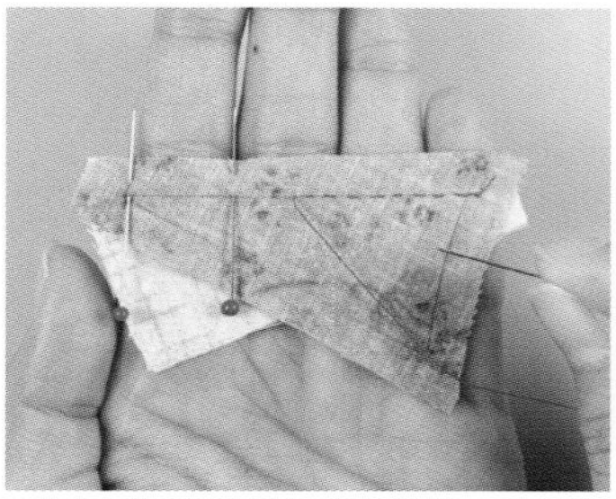

2 Pin pieces A and B right sides together as shown. Sew along the seam line, making an extra stitch at the start and end.

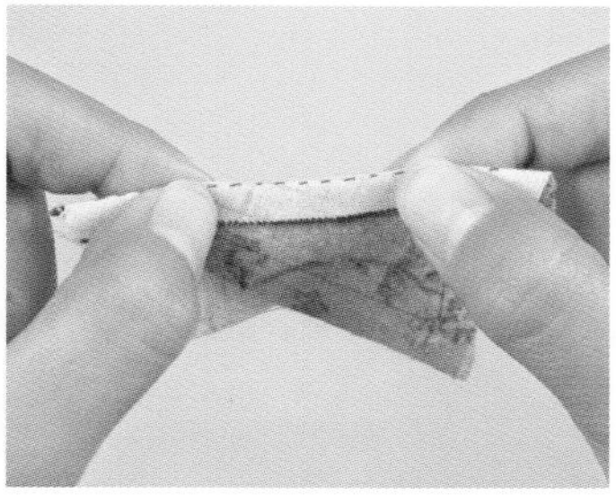

3 Trim the allowance to 6mm, then fold it towards piece A (block 1 complete).

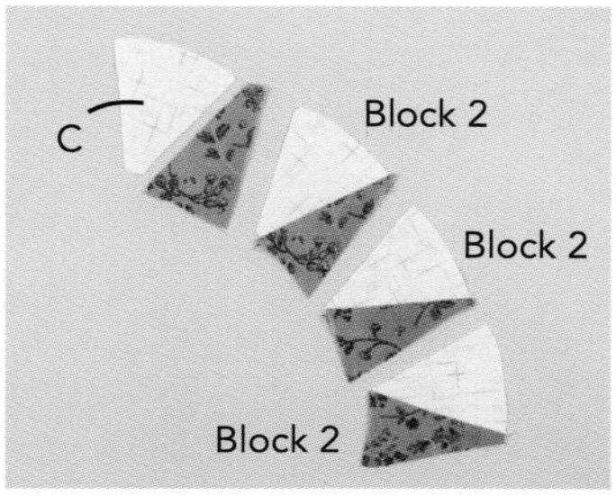

4 Pin one piece A and one piece C right sides together. Sew along the seam line. Fold the allowances towards piece A (block 2 complete). Make four blocks 2.

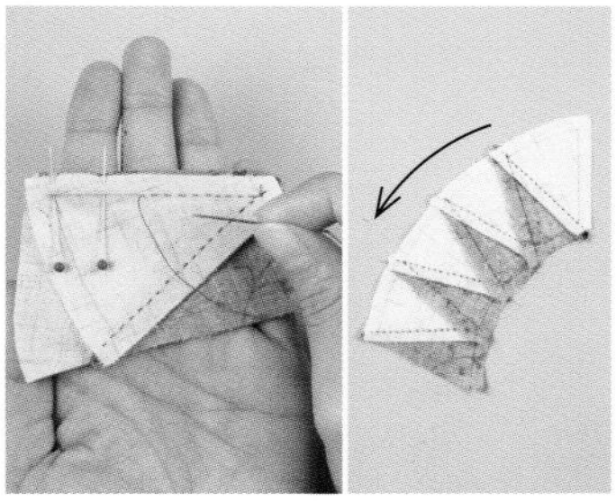

5 Join the blocks 2 together, sewing stitch by stitch on overlapping allowances. Fold the allowances towards the dark pieces (block 3 complete).

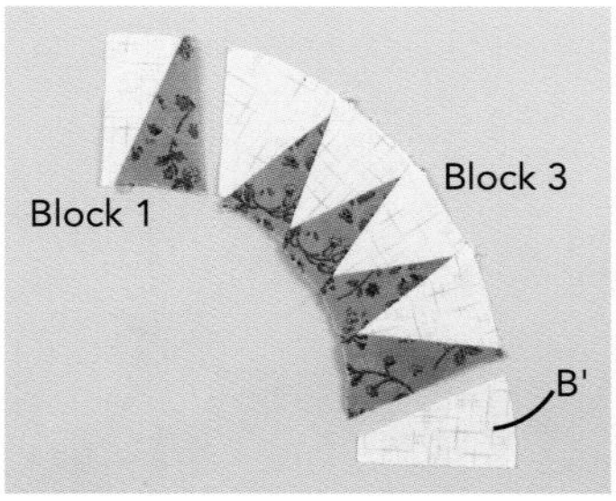

6 Join one block 3, one block 1 and one piece B'. Fold the allowances in one direction (block 4 complete).

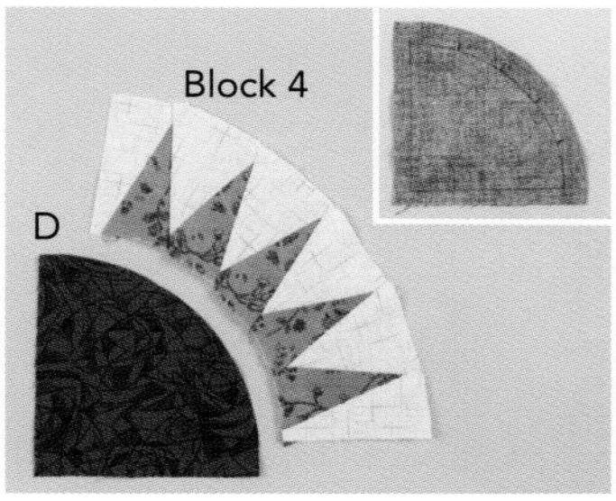

7 Prepare one block 4 and one piece D. Make marks along the curved seam line of D that correspond with the seam junctions of block 1.

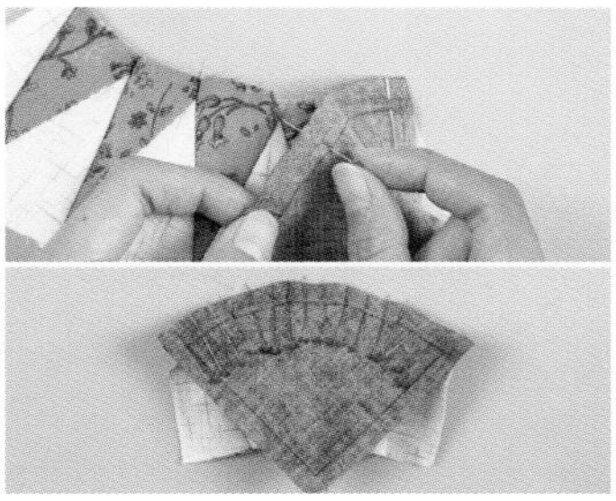

8 Bring block 4 and piece D right sides together and pin, matching up the marks and seam junctions.

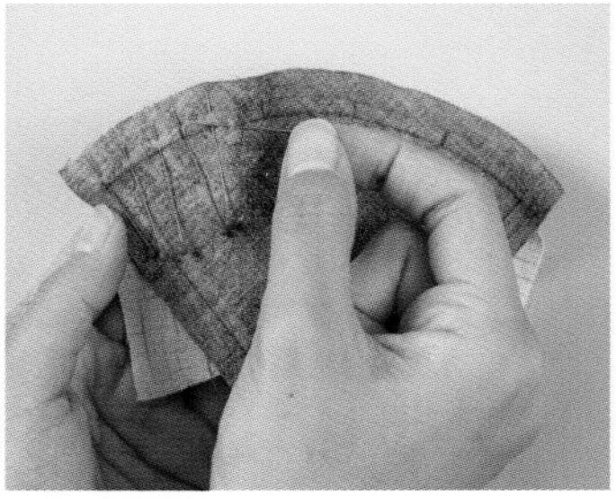

9 Sew along the seam line, working stitch by stitch on overlapping allowances. Fold the allowances towards the dark piece D (block 5 complete).

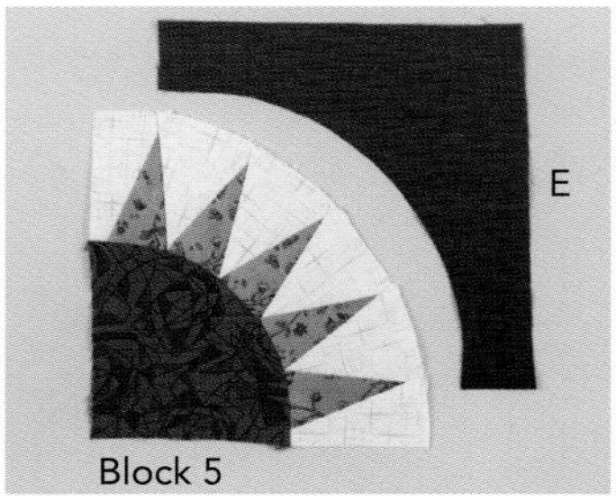

10 Prepare one block 5 and one piece E. Make marks along the curved seam line of E that correspond with the seam junctions of block 1.

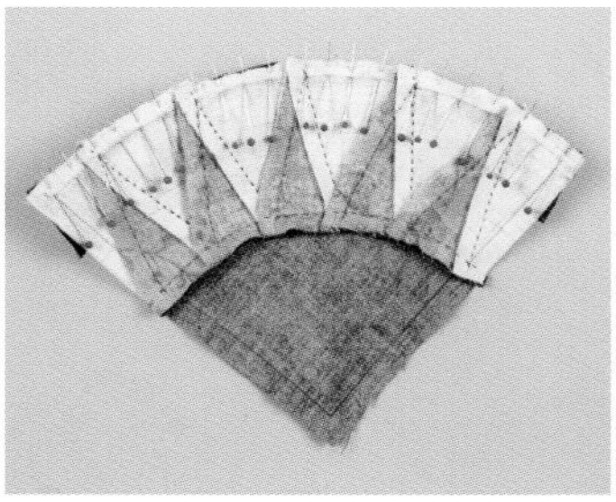

11 Pin block 5 and piece E right sides together, matching up the marks and seam junctions.

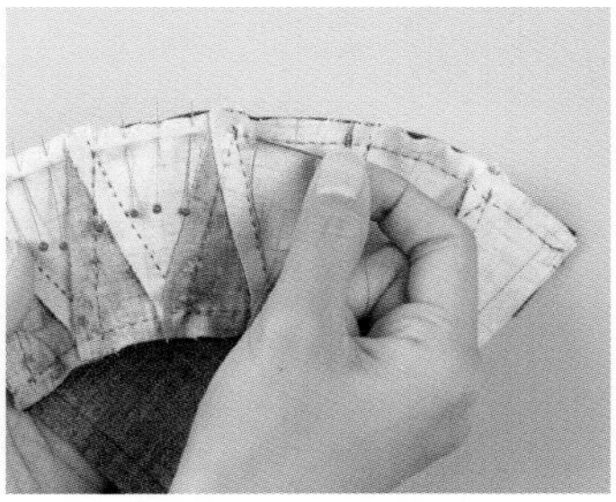

12 Sew along the seam line. Fold the allowances towards block 5.

Charming Puzzle

Level ★★★☆☆

Make the cross-shaped blocks for the corners of this block first then join them with pieces B before sewing the piece C in the centre. When joining on the pieces B and C, sew seams one by one and make extra stitches at corners to avoid gaps forming.

Folding the seam allowances

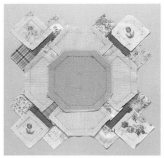

Templates

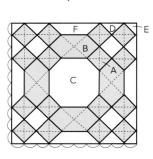

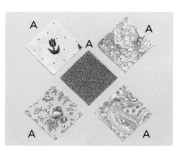

1 Prepare five pieces A.

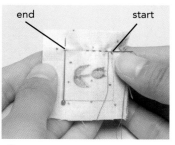

2 Pin two pieces A right sides together as shown. Sew along the seam line, making an extra stitch at the start and end .

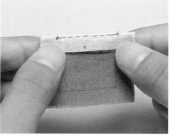

3 Trim the allowance to 6mm, then fold it towards the dark coloured piece.

4 Join on the other pieces A in the same way (block 1 complete).

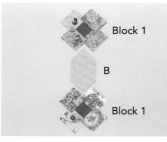

5 Prepare two blocks 1 and one piece B.

6 Bring a block 1 and piece B right sides together and pin along the first edge. Sew, without stitching in the allowances and making an extra stitch at the end.

7 Do not cut the thread. Pin and sew the second edge in the same way. Fold the allowances towards block 1. Join on the other block 1 (block 2 complete).

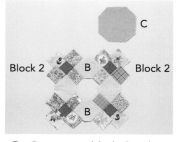

8 Prepare two blocks 2 and two pieces B. Join them in the same way as in steps 6 and 7. Fold the allowances towards the blocks 2 (block 3 complete). Prepare one piece C.

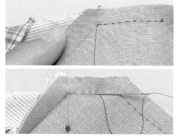

9 Bring the piece C and block 3 right sides together and pin along one edge of C. Sew as in step 6. Join the other edges of C in the same way. Fold the allowances outwards.

*Assembling Several Blocks

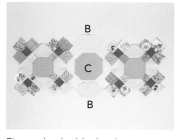

First make the blocks, then use pieces B to join them before finishing with pieces C.

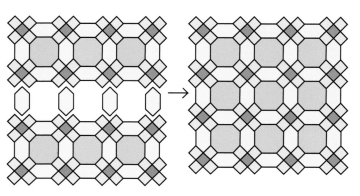

Conifer Tree

✻·✻

Pieces are joined in rows and then combined. As many pieces are cut in symmetry, pay attention to their positioning. Fold seam allowances towards the dark coloured pieces. Combine light and dark fabrics to make the tree, and a light fabric for the background.

Folding the seam allowances

Templates

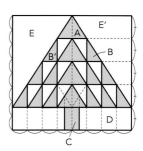

C

Conifer Tree

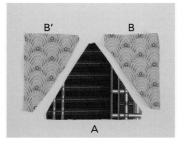

1 Prepare one piece A, one piece B and one piece B'. Lay them out flat to check their positioning.

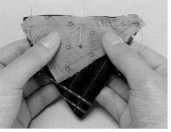

2 Bring pieces A and B right sides together as shown and pin. Sew along the seam.

3 Trim the seam allowance to 6mm, then fold it towards piece B. Join on piece B' in the same way, folding the allowance towards piece B' (block 1 complete). Make three blocks 1.

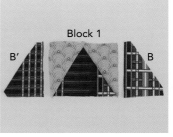

4 Pin block 1 and a piece B and B' right sides together as shown. Sew, then fold the seam allowances towards pieces B and B'. Row 2 is made.

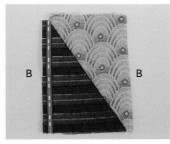

5 Join two pieces B as shown, then fold the seam allowances towards the darker piece (block 2 complete). Join two pieces B' (block 2' complete).

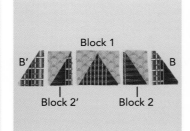

6 Prepare one block 1, one block 2, one block 2', one piece B and one piece B' for row 3. Prepare one block 1, two blocks 2, two blocks 2', one piece B and one piece B' for row 4.

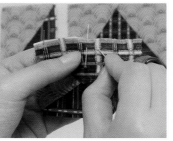

7 Join the pieces for rows 3 and 4, as in step 4. Fold seam allowances towards the darker colour pieces.

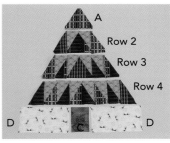

8 Prepare one piece A, one piece C and two pieces D. Lay them out flat with rows 2 to 4 to check their positioning.

9 Pin piece C and a piece D right sides together; sew. Fold the seam allowance towards piece C. Join on the other piece D in the same way

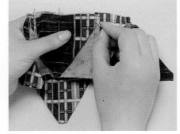

10 Join the piece A to row 2, then join row 3 to the base of row 2, and row 4 to the base of row 3. Join the block made in step 9 to the base of row 4.

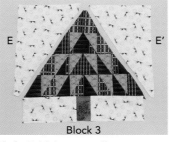

11 Fold the seam allowances towards the darker colours (block 3 complete). Prepare one piece E and one piece E'.

12 Pin piece E and E' to block 3, right sides together and along the long edges; sew. Fold the seam allowances towards block 3.

43

Clamshell

Level ✽ ✽ ✽ ✿ ✿

This block is constructed in a slightly different way: pieces are appliquéd onto a background fabric in rows, working from top to bottom. You need to turn under only the top edge of each piece. Allow pieces to overlap the edges of the background fabric and turn them under when done.

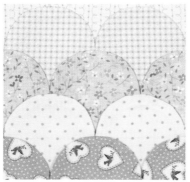

Templates

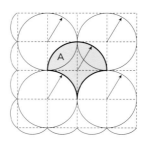

centre point.

Leave a margin.

Leave a margin round the tip of the template to protect it (see page 7).

1 Draw round the template on the wrong side of the fabric, leaving a 7mm seam allowance all round; cut out.

2 Tack around the seam allowance of the top curve. Do not fasten off the thread.

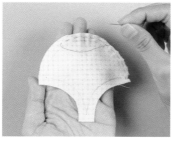

3 Lay the template on the back of the piece, then pull the tacking thread to fold the allowance. Press, then remove the template.

4 Place the template on the right side of the piece as shown, and draw in the seam line. Mark the centre point.

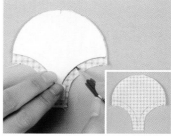

5 Draw a grid of squares on the right side of the background fabric, making two squares the same width as a template. Leave a margin all round the grid.

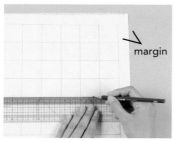

margin

6 Cut out enough pieces to go along the top edge of the background fabric. The pieces of this row do not need preparing as in steps 2 and 3. Make the edges of the piece match up with the grid.

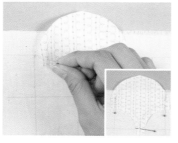

7 Pin the pieces to the background fabric to form the first row. Tack around the seam allowance of the bottom curves of the pieces to hold the pieces in place. Remove the pins.

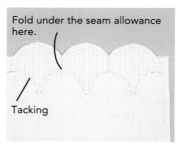

Fold under the seam allowance here.

Tacking

8 Following steps 1 to 4, prepare pieces for the second row. Pin these pieces on top of the first row, so the centre points match the joins between the first row pieces and the top edges overlap the seam allowances. Appliqué in place with slip stitches. Remove the tacking thread.

✽ Assembling A Block

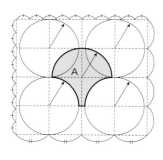

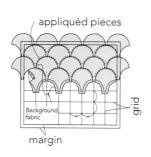

appliquéd pieces

Background fabric

grid

margin

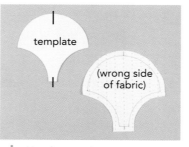

template

(wrong side of fabric)

1 Use the template to cut out enough pieces to cover the background fabric. Prepare each piece following steps 2 to 4.

2 Complete the first row, then pin and sew pieces to the background fabric in rows as in step 8. Where pieces overlap the edges, turn them under and stich in place..

Clover

* *

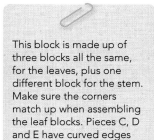

This block is made up of three blocks all the same, for the leaves, plus one different block for the stem. Make sure the corners match up when assembling the leaf blocks. Pieces C, D and E have curved edges so ensure these match up during assembly.

Folding the seam allowances

Templates

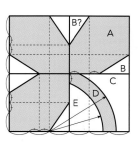

C
Clover

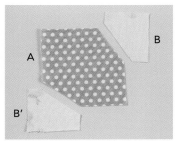

1 Prepare one piece A, one piece B and one piece B'. Lay them out flat to check their positioning.

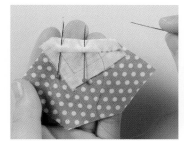

2 Pin the pieces A and B right sides together as shown, then sew along the seam line.

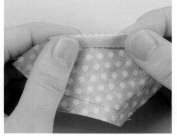

3 Trim the seam allowance to 6mm, then fold it towards piece A. Join on piece B' (block 1 complete). Make two more blocks 1.

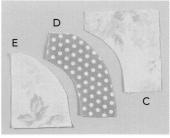

4 Prepare one piece C, one piece D and one piece E. Lay them out flat to check their positioning.

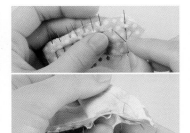

5 Bring piece D and piece C right sides together and pin.

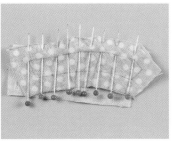

6 Pin closely together so the two pieces don't slip apart as you sew.

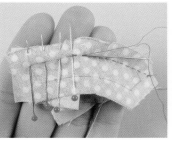

7 Sew along the seam line, making an extra stitch at the start and at the end.

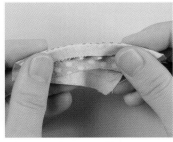

8 Trim the seam allowance to 6mm and fold towards piece D.

9 Join on piece E the same way. Snip into the allowances of piece D and fold them towards piece D (block 2 complete).

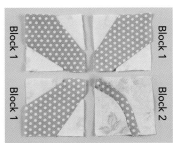

10 Lay out the three blocks 1 and the block 2 flat to check their positioning.

11 Pin the top two blocks 1 right sides together, as shown; sew. Repeat to join the remaining block 1 and block 2.

12 Pin the two strips made in step 11 right sides together. Sew, making extra stitches at the start, end and at the seam junctions.

Clown

Level ★★✿✿✿

✳ ✳

The lozenge-shaped motifs that run across this block are made from several pieces. Once each one is formed, they are joined to each other. Use a different fabric for each lozenge shape, but use the same one for the background shapes (pieces B and B').

Folding the seam allowances

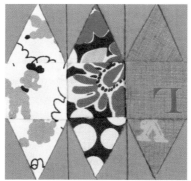

Templates

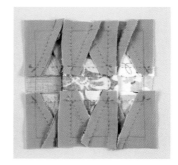

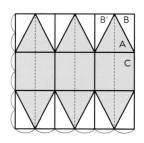

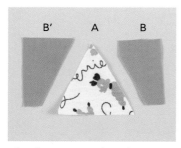

1 Prepare one piece A, one piece B and one piece B'.

2 Pin the pieces A and B right sides together as shown. Sew along the seam line, making an extra stitch at the start and end.

3 Trim the allowance to 6mm, then fold it towards piece A

4 Bring the pieces A and B' right sides together, then pin as in step 2.

5 Sew along the seam line, making an extra stitch at the start and end. Fold the allowances towards piece A (block 1 complete).

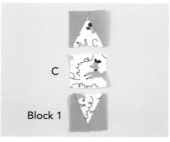

6 Prepare two blocks 1 and one piece C.

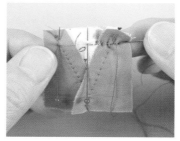

7 Pin one block 1 and piece C right sides together. Sew along the seam line. Join on the other block 1.

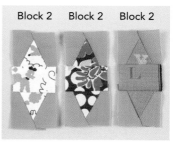

8 Fold back the allowances towards piece C (block 2 complete). Make three blocks 2.

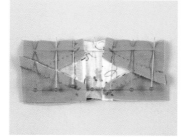

9 Draw a seam line along the length of each block. Pin two blocks 2 right sides together; use a pin to help match up the seam junctions.

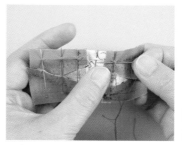

10 Sew along the seam line, making an extra stitch at the seam junctions.

11 Sew stitch by stitch through the overlapping allowances. Fold the seams to one side.

Coffee Cup

❋ ✳ ❋

This figurative block represents a coffee cup and its saucer. The block is composed of straight-edged pieces with the curved shape of the handle appliquéd in place. Choose bold colours for the cup pieces, and set them against a light-coloured fabric background.

Folding the seam allowances

Templates

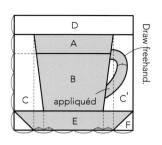

C

Coffee Cup

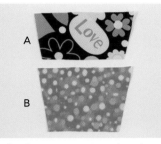

1 Prepare one piece A and one piece B.

2 Pin the pieces A and B right sides together as shown and sew. Fold the allowances towards piece B (block 1 complete).

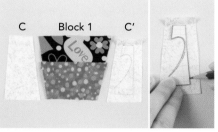

3 Prepare one piece C and one piece C'. As well as drawing in the seam lines, draw the outline of the handle onto the right side of piece C'.

4 Cut out the handle, adding a seam allowance of 3–5mm.

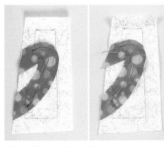

5 Pin the handle onto the right side of piece C' and tack along the centre of the shape.

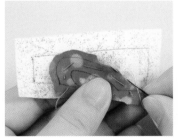

6 Snip into the curved edges. Sew the handle in place, using slip stitch and tucking in the allowance with the tip of the needle as you go.

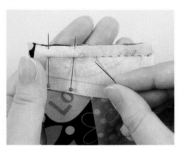

7 Pin block 1 and piece C and C' right sides together; sew.

8 Fold the allowances towards block 1 (block 2 complete).

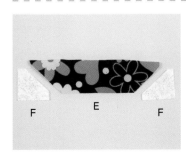

9 Prepare one piece E and two pieces F.

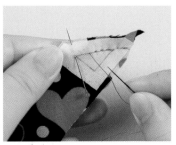

10 Pin the pieces E and F right sides together as shown. Fold the allowances towards piece E (block 3 complete).

11 Prepare one block 2, one block 3 and one piece D.

12 Pin the blocks right sides together, then sew. Join on piece D in the same way.

Colonial Rose

Level ★★★☆☆

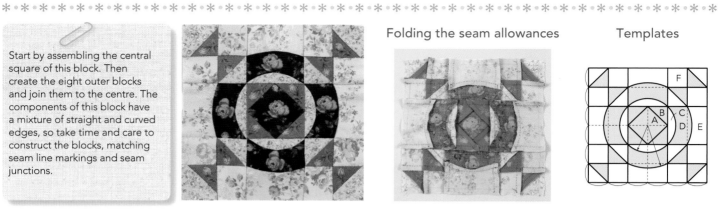

Folding the seam allowances

Templates

Start by assembling the central square of this block. Then create the eight outer blocks and join them to the centre. The components of this block have a mixture of straight and curved edges, so take time and care to construct the blocks, matching seam line markings and seam junctions.

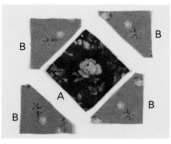

1 Prepare one piece A and 4 pieces B. Lay them out flat to check their positioning. The first step is to join two pieces B on either side of a piece A.

2 Join a piece A and B right sides together, then join on another piece B opposite. Join the other pieces B to the other sides of piece A. Fold the allowances towards piece A.

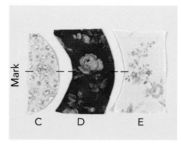

3 Prepare pieces C, D and E and lay them out flat. Mark a central line across the width of each piece.

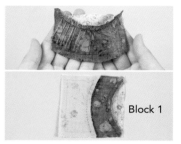

4 Pin and sew the pieces C and D right sides together, matching the centre lines. Add on piece E. Fold back the allowances as shown (block 1 complete). Make four blocks 1.

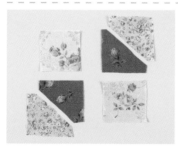

5 Prepare four pieces B and two pieces F. Start by combining the pieces B to make two square blocks.

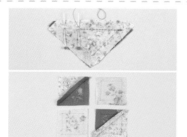

6 Pin and sew two pieces B right sides together as shown. Fold the allowances as shown above.

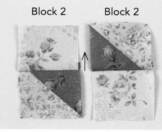

7 Join each block made in step 6 with a piece F. Fold the allowances in the direction of the arrow as shown (block 2 complete).

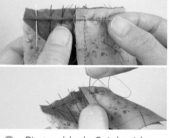

8 Pin two blocks 2 right sides together. Sew stitch by stitch on the overlapping allowances. Fold the allowances outwards (block 3 complete).

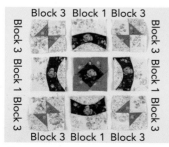

9 Prepare the centre block , four blocks 1 and four blocks 3. Lay them out flat to check their positioning.

10 Pin and sew a block 1 to either side of the centre block to make the central strip. Fold the allowances towards the centre.

11 Join a block 3 to either side of a block 1 to make the top strip. Repeat to make the bottom strip. Fold allowances outwards.

12 Pin and sew the top strip to the central strip, matching up the seam junctions. Repeat to join on the bottom strip.

48

Courthouse Steps

* *

This block is a variation of a log cabin block. There are two ways you can construct the block. The steps here show how strips are joined to a central square and then trimmed to size as you go; but you could cut out the pieces to size before you start and piece in the traditional way.

Folding the seam allowances

Templates

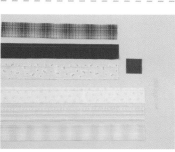

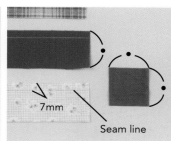

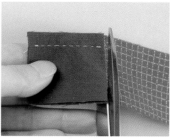

1 Cut out the central square with 7mm seam allowances. Cut out strips of your chosen fabric, the same width as the centre square. Draw the seam line along one edge of each strip.

2 Pin the centre square and one strip right sides together. Sew, making an extra stitch at the start and at the end of the seam.

3 Cut the strip, following the edge of the centre square. Open up the joined pieces.

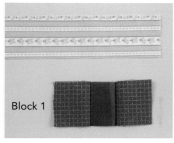

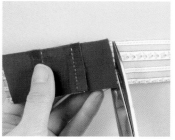

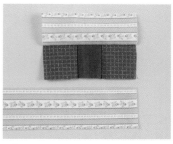

4 Join the rest of the same strip on the other side of the central square in the same way as step 3. Fold the allowances outwards (block 1 complete).

5 Pin block 1 and a second strip right sides together along a long edge; sew. Cut off the excess strip as shown.

6 Open the piece, folding the allowances outward. Join the rest of the strip of the opposite edge in the same way, cutting off the excess.

7 Join another strip on each side of the block from step 6 in the same way. Continue assembling the other strips in the same way.

✳ Variations of the Courthouse steps block

It is possible to enlarge the central square, or to divide it into four triangles.

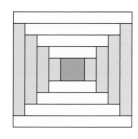

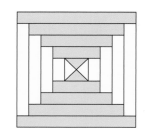

Templates

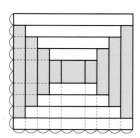

Assembly order

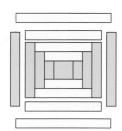

Crocus

Level  ★★★★☆

C

Crocus

Start by making the small block for the top right from pieces A, A' and B. Then combine the pieces with curved edges to form the lower 'petals' of the crocus shape. Make sure seam junctions match up along the centre of the flower motif.

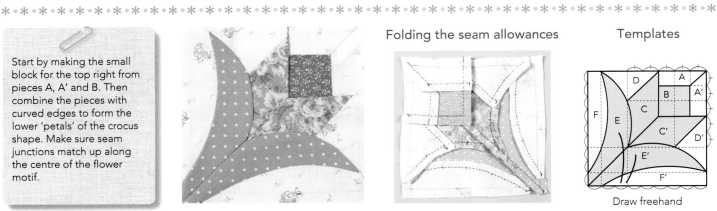

Folding the seam allowances

Templates

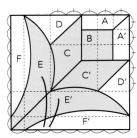

Draw freehand

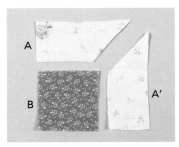

1 Prepare one piece A, one piece A' and one piece B. Lay them out flat to check their positioning.

2 Pin the pieces A and B right sides together, as shown. Sew along the seam line, making an extra stitch at the start and end.

3 Trim the seam allowance to 6mm, then fold it towards piece B.

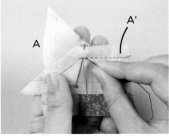

4 Bring pieces A' and B right sides together, then pin the first edge without piercing the edge of piece A; sew.

5 Bring pieces A and A' right sides together, then pin the second edge without piercing the seam allowance of piece B; sew.

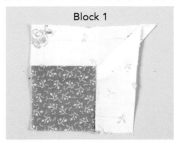

6 Fold the seam allowances towards pieces A' and B (block 1 complete).

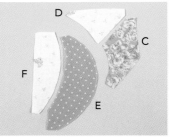

7 Prepare one piece C, one piece D, one piece E and one piece F. Pin pieces C and D right sides together, then sew.

8 Pin pieces E and F right sides together and sew.

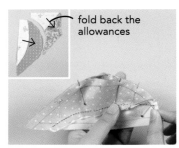

9 Pin the blocks made in steps 7 and 8 right sides together, joining the curved edges, and sew.

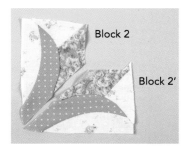

10 Fold the allowances towards piece F (block 2 complete). Using pieces C', D', E' and F' make a symmetrical block (block 2'). Lay them our flat to check their positioning.

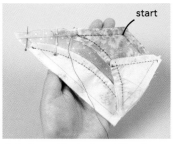

11 Bring blocks 2 and 2' right sides together as shown, then pin. Sew along the seam line.

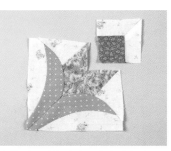

12 Join block 1 and the block from step 11 in the same way as described in steps 4 and 5.

50

Crossroads

* · *

Start by joining pieces A and B to form four cone shapes. Join two of these pieces to a piece C to form a triangle; make four of these triangles, then construct a strip to join them together. Use small stitches as you sew the curves to get neat seams.

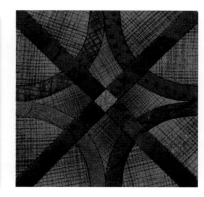

Folding the seam allowances

Templates

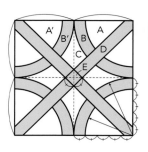

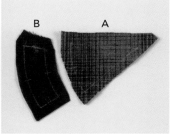

1 Prepare one piece A and one piece B. Mark the marks.

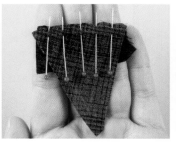

2 Pin pieces A and B right sides together as shown.

3 Sew along the seam line, making an extra stitch at the start and end. Fold the allowance towards piece A (block 1 complete).

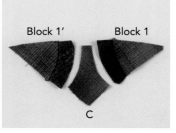

4 Assemble one piece A' and one piece B' in the same way (block 1' complete). Prepare one piece C.

5 Bring block 1 and piece C right sides together, and pin as shown.

6 Sew along the seam line, making an extra stitch at the start and end.

7 Join block 1' to the other side of piece C in the same way (block 2 complete). Make four blocks 2.

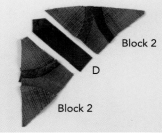

8 Lay out two blocks 2 and one piece D flat to check their positioning.

9 Pin a block 2 and piece D right sides together; sew. Join on the other block 2. Fold back the allowances towards piece D (block 3 complete).

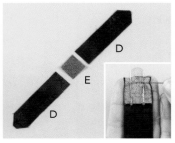

10 Pin two pieces D and one piece E right sides together; sew. Fold the allowances towards piece D (block 4 complete).

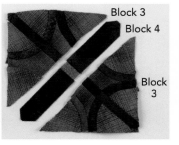

11 Prepare another block 3. Lay it and the block 4 out flat to check their positioning.

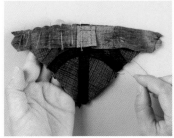

12 Pin a block 3 and 4 together along the long edge; sew. Join on the remaining block 3 in the same way.

Daddy's Joy

Level ★ ★ ☆ ☆ ☆

* • *

This block is made up of four smaller blocks; you need to combine at least four to get the effect of overlapping rings. There are many curved edges so match up any marks and seam junctions and use plenty of pins. Trim the allowances of curved seams to 5mm for a fine finish.

Folding the seam allowances

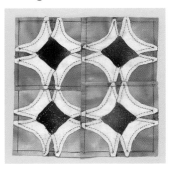

Templates

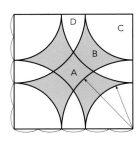

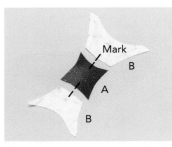

1 Prepare one piece A and two pieces B. Make marks in the centres of the curved edges as shown.

2 Pin a piece A and B right sides together, matching marks. Sew along the seam line. Join on the other piece B.

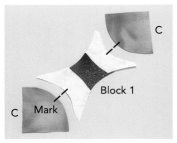

3 Fold the allowances towards piece B (block 1 complete). Prepare two pieces C, marking the curved edges as shown.

4 Pin block 1 and a piece C right sides together, matching marks. Sew along the seam line. Join on the other piece C (block 2 complete).

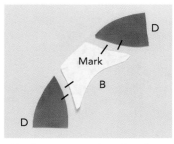

5 Prepare one piece B and two pieces D, marking the edges as shown. Join them, then fold the allowances towards pieces D (block 3 complete).

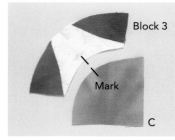

6 Prepare one block 3 and one piece C. Make marks in the centres of the curved edges as shown.

7 Pin block 3 and piece C right sides together, matching the marks. Sew from the end to the centre mark. Pin and sew the other half of the seam.

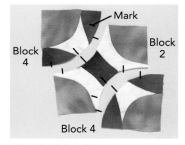

8 Fold the allowances towards piece C (block 4 complete). Prepare one block 2 and two blocks 4. Mark the curved edges as shown.

9 Bring a block 2 and 4 right sides together and pin at the ends of the seams, at the marks and in between.

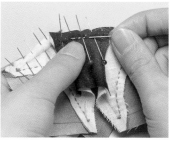

10 Sew along the seam line, making an extra stitch at the seam junctions. Join on the other block 4 (block 5 complete).

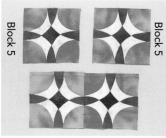

11 Prepare four blocks 5. Assemble them in pairs to get two strips. Fold the allowances in alternate directions. Join them, sewing along the seam line.

Dahlia

* · *

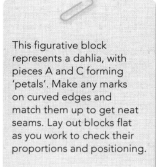

This figurative block represents a dahlia, with pieces A and C forming 'petals'. Make any marks on curved edges and match them up to get neat seams. Lay out blocks flat as you work to check their proportions and positioning.

Folding the seam allowances

Templates

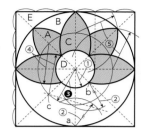

Draw the curves from points a and b to obtain point c.

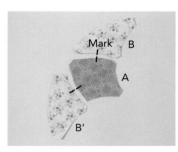

1 Prepare one piece A, one piece B and one piece B'. Mark the curved edges as shown.

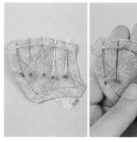

2 Pin the pieces A and B (then B') right sides together as shown. Sew along the seam line making an extra stitch at the start and end (block 1 complete).

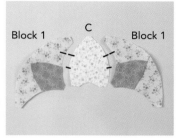

3 Make another block 1. Prepare two blocks 1 and one piece C. Mark the curved edges as shown.

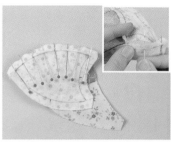

4 Pin block 1 and piece C right sides together as shown, using plenty of pins to keep the pieces secure.

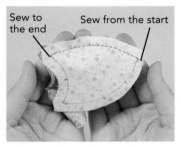

5 Sew along the seam line. Fold the allowances towards piece C. Join on the other block 1 in the same way (block 2 complete). Make two blocks 2.

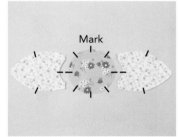

6 Prepare two pieces C and one piece D. Make eight evenly spaced marks around the diameter of piece D. Mark the curved edges on pieces C as shown.

7 Pin the pieces C and D right sides together, matching marks. Sew along the seam line making an extra stitch at the start and end (block 3 complete).

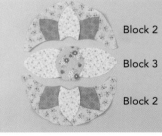

8 Prepare two blocks 2 and one block 3.

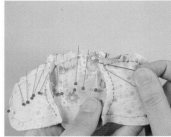

9 Pin blocks 2 and 3 right sides together, without piercing the allowances. Sew from the end to the seam junction, then make an extra stitch.

10 Push the needle into the next piece without piercing the allowances. Continue sewing in the same way, making an extra stitch at the end of the seam.

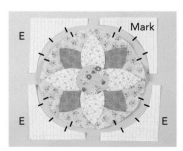

11 The central block is finished. Prepare four pieces E and mark their curved edges and the outer edge of the central block as shown.

12 Pin and sew the pieces E to the block one at a time and matching up marks. Sew along the seam line making an extra stitch at the start and end.

Daisy Chain

* · *

The six pieces A represent the petals of a daisy. One piece A and one piece B are joined to make a small block. All the pieces have curved edges, so transfer any marks and match them up; and use plenty of pins to keep edges neatly aligned. The daisy centre is appliquéd in place.

Folding the seam allowances

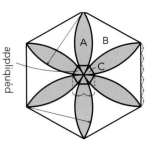

Templates

See page 87 for a hexagonal template.

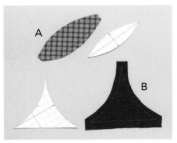

1 Prepare one piece A and one piece B. Mark with seam lines and the guides indicated above.

2 Bring piece A and piece B right sides together.

3 Pin the ends of the seam line and at the mark, then pin from the start of the seam to the mark.

4 Sew along the seam line, making an extra stitch at the start and at the mark.

5 Pin to the other end of the seam line, making an extra stitch at the end.

6 Trim the allowance to 6mm, then fold it towards piece A (block 1 complete).

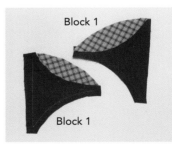

7 Make five blocks 1.

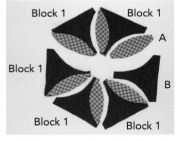

8 Prepare two large blocks: join two blocks 1 and one piece A; join three blocks 1 and one piece B.

9 Bring the blocks as detailed in step 8 right sides together, then pin and sew as in steps 3 to 5.

10 The two large blocks are made.

11 Pin the two blocks from steps 9 and 10 right sides together. Sew to the centre, make an extra stitch, then sew to the end of the seam line.

12 Fold the allowances in a spiral shape. Turn under the edges of piece C and sew to the centre of the block using slip stitches.

D
Daisy Chain

Dandelion

* ✶ * ✶ * ✶ * ✶ * ✶ * ✶ * ✶ * ✶ * ✶ * ✶ * ✶ * ✶ * ✶ * ✶ * ✶ * ✶ * ✶ * ✶ * ✶ *

The stem and base of the dandelion are appliquéd in place. Use the template to cut out the flower base. For the stem, cut out a bias strip twice the width of the template; the seam allowances are half the width of the template. Use the stem template to mark its position on the block.

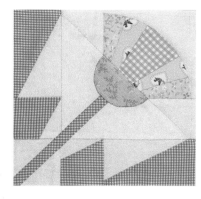

Folding the seam allowances

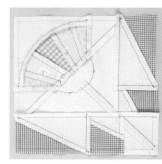

Templates

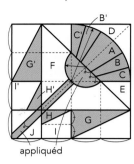

appliquéd

D

Dandelion

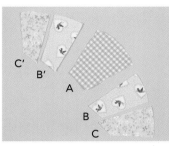

1 Prepare one piece A, one piece B, one piece B', one piece C and one piece C' for the flower.

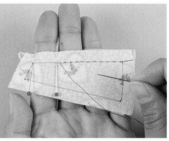

2 Pin and sew the pieces B and C (and B' and C') right sides together. Join these blocks to the either sides of piece A.

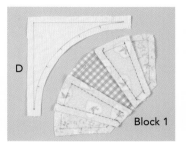

Block 1

3 Fold the allowances towards pieces A, and towards C and C' (block 1 complete). Prepare one block 1 and one piece D. Mark the seam lines.

4 Pin block 1 towards piece D right sides together and sew along the seam line. Fold the allowances towards block 1 (block 2 complete).

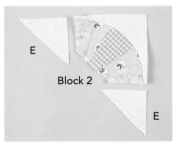

Block 2

5 Prepare one block 2 and two pieces E. Lay them out flat to check their positioning.

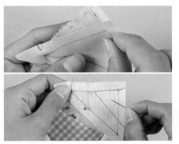

6 Pin block 2 and a piece E right sides together as shown. Sew along the seam line. Join on the other piece E. Fold the allowances towards pieces E (block 3 complete).

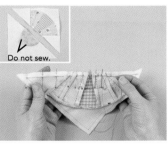

Do not sew.

7 Appliqué the base of the flower towards piece F, leaving a gap at the base for the stem. Join the piece to block 3 (block 4 complete).

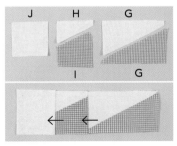

8 Join two pieces G and the pieces H and I. Then join on piece J, as shown. Fold the allowances as shown. Join the pieces G' to I' in the same way (blocks 5 and 5' complete).

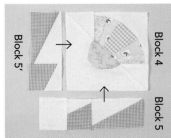

9 Lay the blocks out flat to check their positioning.

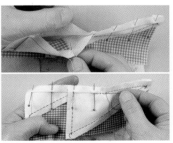

10 Bring the blocks 4 and 5' right sides together and pin. Sew along the seam line.

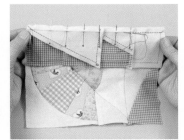

11 Pin block 5 and the block made in step 10 right sides together. Sew along the seam line. Make extra stitches at the seam junctions.

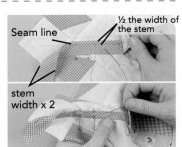

½ the width of the stem

Seam line

stem width x 2

12 Prepare the stem (see above) and pin in position, with one end under the flower base. Turn under the edge and slip stitch in place. Finish the sewing the flower base.

Desert Rose

Level ★★☆☆☆

✳·✳

Six pieces B are assembled around the central hexagonal piece A to get a star. The diamond-shaped pieces C are added around the edge to form a large hexagonal block. Make extra stitches where corners join to avoid any gapping.

Folding the seam allowances

Templates

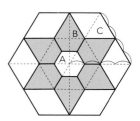

See page 87 for a hexagonal template.

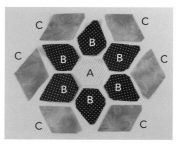

1 Prepare one piece A, six pieces B and six pieces C.

2 Pin a pieces A and B right sides together as shown. Sew along the seam line, making an extra stitch at the start and end.

3 Trim the allowance to 6mm, then fold it towards piece B.

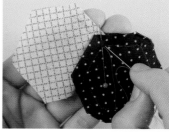

4 Bring the piece B from steps 2 and 3 and another piece B right sides together. Pin the short edge, then sew to the corner without piercing the allowances. Make an extra stitch.

5 Pin the next edge and piece A right sides together, then sew to the corner without piercing the allowances. Fold the allowances in one direction.

6 Join on the other pieces B as in steps 4 and 5. Pin the first edge of the last piece B, then sew to the mark.

7 Pin and sew the second edge of piece A, then sew the third edge, making an extra stitch at the end (block 1 complete).

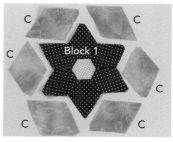

8 Assemble one block 1 and six pieces C.

9 Pin a piece C to one of the points of block 1, right sides together and along the first edge. Sew along the seam line; do not cut the thread.

10 Pin then sew along the second edge. Join on the five other pieces C in the same way. Fold the allowances in one direction.

✳ Assembling Several Blocks

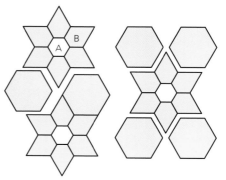

Use hexagonal pieces instead of the diamond-shaped pieces C to join together blocks 1.

Diamond Flower

* *

The pieces A and A' are joined together to form the 'petals' for this block and they are joined to a central square piece B to make the flower. Pieces C and D form the corners and edges. A floral fabric makes a good choice for the 'petal' pieces; choose different fabrics for the centre and edges.

Folding the seam allowances

Templates

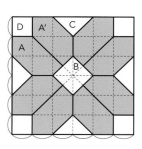

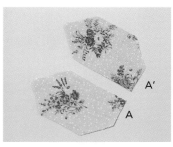

1 Prepare one piece A and one piece A'.

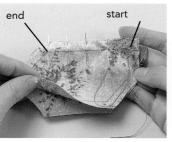

2 Pin the pieces A and A' right sides together as shown. Sew along the seam line making an extra stitch at the start and end.

3 Trim the allowance to 6mm, then fold it towards piece A' (block 1 complete).

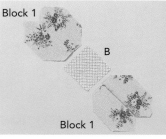

4 Prepare two blocks 1 and one piece B.

5 Pin a block 1 and piece B right sides together. Sew along the seam line making an extra stitch at the start and end.

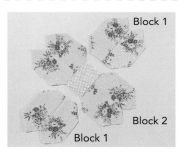

6 Fold the allowances towards towards piece B (block 2 complete). Prepare two more blocks 1 and lay them out flat with block 2 to check their positioning.

7 Pin blocks 1 and 2 right sides together along the first edge without piercing the allowances. Sew along the seam line without stitching in the allowances. Make an extra stitch; do not cut the thread.

8 Pin along the second edge and sew along the seam line, making an extra stitch at the end; do not cut the thread.

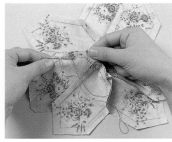

9 Pin and sew the third edge in the same way, making an extra stitch at the end. Fold the allowances in one direction (block 3 complete).

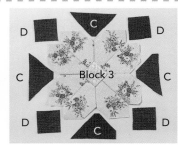

10 Prepare one block 3 , four pieces C and four pieces D and lay them out flat to check their positioning.

11 Pin block 3 and piece C right sides together along the first edge without piercing the allowances. Sew along the seam line, making an extra stitch at the end; do not cut the thread.

12 Pin and sew the second edge in the same way. Join the other pieces C and D to block 3 in the same way.

Diamond Star

Level ★★★☆☆

D

Diamond Star

Join the pieces A and B to form the star shape, then add the piece C to make the central block. Combine D and D' pieces to form the corner sections. Choose four different colours for pieces A to D; pick them with care to get the maximum effect for the star shape.

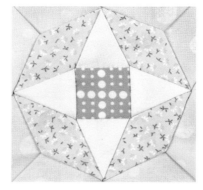

Folding the seam allowances

Templates

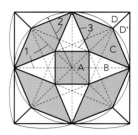

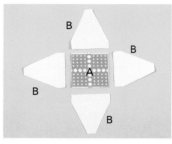

1 Prepare one piece A and four pieces B.

2 Pin a piece A and B right sides together as shown. Sew along the seam line. Fold the allowance towards piece A.

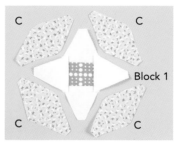

3 Join on the other three pieces B, starting with the piece opposite the first piece B (block 1 complete). Prepare one blocks 1 and four pieces C.

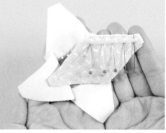

4 Bring the block 1 and a piece C right sides together, then pin along the first edge without piercing the allowances.

5 Sew along the seam line. Make an extra stitch at the end; do not cut the thread.

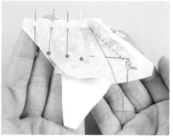

6 Pin the second edge in the same way as the first edge.

7 Sew along the seam line, making an extra stitch at the end.

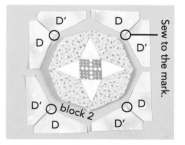

8 Join on the other three pieces C as in steps 4 to 7 (block 2 complete). Prepare four pieces D and four pieces D'.

9 Pin the pieces D and D' right sides together as shown. Sew along the seam line, making an extra stitch at the start and end. Fold the allowances to one side (block 3 complete).

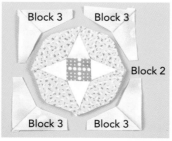

10 Prepare one block 2 and four blocks 3.

11 Pin the first edge of a block 3 to block 2. Sew along the seam line. Make an extra stitch at the end; do not cut the thread.

12 Pin and sew the second edge as in step 6. Join on the other blocks 3 in the same way.

Dianthus

Start by making small blocks from pieces A, B, C, C' and D, then join together with pieces E to form two semi-circles. Join these with pieces F to form the block. The centre piece G is appliquéd in place. Sew only along the seam lines of pieces to make it easier to fold allowances.

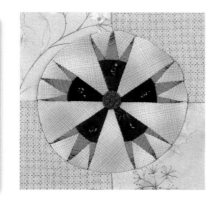

Folding the seam allowances

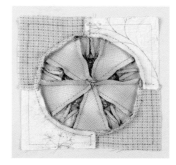

Templates

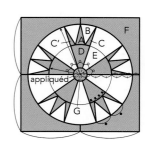

D — Dianthus

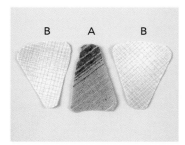

1 Prepare one piece A and two pieces B.

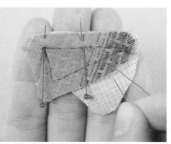

2 Bring piece A and B right sides together, then pin. Sew along the seam line, making an extra stitch at the start and end.

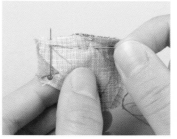

3 Trim the allowance to 6mm, then fold it towards piece A. Join on the other piece B in the same way.

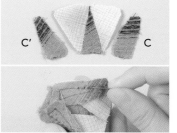

4 Prepare one piece C and one piece C'. Join these to the pieces B, sewing along the seam lines only.

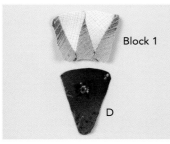

5 Fold the allowances towards pieces C and C' (block 1 complete). Prepare one piece D and mark with the seam line.

6 Pin block 1 and piece D right sides together, then sew along the seam line (block 2 complete).

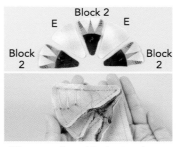

7 Join three blocks 2 and two pieces E to obtain a semi-circle. Join two blocks 2 and three pieces E to make another semi-circle. Fold the allowances towards blocks 2.

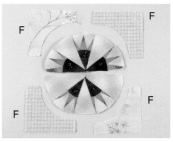

8 Prepare the two semi-circles and four pieces F.

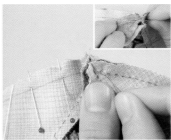

9 Pin the two semi-circles right sides together. Sew along the seam line making an extra stitch at the seam junctions.

10 Join the four pieces F as shown to form a frame.

11 Pin the edge of the circle and the inner edge of the frame right sides together. Sew, using small stitches and making an extra stitch at seam junctions.

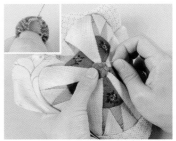

12 Sew around the allowance of piece G. Pull on the thread to fold under the allowance. Appliqué the piece in the centre of the block.

Dog

✳·✳

This block is good for beginners as all pieces are joined along straight edges. For the ground on which the dog stands, choose a brown or green fabric. Here, the ear and tail use a different fabric from the body; the collar uses another. Both the ear and the collar pieces are appliquéd in place.

Folding the seam allowances

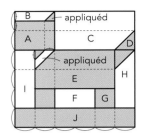

Templates

B appliquéd
A C D
appliquéd
I E H
F G
J

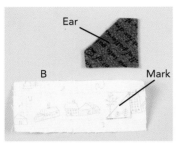

1 Prepare the piece of fabric for the ear and for B. Using the template as a guide, mark the position of the ear on fabric piece B.

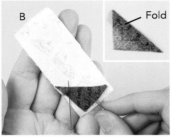

2 Fold the seam allowance along the long edge of the ear piece to the wrong side. Pin it to the marked position and slip stitch in place.

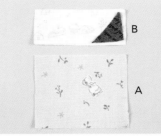

3 Prepare one piece A.

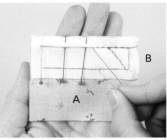

4 Pin pieces A and B right sides together, as shown. Sew along the seam, then press it towards piece A (block 1 complete).

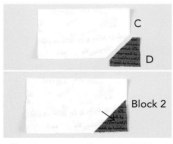

5 Join pieces C and D. Fold the seam allowance towards the darker fabric (block 2 complete).

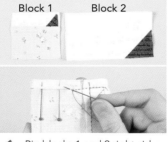

6 Pin blocks 1 and 2 right sides together along the short edges shown. Sew along the seam and fold it towards block 1.

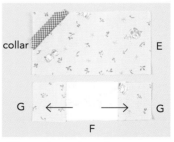

7 Appliqué the collar onto piece E as shown. Join one piece F with two pieces G. Fold the allowances towards piece G (block 3 complete). Join piece E and block 3 (block 4 complete).

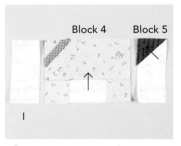

8 Join a piece D and a piece H to form block 5, then join it to block 4 as shown. Join a piece I to the other side of block 4. Fold the seam allowances towards block 4.

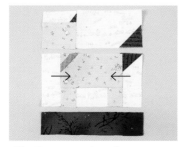

9 Prepare a piece J.

10 Pin the completed strips right sides together.

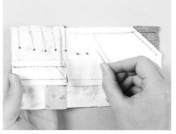

11 Sew, making an extra stitch at the beginning and end of the seam.

12 Sew stitch by stitch through overlapping allowances. Join piece J to the bottom.

Dogwood

* *

A large part of this block is appliquéd in place, but what makes it unusual is that the outer parts of the petals are double layered. These sections are lightly stuffed and left unstitched so as to create a 3D effect. The centre is also appliquéd in place.

Folding the seam allowances

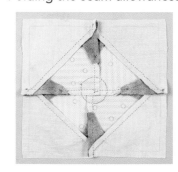

Templates

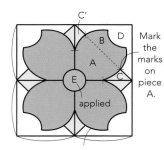

Mark the marks on piece A.

applied

Draw curves freehand.

D
Dogwood

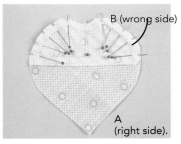

B (wrong side)

A (right side).

1 Prepare one piece A and one piece B. Mark the wrong side of piece A (see template). Pin pieces A and B right sides together, using plenty of pins.

2 Sew along the seam line, making an extra stitch at the start and end.

3 Snip into the allowance on the inward curving section at the top of the petal (block 1 complete).

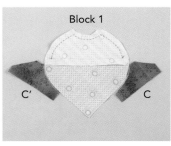

Block 1

C'   C

4 Prepare one block 1, one piece C and one piece C'.

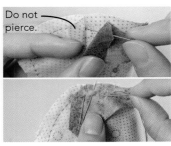

Do not pierce.

5 Pin the pieces A and C right sides together, without piercing the allowance. Sew along the seam line. Fold the allowances towards block 1. Join on C' (block 2 complete).

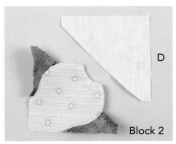

D

Block 2

6 Turn piece B to the right side to form the petal shape. Prepare one piece D.

Allowance of piece B

7 Pin block 2 and piece D right sides together. Sew along the seam line. Trim the allowances and fold them towards block 2 (block 3 complete).

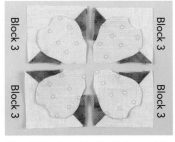

Block 3   Block 3

Block 3   Block 3

8 Make four blocks 3. Assemble them in pairs to get two strips.

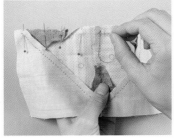

9 Pin the two strips right sides together. Sew along the seam line, making an extra stitch at the seam junctions.

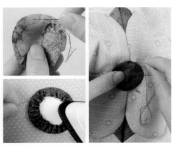

10 Prepare a piece E. Tack around the seam allowance. Pull the thread to fold under the allowance. Appliqué the piece to the centre of the block.

11 Turn the block to the wrong side and pad the tips of the petals with a little stuffing.

* Embroidery

It is possible to secure the tips of the petals to the background by using an embroidery stitch such as blanket stitch.

Dolly's Pleasure

* · *

Choose a bright colour for the centre of this block and contrasting colours for the shapes around it to represent the star. Match up corners carefully and make extra stitches at the seam junctions to avoid any mismatch.

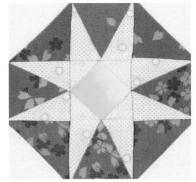

Folding the seam allowances

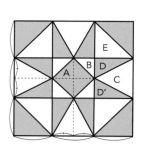

Templates

1 Transfer the templates to the wrong side of your fabrics. Add 7mm seam allowances, and cut out.

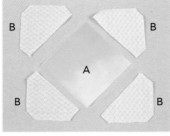

2 Prepare one piece A and four pieces B.

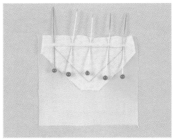

3 Pin pieces A and B right sides together as shown.

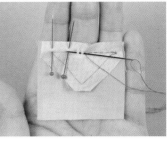

4 Sew along the seam line, making an extra stitch at the start and end.

5 Trim the allowance to 6mm, then fold it towards piece A. Join on the other pieces B in the same way (block 1 complete).

6 Fold the allowances towards piece A.

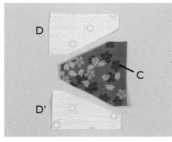

7 Prepare one piece C, one piece D and one piece D'.

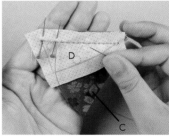

8 Join piece C towards piece D. Join on the piece D' (block 2 complete). Make four blocks 2.

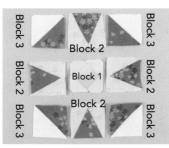

9 Join two pieces E (block 3 complete). Make four blocks 3. Lay out the blocks 1 to 3 flat to check their positioning.

10 Join the blocks in the rows shown in step 9 so you have three strips.

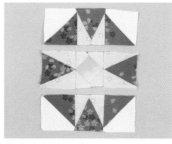

11 Fold the allowances towards the blocks 2.

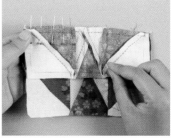

12 Pin the top and centre strips right sides together. Sew along the seam line, then fold the allowances towards the central strip. Join on the bottom strip.

Double Sawtooth

✻ ∙ ✻

The pieces that combine to form the outer edges of this block are joined first. They are then sewn around the central piece B. Try to be accurate when joining the triangular pieces so as to achieve the perfect zigzag pattern on the outer strips.

Folding the seam allowances

Templates

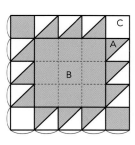

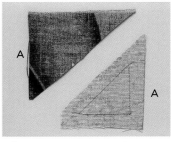

1 Prepare two pieces A.

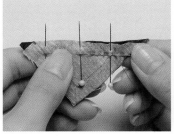

2 Pin the two pieces A right sides together as shown. Sew along the seam line, making an extra stitch at the start and end.

3 Trim the allowance to 6mm, then fold it towards the dark coloured piece (block 1 complete).

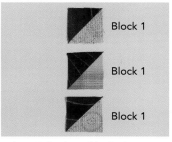

4 Make three blocks 1.

5 Pin two blocks 1 right sides together. Sew along the seam line. Fold the allowances towards the dark colour piece. Join on the other block 1 (block 2 complete).

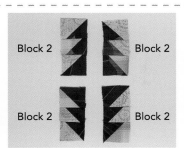

6 Make four blocks 2. Lay them out in symmetrical pairs to check their positioning.

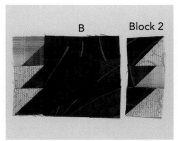

7 Pin a block 2 and piece B right sides together, then sew along the seam line. Join on the other block 2 (Block 3 complete).

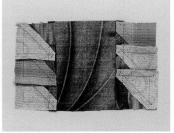

8 Fold the allowances towards piece B as shown.

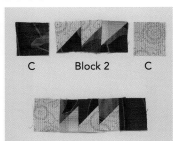

9 Pin one piece C and a block 2 right sides together. Sew along the seam line. Join on another piece C (block 4 complete).

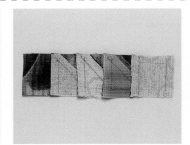

10 Fold the allowances towards darker coloured pieces as shown.

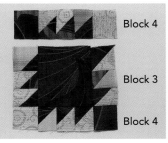

11 Lay out one block 3 and two blocks 4 flat to check their positioning.

12 Pin a block 3 and 4 right sides together. Sew, making an extra stitch at the seam junctions. Sew stitch by stitch on overlapping allowances. Join on the other block 4.

Double Wedding Ring

Level ★★★★☆

D

The small pieces A, B and B' are joined into a strip, as are pieces A, B, B', C and C'. The curved strips are joined together with pieces D to make eye-like shapes; these are then joined with a piece E. Cut out pieces accurately and match up any marks to ensure the finished block has neat seams.

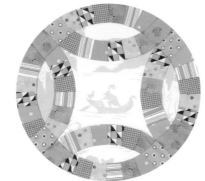

Folding the seam allowances

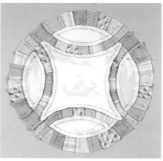

Templates

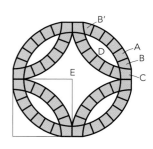

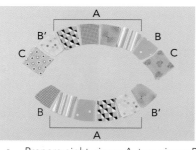

1 Prepare eight pieces A, two pieces B, two pieces B', two pieces C, one piece D and one piece E for one small block. Mark seam lines on pieces D and E. Lay out the pieces flat to check their positioning.

① Draw a square with sides the same width as the radius of the circle. Place the tip of a compass on points B then C, and draw the curves as shown.

② Divide up the curved sections as shown.

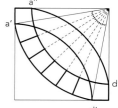

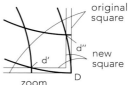

original square

new square

zoom

2 Pin two pieces A right sides together. Sew along the seam line, making an extra stitch at the start and end. Join on two pieces B and two pieces B' at either end.

Sew along the seam line

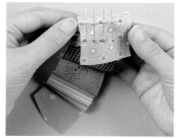

3 Join on a piece C at either end in the same way. Make another strip the same way, but omitting the pieces C.

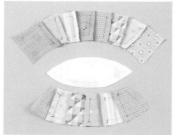

4 Two curved strips have been made. Fold the allowances in one direction, alternating the direction between the two strips.

5 Pin the short strip and piece D right sides together up to the centre of the curved edge; sew. Pin and sew the rest of the curved edge of D.

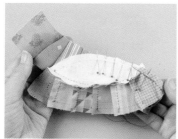

6 Pin the block from step 5 and the long strip right sides together. Sew as in step 5, making an extra stitch at the junctions.

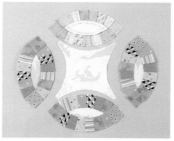

7 Fold the allowances towards the strips. Prepare four identical small blocks and one piece E.

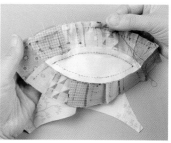

8 Join a block and piece E right sides together as in step 5. Join on the remaining blocks in the same way.

Grape Bunches

* *

The curved strips of this block are cut in one piece. The fewer pieces make this easier than the previous block. Match up seam lines and marks on curves, and sew the curved edges with small stitches for a neat finish. Make four small blocks, then join them to a piece D.

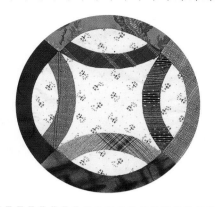

Folding the seam allowances

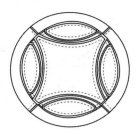

Templates

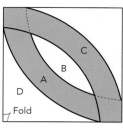

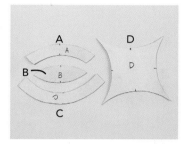

1 Prepare the templates and mark the centre point on each curved edge. Use to cut out fabric pieces, transferring the marks.

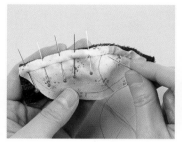

2 Pin the pieces A and B right sides together as shown. Sew along the seam line making an extra stitch at the start and end.

3 Snip into the allowances up to 3mm from the stitching, then fold them towards piece A (block 1 complete).

4 Pin block 1 and piece C right sides together, then sew as in step 2. Snip into the allowances and fold them towards piece C (block 2 complete).

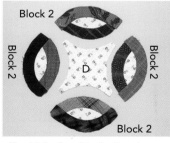

5 Make four blocks 2 and prepare one piece D.

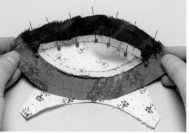

6 Bring a block 2 and piece D right sides together and pin, matching marks and seam lines; sew. Fold the allowances towards block 2. Join on the other blocks 2 in the same way.

✱ Alternative option for seam allowances

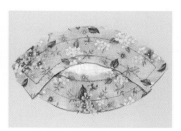

Fold the allowances towards piece B without notching the allowances.

✱ Adding a piece at the crossing points

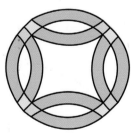

It is possible to add in small pieces to at the crossing points between pieces A and C.

✱ Assembling more blocks

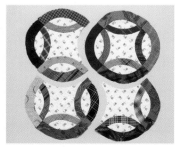

Make several small blocks, then assemble them as shown above.

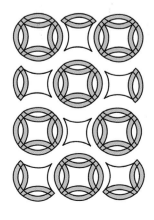

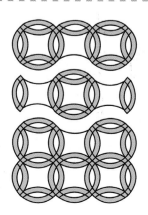

It is possible to combine pieces in a variety of ways over several rows.

Dresden Basket

* *

Make this block in two parts: assemble the pieces for the 'basket' in a triangular block; join the pieces for the 'handle' into a second triangle. Join the two triangles. Match up corners and seam junctions for a neat and accurate finish.

Folding the seam allowances

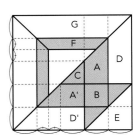

Templates

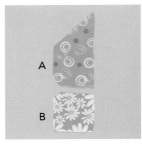

1 Prepare one piece A and one piece B.

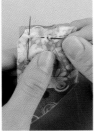

2 Pin the pieces A and B right sides together as shown. Sew along the seam line, making an extra stitch at the start and end. Fold the allowances towards piece B.

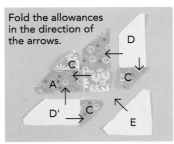

Fold the allowances in the direction of the arrows.

3 Join pieces A' and C, C and D and C and D'. Join these with the A and B block (block 1 complete). Prepare one piece E.

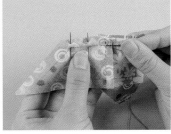

4 Pin block 1 and piece E right sides together. Sew, making an extra stitch at the seam junctions (block 2 complete).

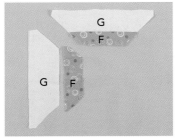

5 Join one piece F and one piece G, then fold the allowances towards piece F (block 3 complete). Make another block 3.

6 Pin the two blocks 3 right sides together as shown. Sew along the seam line, making an extra stitch at the start and end (block 4 complete).

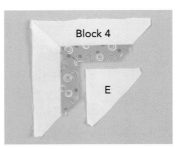

7 Fold the allowances to one side. Prepare one piece E.

8 Bring the block 4 and piece E right sides together, and pin along the first edge without piercing the allowances. Sew along the seam line to the corner of piece E.

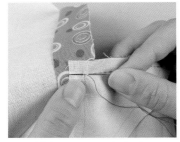

9 Make an extra stitch; do not cut the thread. Pin the second edge without piercing the allowances.

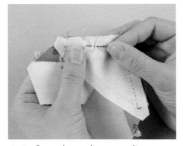

10 Sew along the seam line, making an extra stitch at the end. Fold the allowances towards block 4 (block 5 complete).

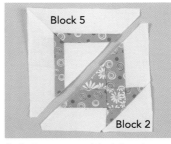

11 Prepare one block 2 and one block 5.

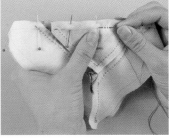

12 Bring blocks 2 and 5 right sides together and pin along the long edges. Sew, working stitch by stitch on the overlapping allowances.

Dresden Plate

✳ ✳

This block has two versions: the tips of the 'petals' are either curved or pointed. Join together the 'petals' (pieces A) in a ring and sew this to the background fabric, before appliquéing on the central piece. The background fabric is cut away behind the flower shape so the block touches any padding when you quilt it.

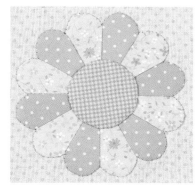

Folding the seam allowances

Templates

Curved petals

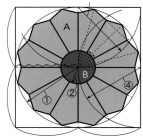

appliquéd

Pointed petals

The number of pieces A and the size of piece B vary depending on the design.

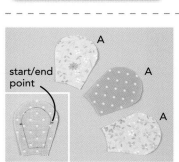

start/end point

1 Prepare three pieces A. Mark with seam lines and the start and end points of the straight seams as shown.

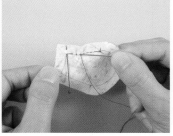

2 Pin two pieces A right sides together. Sew along the straight side seam line making an extra stitch at the start and end.

3 Trim the allowance to 6mm, then fold it towards the left.

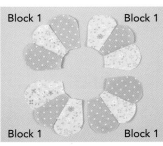

4 Join on the other piece A in the same way (block 1 complete). Make three more blocks 1. Join them in pairs, then join these together to form a ring.

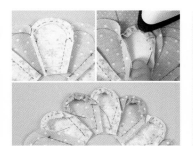

5 Stitch around the seam allowance of each curved edge. Place the template on each piece and pull on the thread to draw up the allowances and turn them under; press.

6 Pin the ring of blocks to the background fabric and sew in place using slip stitches and a matching colour of thread.

7 Prepare a piece B. Sew around the seam allowance Put the template on the wrong side and pull the thread to turn under the allowance. Press and remove the template.

8 Pin piece B to the centre of the ring. Sew in place with slip stitches. Do not stitch into the background fabric.

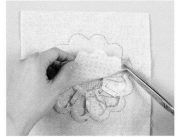

9 Turn the block over and cut away the background fabric behind the flower shape, leaving a 6mm allowance.

✳ Pointed Petals

Join the pieces A as in steps 1 to 4 (you can make two semi-circles instead of a ring). Turn under the pointed edges and press.

Pin the block to the back-ground fabric, then appliqué in place with slip stitches.

Daisy Path

Level ★★☆☆☆

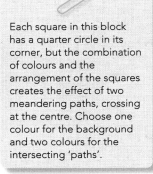

Each square in this block has a quarter circle in its corner, but the combination of colours and the arrangement of the squares creates the effect of two meandering paths, crossing at the centre. Choose one colour for the background and two colours for the intersecting 'paths'.

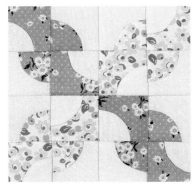

Folding the seam allowances

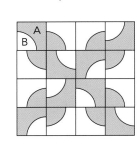

Templates

A
B

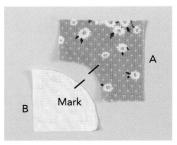

1 Prepare one piece A and one piece B. Mark the centre point on the curved edges of each piece.

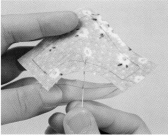

2 Bring the pieces A and B right sides together, using a pin to help you match the centre points.

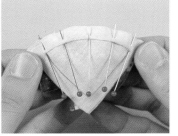

3 Pin at the centre point, at either end of the seam and in between.

4 Sew along the seam line, using small stitches and making an extra stitch at the start and end. Fold the allowances towards piece B (block 1 complete).

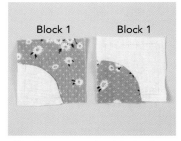

5 Prepare another block 1 but reversing the colours.

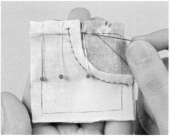

6 Pin the two blocks 1 right sides together. Sew along the seam line (block 2 complete). Make two blocks 2.

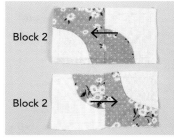

7 Pin the two blocks 2 right sides together. Sew point along the seam line, making an extra stitch at the junctions. Fold the allowances in the direction of the arrows (block 3 complete).

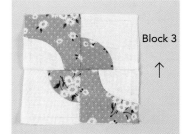

8 Fold the allowances to one side. Make one more block 3 in the same colour way; make two blocks three in a different colour way.

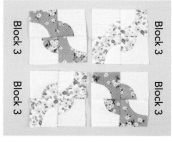

9 Lay out the four blocks 3 flat to check their positioning.

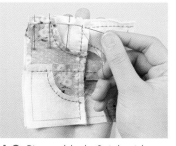

10 Pin two blocks 3 right sides together. Sew as in step 7. Join the other two blocks 3. Fold the allowances in opposite directions.

11 Pin the two pieces right sides together. Sew along the seam line making an extra stitch at the seam junctions.

68

Dutch Windmill

✳ ✳

Start by joining pieces A, B, C and D to form a square, then assemble the strips composed of pieces E, F, F' and G. Choose strong colours for the fabric pieces B, F and F' to represent the sails of the windmill.

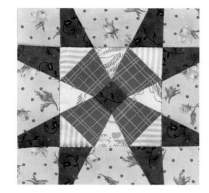

Folding the seam allowances

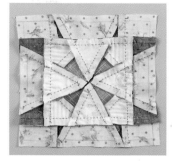

Templates

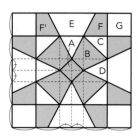

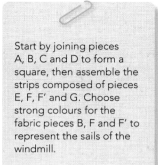

1 Prepare one piece A and one piece B.

2 Pin the pieces A and B right sides together, as shown. Sew along the seam line, making an extra stitch at the start and end of the seam.

3 Trim the seam allowance to 6mm, then fold it towards piece A.

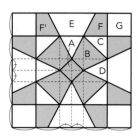

4 Join another piece B to the opposite edge of piece A (block 1 complete). Fold the seam allowance towards piece A. Prepare two pieces C.

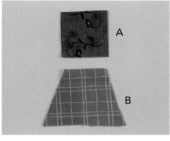

5 Pin block 1 and one piece C right sides together. Sew along the seam line. Fold the seam allowance towards piece B. Join on the other piece C (block 2 complete).

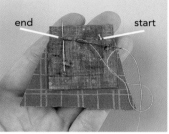

6 Pin a piece B and and a piece C right sides together, then sew. Fold the seam allowance towards piece B. Join on two pieces D (block 3 complete). Make two blocks 3.

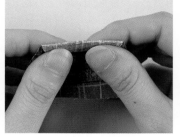

7 Lay one block 2 and two blocks 3 out flat to check their positioning.

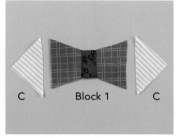

8 Pin the first straight edges of block 2 and a block 3 right sides together, then sew along the seam line. Pin and sew the second edge. Do not sew into the allowances of pieces A and B. Fold the allowances towards block 2. Join on the other block 3 (block 4 complete).

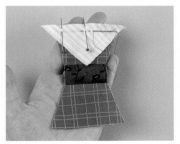

9 Prepare one piece E, one piece F, one piece F' and two pieces G. Join the pieces together as shown above to form a strip. Fold the allowances towards pieces F and F'. Make another strip the same way.

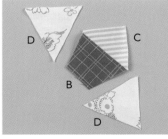

10 Make two short strips composed of one piece E, one piece F and one piece F'. Place the strips from around block 4.

11 Pin the block 4 and a short strip right sides together, matching up the junction points. Sew the seam. Fold the allowances towards the strip. Join on the other short strip.

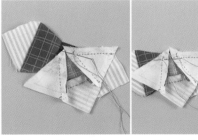

12 Pin block 4 and one long strip right sides together, matching up the junction points. Sew the seam. Fold the allowances towards the strip. Join on the other long strip.

Eight Petals

Join pieces A, B, C and D to form a small block. Then make three more blocks and join all four to make the final block. Match up any marks to sew the curved edges correctly and avoid any gapping. Choose two different colours for pieces A and B to represent overlapping petals.

Folding the seam allowances

Templates

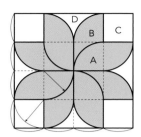

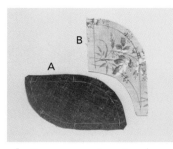

1 Prepare one piece A and one piece B. Mark the length of the adjacent seam line of piece B on the edge of A as shown.

2 Bring piece A and piece B, right sides together as shown, then pin along the seam to the mark.

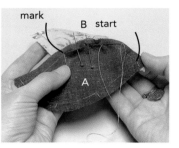

3 Sew along the seam, making an extra stitch at the start and at the mark.

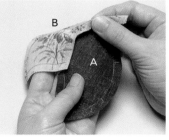

4 Trim the seam allowance to 6mm, then fold it towards piece A.

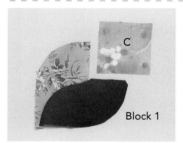

5 Turn the pieces to the right side (block 1 complete). Prepare piece C.

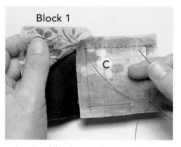

6 Pin block 1 and piece C right sides together along the first edge as shown. Sew without stitching in the seam allowance of piece B. Make an extra stitch.

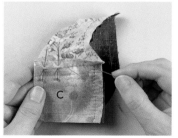

7 Do not cut off the thread. Pin along the second edge, then sew along the seam (block 2 complete).

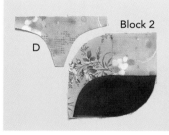

8 Fold the seam allowances in one direction. Prepare a piece D.

9 Pin block 2 and piece D right sides together, aligning the curves of pieces B and D. Sew along the seam without stitching into the seam allowance of piece C (block 3 complete).

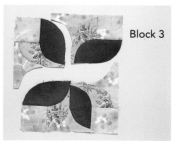

10 Make three more blocks 3.

11 Bring two blocks 3 right sides together as shown, and pin. Sew, making an extra stitch at the start and end of the seam (block 4 complete). Make another block 4.

12 Pin the blocks 4 right sides together. Sew without stitching through the centre seam allowances. Fold down the centre allowances in a spiral.

Eight-Pointed Star

One square and eight triangles are joined to form a star. It is essential to get neat points on the triangles to succeed with this block. Match the corners and pin them before joining. Choose contrasting colours for the star and the background.

Folding the seam allowances

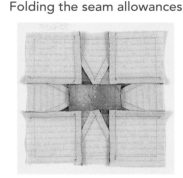

Templates

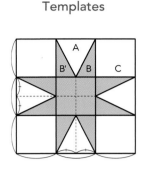

1 Prepare one piece A, one piece B and one piece B'.

2 Pin pieces A and B right sides together as shown. Sew along the seam, making an extra stitch at the start and end.

3 Trim the seam allowance to 6mm, then fold it towards B (block 1 complete).

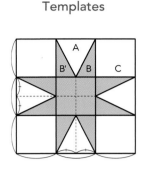

4 Pin block 1 and piece B' right sides together as shown. Sew the seam, then fold the allowance towards piece B' (block 2 complete). Make three more blocks 2.

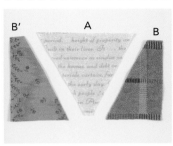

5 Prepare two pieces C.

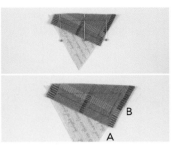

6 Pin block 2 and piece C right sides together. Sew along the seam line.

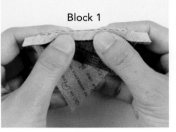

7 Join on the other piece C in the same way. Fold the seam allowances towards block 2 (block 3 complete). Make one more block 3.

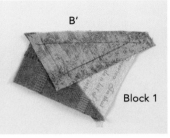

8 Prepare two more blocks 2 and the central piece C. Make the marks on piece C as indicated.

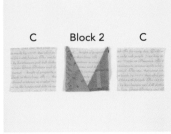

9 Pin a block 2 and the piece C right sides together, then pin, matching the point of piece A with the mark on the piece C seam line.

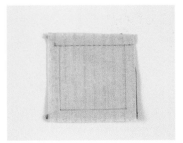

10 Draw the seam line across piece A for ease. Sew along it. Repeat to join the other block 2 to piece C (block 4 complete).

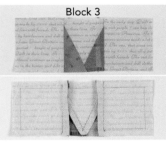

11 Fold the seam allowances of block 4 outwards, towards the blocks 2.

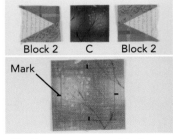

12 Pin blocks 3 and 4 right sides together. Sew along the seams and fold the allowances towards block 4.

English Ivy

* *

This block is made up of several triangular pieces so it is important to get neat points. Pin the pieces together by making the corners match up to avoid any gapping. Choose contrasting colours for the pattern and background fabrics.

Folding the seam allowances

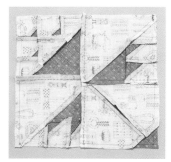

Templates

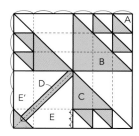

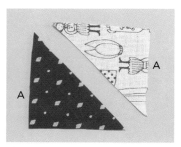

1   Prepare two pieces A.

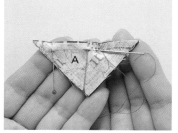

2   Pin the two pieces A right sides together. Sew along the seam, making an extra stitch at the start and end.

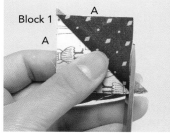

3   Trim the seam allowance to 6mm, then fold it towards the darker fabric (block 1 complete).

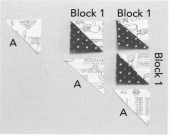

4   Prepare two more blocks 1 and three additional pieces A.

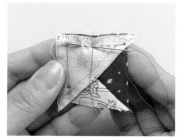

5   Pin the pieces from step 4 right sides together, then sew along the seams. Fold the seam allowances towards the dark coloured pieces (block 2 complete).

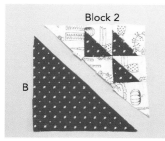

6   Pin block 2 and piece B right sides together along the long edges. Sew along the seam. Fold the allowances towards the dark piece B (block 3 complete).

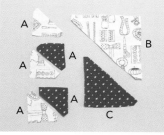

7   Prepare five pieces A, one piece B and one piece C. Join the pieces A as arranged above, then join on the piece C, and finally the piece B (block 4 complete). Make a symmetrical block 4.

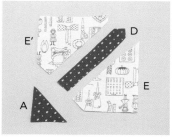

8   Join a piece E and and a piece E' to either side of a piece D. Fold the seam allowances towards piece D.

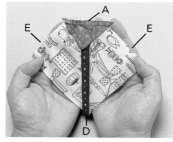

9   Pin the piece from step 8 and one piece A right sides together. Sew along the seam as shown. Fold the seam allowances towards piece A (block 5 complete).

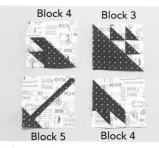

10   The four component blocks are complete. Lay them out as shown to check their positioning.

11   Pin two blocks right sides together, then sew along one seam. Fold the allowances to one side. Repeat to join the other two blocks.

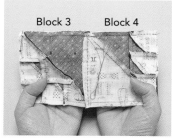

12   Pin the two strips right sides together and stitch along the seam. Fold the allowance to one side.

Evergreen Tree

* · *

This block is composed of several strips. Join pieces A into strips and then join them with B and C strips. Be careful, one of them is assembled in reverse. Mark the positions of seam junctions on pieces B and C then match them up when sewing to keep seams neat.

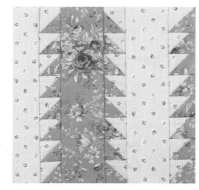

Folding the seam allowances

Templates

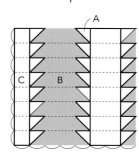

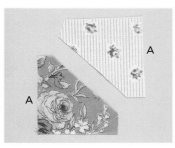

1 Prepare two pieces A.

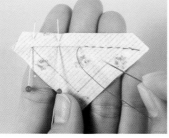

2 Pin the pieces A right sides together as shown. Sew along the seam line, making an extra stitch at the start and end.

3 Trim the allowance to 6mm, then fold it towards the dark coloured piece (block 1 complete).

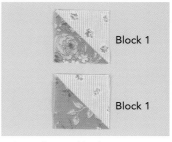

4 Make two blocks 1.

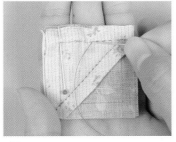

5 Pin the two blocks 1 right sides together. Sew along the seam line, making an extra stitch at the start and end.

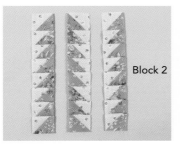

6 Continue to make blocks 1 and join them into strips of eight blocks each, as shown. Note that the arrangement of the centre strip is reversed (three blocks 2 complete).

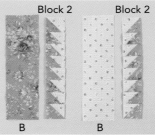

7 Prepare two pieces B and lay them out flat with two blocks 2. Mark the pieces B with seam lines.

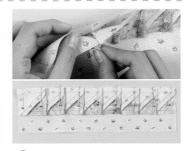

8 Bring a block 2 and piece B right sides together, then pin at the start and end of the seam, and at the seam junctions.

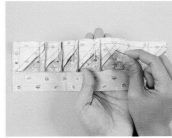

9 Sew along the seam line, making an extra stitch at the start and end. Fold the allowances towards piece B. Join the other pieces from step 7 in the same way (two blocks 3 complete).

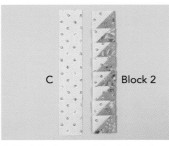

10 Join the remaining block 2 and one piece C as in steps 8 and 9 (block 4 complete).

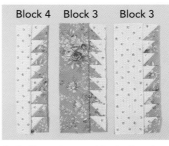

11 Place the two blocks 3 and one block 4 flat to check their positioning.

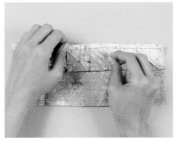

12 Pin and sew blocks 3 and 4 right sides together. Join the other block 3 to the opposite side. Fold the allowances towards the pieces B and C.

Evening Star

* *

Start by forming a central strip. Join pieces A, B and C, then pieces A, B and D to obtain the upper and lower strips, then join together these three strips. Match the corners of the pieces accurately to obtain nice points. Straight edges make these pieces easy to assemble.

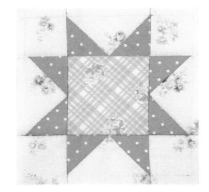

Folding the seam allowances

Templates

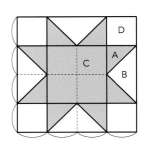

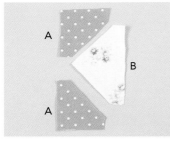

1 Prepare two pieces A and one piece B.

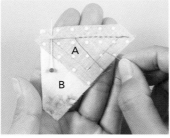

2 Pin the piece B and a piece A right sides together. Sew along the seam, making an extra stitch at the beginning and end.

3 Trim the seam allowance to 6mm, then fold it towards to piece A

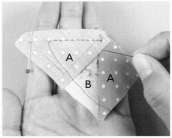

4 Add on the other piece A in the same way. Fold the seam allowance towards piece A (block 1 complete). Make three more blocks 1.

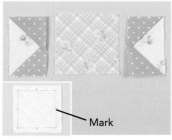

5 Make marks on piece C as shown.

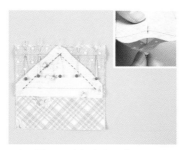

6 Pin one block 1 and piece C right sides together as shown.

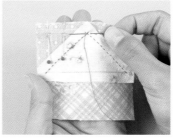

7 Sew along the seam, making an extra stitch at the beginning and end. Fold the allowances towards block 1. Join on the other block 1 (block 2 complete).

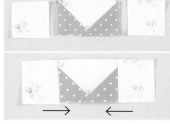

8 Pin two pieces D to one block 1 as shown. Sew along the seams then fold the allowances towards block 1 (block 3 complete). Make another block 3.

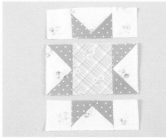

9 One block 2 and two blocks 3 have been completed. Lay them out as shown as a guide to positioning.

10 Bring the top block 3 and the central block 3 right sides together.

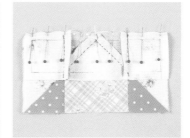

11 Pin along the seam.

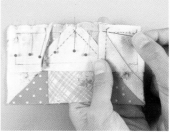

12 Sew along the seam, making an extra stitch at the start and end and at the seam junctions. Fold the allowances towards block 2. Join on the other block 3 in the same way.

Fan

* ❋ *

The fan section of this block is made up of pieces A; these are joined together first. The quarter-circle piece B is added next and then the outer section, piece C. If you mark the curved edges of pieces B and C with the postions of the seam junctions on the fan, it will make for a neater finish.

Folding the seam allowances

Templates

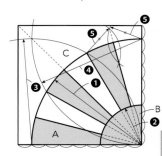

1   Draw around the templates on the wrong side of the fabric, adding a 7mm seam allowance all round; cut out.

2   Prepare two pieces A. Lay them out flat to check their positioning.

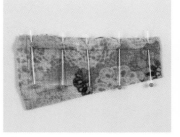

3   Bring two pieces A right along the seam line.

4   Sew along the seam line, making an extra stitch at the start and end.

5   Trim the allowance to 6mm, then fold it towards the lower piece.

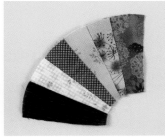

6   Join on the other four pieces A as in steps 3 to 5. Fold the allowances downwards (block 1 complete).

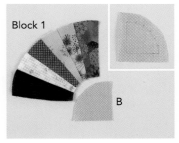

7   Prepare one block 1 and one piece B. Make marks along the curved seam line of B that correspond with the seam junctions of block 1.

8   Bring block 1 and piece B right sides together and pin, matching up the marks and seam junctions.

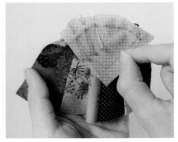

9   Sew along the seam line, making an extra stitch at the start and end. Fold back the allowances towards piece B (block 2 complete).

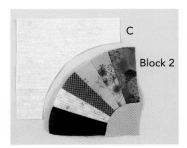

10   Prepare one block 2 and one piece C. Make marks along the curved seam line of C that correspond with the seam junctions of block 1.

11   Pin block 2 and piece C right sides together.

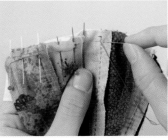

12   Sew along the seam line making an extra stitch at the seam junctions. Fold the allowances towards the pieces A.

Fanfare

Level ★ ★ ☆ ☆ ☆

Make four small blocks with pieces A, B and B'. These are joined with pieces C, D and E to obtain three larger blocks. Choose two different colours for the rays of the central motif and alternate between them for pieces A, B, B' and D. Use different fabrics for the corner and centre.

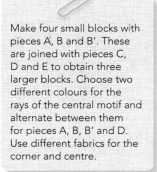

Folding the seam allowances

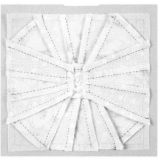

Templates

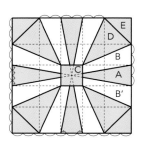

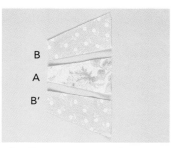

1   Prepare one piece A, one piece B and one piece B'.

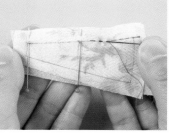

2   Pin pieces A and B right sides together as shown. Sew along the seam line, making an extra stitch at the start and end.

3   Trim the allowance to 6mm, then fold it towards piece B.

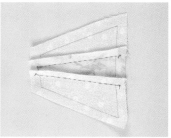

4   Join on piece B' in the same way. Fold the allowance towards piece A (block 1 complete). Make four blocks 1.

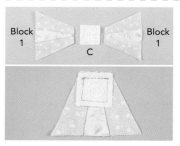

5   Join two blocks 1 and one piece C. Fold the allowances towards piece C (block 2 complete).

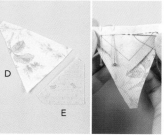

6   Pin one piece D and one piece E right sides together. Sew along the seam line, making an extra stitch at the start and end. Fold the allowances towards piece E (block 3 complete).

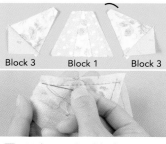

7   Make another block 3. Join one block 1 and two blocks 3, making extra stitches at the start and end of the seam (block 4 complete).

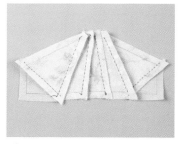

8   Make another block 4 in the same way. Fold the allowances in the same direction as for block 1.

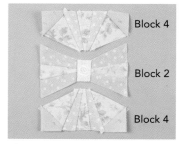

9   Lay out the block 2 and two blocks 4 flat to check their positioning.

10   Pin the blocks 2 and 4 right sides together along the first edge and sew. Make an extra stitch, then take the needle through to next edge.

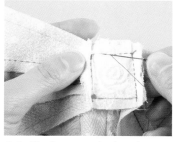

11   Pin the second edge, then sew without piercing the allowances; make an extra stitch.

12   Pin the third edge, then sew to the end. Join on the other block 4 in the same way.

Farmer's Daughter

Make upper and lower strips with pieces A, B, B' and C and a central strip composed of three pieces A and two pieces C. Despite the large number of pieces, this block is not difficult to make. Choose a coloured fabric for the cross that makes the motif stand out.

Folding the seam allowances

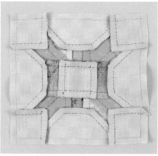

Templates

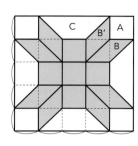

1 Prepare one piece A, one piece B and one piece B'. Mark with seam lines.

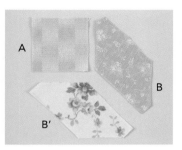

2 Pin pieces A and B right sides together as shown. Sew along the seam line, making an extra stitch at the start and end.

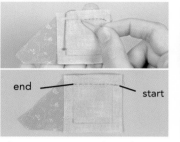

3 Trim the allowance to 6mm, then fold it towards piece B

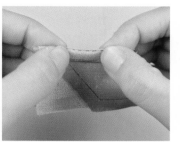

4 Bring the piece B' and A right sides together and pin along the first edge. Sew along the seam line, making an extra stitch at the end. Do not cut the thread.

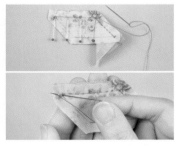

5 Pin along the second edge, then sew to the end. Make an extra stitch (block 1 complete).

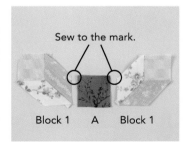

6 Make another block 1. Join the two blocks 1 and one pieces A. Fold the allowances towards piece A (block 2 complete).

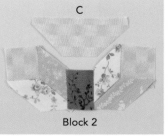

7 Prepare one block 2 and one piece C. Lay them out flat to check their positioning.

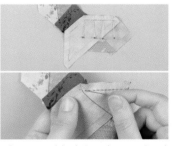

8 Bring block 2 and piece C right sides together and pin along the first edge. Sew along the seam line without piercing the allowance of piece A.

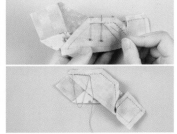

9 Pin and sew the second and third edges in the same way, making an extra stitch at each corner (block 3 complete). Make two blocks 3.

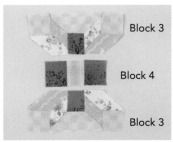

10 Join three pieces A (block 4 complete).

11 Pin blocks 3 and 4 right sides together. Sew along the seam line, working stitch by stitch on overlapping allowances.

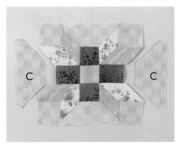

12 Fold the allowances outward. Join on two pieces C in the same way as described in steps 8 and 9.

Firewood Bucket in the Kitchen

* *

Start by joining the trapezoid-shaped pieces A in pairs to form four blocks. These are joined to a piece B, and then triangular pieces C are added at the corners to form the block. Use shades of brown and tan to suggest the theme of this square.

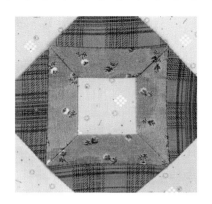

Folding the seam allowances

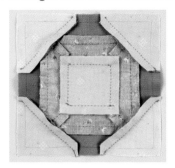

Templates

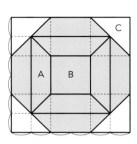

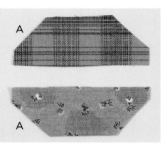

1   Prepare two pieces A cut from different fabrics.

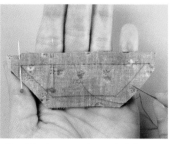

2   Pin the two pieces A right sides together as shown. Sew along the seam line making an extra stitch at the start and end.

3   Trim the allowance to 6mm, then fold it towards the outer piece (block 1 complete).

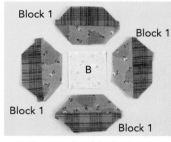

4   Prepare four blocks 1 and one block B.

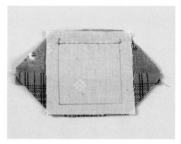

5   Pin a block 1 and piece B right sides together as shown. Sew along the seam line. Fold the allowances towards block 1.

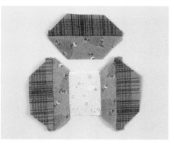

6   Join another block 1 to the opposite side of the piece B (block 2 completed).

7   Pin the first edge of a block 1 to block 2 right sides together. Sew along the seam line without piercing the allowances. Make an extra stitch; do not cut the thread.

8   Pin along the second edge, then sew along the seam line without stitching in the allowances. Make an extra stitch; do not cut the thread.

9   Pin and sew the third edge in the same way, making an extra stitch at the end.

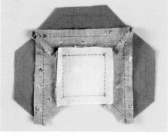

10   Fold the allowances as shown.

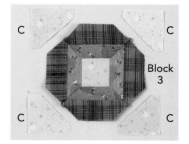

11   Join on the fourth block 1 in the same way (block 3 complete). Prepare four pieces C.

12   Pin block 3 and a piece C right sides together as shown. Sew, working stitch by stitch through the allowances. Join on the other pieces C.

Fireworks

* • *

Start by making a strip from pieces A, B and C that goes across the centre. Then make triangular blocks from pieces A, B, C and D. Join the three blocks to finish. Make sure that corners match up and make extra stitches at seam junctions to avoid gaps forming.

Folding the seam allowances

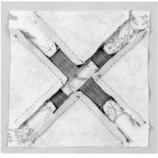

Templates

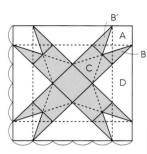

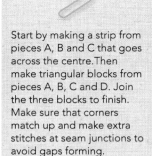

1 Prepare one piece A, one piece B and one piece B'.

2 Pin pieces A and B right sides together as shown. Sew along the seam line, making an extra stitch at the start and end.

3 Trim the allowance, then fold it towards piece B.

4 Join the pieces A and B' in the same way (block 1 complete). Make three more blocks 1.

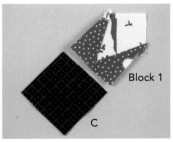

5 Prepare one block 1 and one piece C.

6 Pin block 1 and piece C right sides together. Sew along the seam line. Fold the allowances towards piece C (block 2 complete).

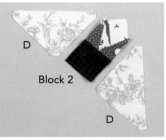

7 Prepare one block 2 and two pieces D.

8 Pin block 2 and piece D right sides together. Sew along the seam line. Join the other piece D. Fold the allowances towards block 2 (block 3 complete). Make another block 3.

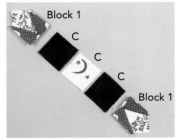

9 Prepare two blocks 1 and three pieces C.

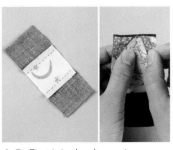

10 First join the three pieces C. Fold the allowances outwards. Join on the two blocks 1. Fold the allowances towards the pieces C (block 4 complete).

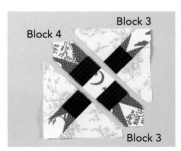

11 Lay out two blocks 3 and one block 4 flat to check their positioning.

12 Pin a block 3 and 4 right sides together. Sew along the seam line, making an extra stitch at the seam junctions. Join on the other block 3.

Fish

* · *

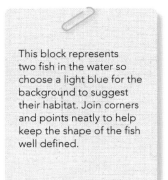

This block represents two fish in the water so choose a light blue for the background to suggest their habitat. Join corners and points neatly to help keep the shape of the fish well defined.

Folding the seam allowances

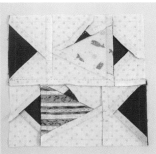

Templates

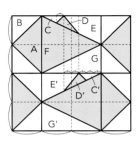

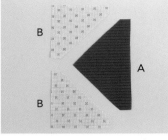

1 Prepare one piece A and two pieces B.

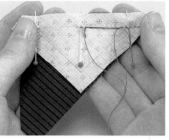

2 Pin pieces A and B right sides together as shown. Sew along the seam line, making an extra stitch at the start and end.

3 Trim the allowance to 6mm, then fold it towards piece A. Join on the other piece B (block 1 complete). Make two blocks 1.

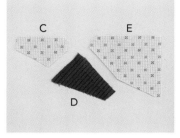

4 Prepare one piece C, one piece D and one piece E.

5 Pin the pieces C and D right sides together. Sew along the seam line. Fold the allowances towards piece D.

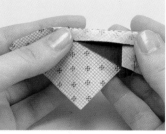

6 Join on piece E, sewing along the seam line. Fold the allowances towards piece D. Trim the excess allowances (block 2 complete)

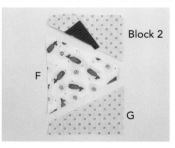

7 Prepare a block 2, one piece F and one piece G. Join the pieces F and G (block 3 complete).

8 Pin blocks 2 and 3 right sides together. Sew along the seam line. Fold the allowances towards piece F (block 4 complete).

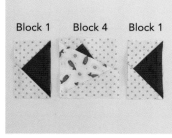

9 Lay out the two blocks 1 and one block 4 flat to check their positioning.

10 Pin two blocks right sides together. Sew along the seam line. Join on the other block in the same way (block 5 complete).

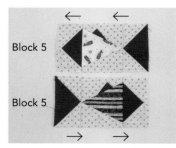

11 Make a symmetrical block 5. Fold the allowances in the directions of the arrows.

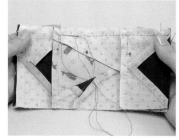

12 Pin the two blocks 5 right sides together. Sew along the seam line, making extra stitches at the seam junctions.

Florida

Level ★★★☆☆

To form this hexagonal block make six triangles and join them together. Each triangle is surrounded by fabric strips, joined at the corner with diamond shapes. Where the triangles meet at the middle, the diamond shapes form a star.

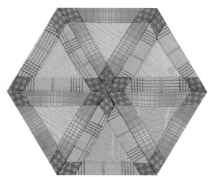

Folding the seam allowances

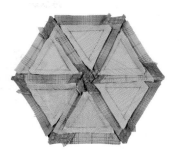

Templates

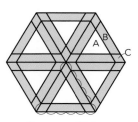

See page 87 for a hexagonal template.

F
Florida

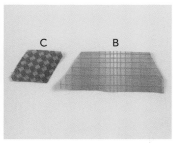

1 Prepare one piece B and one piece C.

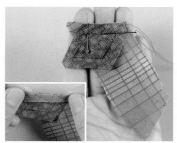

2 Pin pieces B and C right sides together as shown. Sew along the seam line, making an extra stitch at the start and end. Fold the allowances towards piece C (block 1 complete).

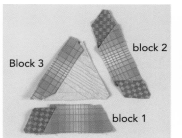

3 Join one piece B and two pieces C (block 2 complete). Join one piece A and one piece B. Fold the allowances towards piece B (block 3 complete).

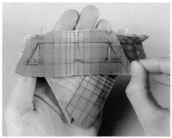

4 Bring blocks 1 and 3 right sides together, matching the seam junctions; pin. Sew along the seam line without sewing through the allowance.

5 Join block 2 and the block from step 4 in the same way. Fold the allowances to one side, either outwards or inwards (block 4 complete).

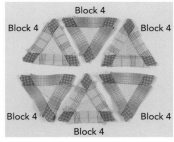

6 Make six blocks 4. Lay them out flat to check their positioning.

7 Pin two blocks 4 right sides together. Sew along the seam line, making an extra stitch at the junctions.

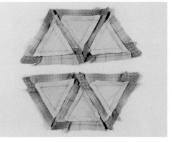

8 Assemble the other blocks 4 to form two strips of three.

✳ Assembling several blocks

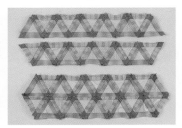

1 You can join blocks 4 into strips and then join these together.

2 Pin two strips right sides together. Sew along the first seam line. Make an extra stitch on the junction of the corners of the six pieces; insert the needle through the corner of all the pieces .

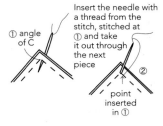

① angle of C

Insert the needle with a thread from the stitch, stitched at ① and take it out through the next piece

②

point inserted in ①

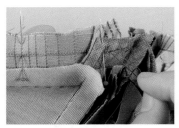

3 Pull the thread through, make an extra stitch, then continue sewing.

Flying Geese

Level ★★ ✿ ✿ ✿

The triangular pieces of this block are meant to represent geese in flight. Small triangles are combined to make two strips; these are set on either side of a plain strip of fabric. Use a light fabric for the pieces B that are the background to the pieces A.

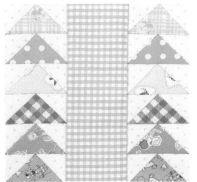

Folding the seam allowances

Templates

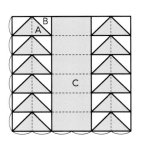

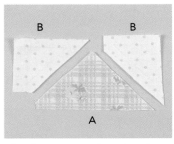

1 Prepare one piece A and two pieces B. Mark the seam lines.

2 Pin pieces A and B right sides together as shown. Sew along the seam line, making an extra stitch at the start and end.

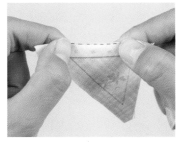

3 Trim the allowance to 6mm, then fold it towards piece A

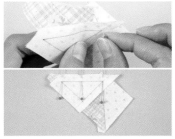

4 Join on the other piece B in the same way (block 1 complete).

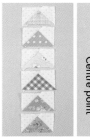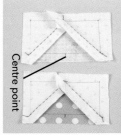

5 Prepare six blocks 1. Lay them out flat to check their positioning. Mark the centre point of the bottom edge of each piece A. Pin two blocks 1 right sides together, matching the top of the piece A on one block to the centre point of the piece A on the next block.

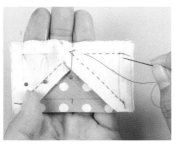

6 Sew along the seam line, making an extra stitch at the start, end and seam junction. Join the other blocks 1 in the same way (block 2 complete).

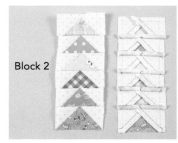

7 Make two blocks 2. Fold the allowances upwards.

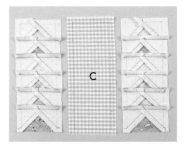

8 Prepare two blocks 2 and one piece C. Lay them out flat, wrong sides up so you can mark the positions of the seam junctions on blocks 2 on the long edges of piece C.

9 Pin block 2 and piece C right sides together, matching up the marks and seam junctions.

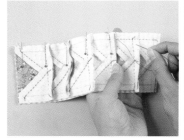

10 Sew along the seam line, working stitch by stitch on overlapping allowances.

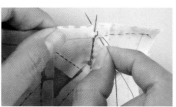

Formal Garden

Make four small blocks from pieces A and B, then join them with a piece C. The pieces B create the paths of the garden, so make them from fabrics that contrast with the background colour of the pieces A. Use a different fabric for the centre piece C.

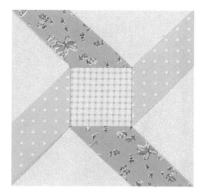

Folding the seam allowances

Templates

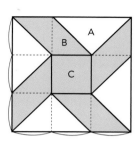

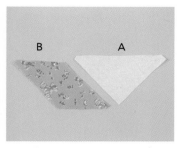

1 Prepare one piece A and one piece B

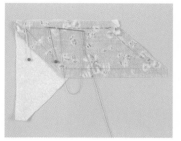

2 Pin pieces A and B right sides together as shown. Sew along the seam line, making an extra stitch at the start and end.

3 Trim the allowance to 6mm, then fold it towards piece B (block 1 complete). Make four blocks 1.

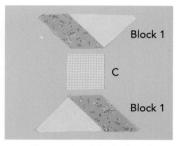

4 Prepare two blocks 1 and one piece C.

Sew along the seam line

5 Pin block 1 and piece C right sides together. Sew along the seam line. Join on the other block 1 in the same way (block 2 complete).

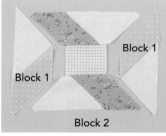

6 Fold the allowances towards the blocks 1. Prepare two blocks 1 and one block 2.

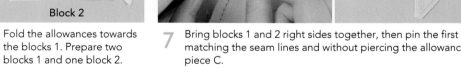

7 Bring blocks 1 and 2 right sides together, then pin the first edge, matching the seam lines and without piercing the allowances of piece C.

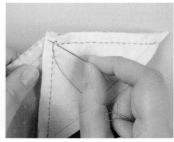

8 Sew along the first edge. Make an extra stitch in the allowance of piece C. Do not cut the thread.

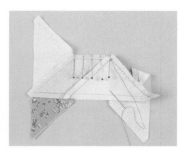

9 Pin the second edge, then sew along the seam line without stitching in the allowances.

10 Make an extra stitch at the corner.

11 Pin and sew the the third edge in the same way. Join on the other block 1 in the same way.

Garden Maze

Level ✿✿✾✾✾

Choose a dark coloured fabric for pieces B, C and D which represent the labyrinth. The 'flower' at the centre of the maze is appliquéd on – you can choose which design to use. Alternatively, pick a different fabric with a large floral design.

Folding the seam allowances

Templates

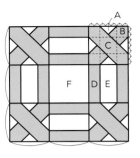

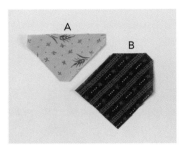

1 Prepare one piece A and one piece B.

2 Pin pieces A and B right sides together as shown. Sew along the seam line, making an extra stitch at the start and end.

3 Trim the allowance to 6mm, then fold it towards piece B.

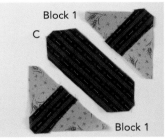

4 Join on another piece A (block 1 complete). Fold the allowances towards piece B. Make two blocks 1 and prepare one piece C.

5 Pin block 1 and piece C right sides together. Sew along the seam line. Fold the allowances towards piece C. Join on the other block 1 (block 2 complete).

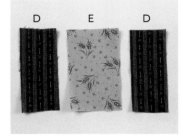

6 Join two pieces D and one piece E, sewing along the seam lines. Fold the allowances towards pieces D (block 3 complete).

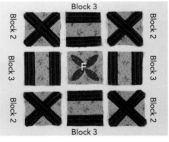

7 Make four blocks 2 and four blocks 3. Prepare one piece F. Appliqué a motif of your choice on piece F.

8 Pin a block 2 and 3 right sides together. Sew along the seam line, making an extra stitch at the seam junctions.

9 Join the blocks in strips as shown. Fold the allowances outward.

10 Pin two strips right sides together. Sew along the seam line, making an extra stitch at the seam junctions. Fold the allowances outward.

* Assembling several blocks

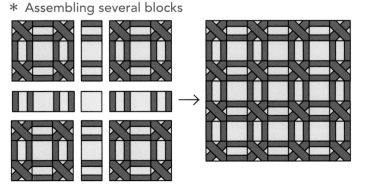

Arrange your finished blocks, then make extra strips from blocks 3 and pieces F and use them, with a piece F at the centre, to join the blocks.

Glorified Nine Patch

* *

Join pieces A and B into strips, then add pieces B and C to form the nine patch sections. Then add pieces D and E to make the block. Match up the marks to get a neat finish. Fold down the central seam allowances in a spiral shape. Choose colours in different shades for the nine patch sections.

Folding the seam allowances

Templates

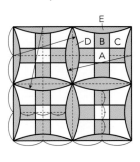

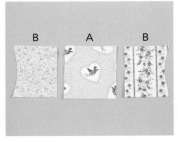

1 Prepare one piece A and two pieces B. Lay them out flat to check their positioning.

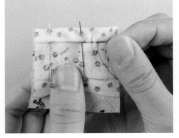

2 Pin the pieces A and B right sides together. Sew, making an extra stitch at the start and end of the seam. Join on the other piece B.

3 Trim the seam allowances to 6mm, then fold them towards piece B (central block complete).

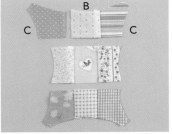

4 Join one piece B and two pieces C in the same way to make the top and bottom strips. Fold the seam allowances towards piece B.

5 Pin the central strip and one strip from step 4 right sides together. Sew, making extra stitches at the seam junctions. Join on the remaining strip on the opposite side.

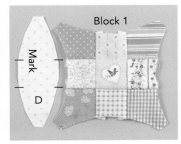

6 Fold the seam allowances towards the central strip (block 1 complete). Prepare one piece D and mark as shown.

7 Pin block 1 and piece D right sides together, making sure the marks and junctions coincide. Sew along the seam line.

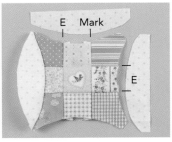

8 Fold the seam allowances towards piece D. Prepare two pieces E and mark as shown.

9 Join the pieces E to block 1 making sure the marks and junctions coincide. Sew along the seam line (block 2 complete).

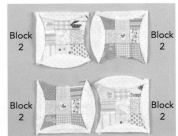

10 Make four blocks 2. Lay them out flat to check their positioning, as shown.

11 Join together the adjacent blocks in pairs to make two strips.

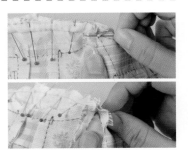

12 Pin the two strips right sides together, without piercing the seam allowances; sew.

Goose in the Pond

* · *

Make up small blocks, then join them together into strips. As there are a large number of pieces, lay them out flat to check their positioning at each stage. All the pieces have straight edges. Choose contrasting colours and patterns to highlight the design.

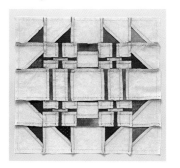

Folding the seam allowances

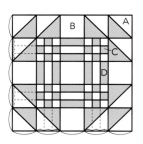

Templates

1 Prepare two pieces A.

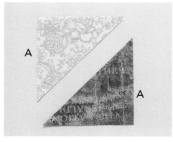

2 Pin the two pieces A right sides together along the long edges, then sew in place.

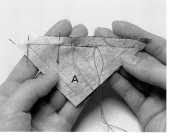

3 Trim the seam allowance to 6mm, then fold it towards the darker coloured piece (block 1 complete).

4 Prepare three more blocks 1 and one piece B.

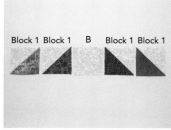

5 Pin the blocks from step 4 right sides together and sew along the seams (block 2 complete). Make another block 2.

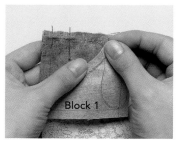

6 Prepare nine pieces C. Join them in sets of three, alternating the colours. Fold the seam allowances towards the darker coloured pieces (three blocks 3 complete).

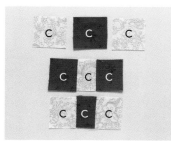

7 Pin the blocks 3 right sides together and sew along the seams. Fold the allowances inwards (block 4 complete). Prepare three more blocks 4.

8 Prepare three pieces D. Pin them right sides together and sew the seams. Fold the allowances towards the dark coloured pieces (block 5 complete). Prepare two blocks 5.

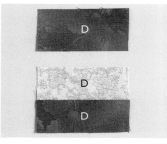

9 Pin together two blocks 1, two blocks 4 and one block 5, then sew. Fold the seam allowances towards blocks 1 and 5.

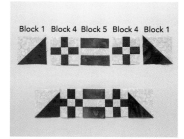

10 Pin together three pieces B and two blocks 5 as shown. Sew along the seams. Fold the seam towards the blocks 5.

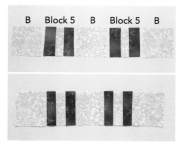

11 The five strips are complete.

12 Pin the strips right sides together and sew along the seams.

Grandmother's Flower Garden

Level ✿✿✿✿✿

✳·✳

This block composed of seven hexagons is a classic patchwork motif. The central piece represents the heart of the flower and the other six pieces the petals. Make any marks match up and sew one edge after the other.

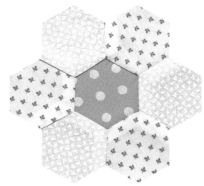

Folding the seam allowances

Templates

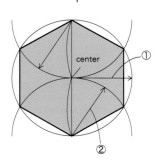

1 Place the template on the wrong side of the fabric and draw around it. Adding 7mm for a seam allowance, cut out the shape.

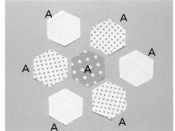

2 Prepare seven pieces A. Lay them out flat to check the arrangement of your colours.

3 Bring the central piece A and another piece right sides together. Pin the start and end of one straight edge, then sew along the seam.

4 Join on two other pieces A in the same way. Trim the seam allowances to 6mm, then fold them outwards.

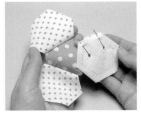

5 Pin a straight edge of one piece A to the straight edge of one of the outer pieces A, right sides together, as shown.

6 Sew along the seam, making an extra stitch at the start and end, and without stitching into the other seams. Do not cut the thread.

7 Pin the next edge of the piece A to the next edge of the other piece, right sides together. Sew without stitching into the other seams.

8 Pin the third edges of the pieces right sides together. Sew the seam. Fold the seam allowances of the outer pieces A in one direction.

✳ Another way to fold the seam allowances

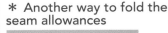
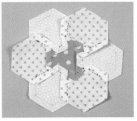

It is possible to fold the seam allowances in a spiral shape.

✳ Assembling blocks

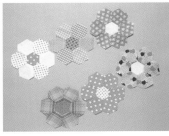

1 Join blocks together into strips. Lay out strips flat to check the arrangement of the different colours.

2 Pin the strips right sides together, then sew along the seam lines. Do not stitch through the overlapping seam allowances.

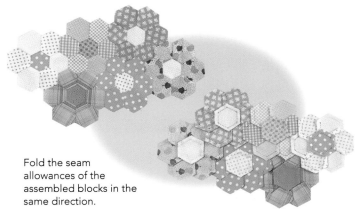

Fold the seam allowances of the assembled blocks in the same direction.

Grace's Windmill

·

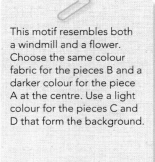

This motif resembles both a windmill and a flower. Choose the same colour fabric for the pieces B and a darker colour for the piece A at the centre. Use a light colour for the pieces C and D that form the background.

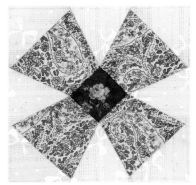

Folding the seam allowances

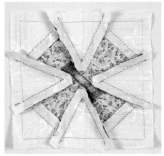

Templates

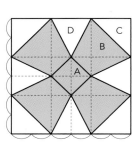

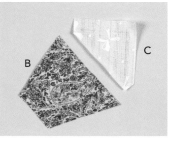

1 Prepare one piece B and one piece C.

2 Pin pieces B and C right sides together, as shown; sew. Fold the seam allowance towards piece B (block 1 complete).

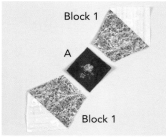

3 Make four blocks 1 and prepare one piece A. Lay them out flat to check their positioning.

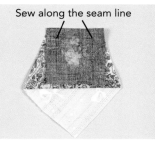

4 Pin one block 1 and piece A right sides together; sew. Fold the allowance towards piece B. Join on another block 1 (block 2 complete).

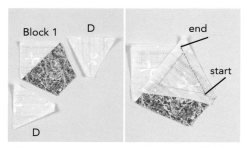

5 Join together one block 1 and two blocks D as shown. Fold the seam allowances towards the dark piece B (block 3 complete).

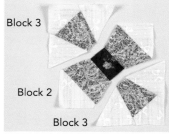

6 Make another block 3. Lay out all the blocks to check their positioning

7 Bring blocks 2 and 3 right sides together. Pin along the first edge without piercing the seam allowances.

8 Sew along the seam line, making an extra stitch at the end. Do not cut the thread.

9 Pin along the second edge.

10 Continue sewing along the second edge, making an extra stitch at the end. Do not cut the thread.

11 Pin and sew the third edge. Fold the seam allowances towards block 2. Join on the other block 3 in the same way.

Guiding Star

* • *

Make four small blocks with pieces A and B. Then assemble them in pairs to make the star shape. Then add on the pieces C and C'. Match up seams when joining smaller blocks to help get a neat finish.

Folding the seam allowances

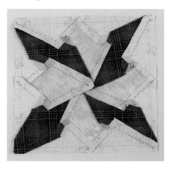

Templates

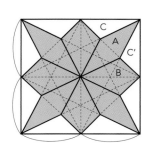

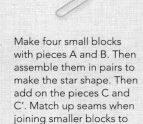

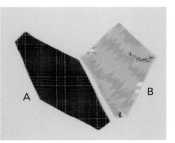

1 Prepare one piece A and one piece B, with piece B placed to the right of piece A.

2 Pin pieces A and B right sides together as shown. Sew along the seam line, making an extra stitch at the start and end.

3 Trim the seam allowance to 6mm, then fold it towards to piece A (block 1 complete).

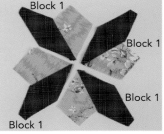

4 Make four blocks 1. They form the centre of the final block. Lay them out flat to check their positioning.

5 Bring two blocks 1 right sides together. Pin along the seam line, using a pin to help you match up the junctions between seams; sew.

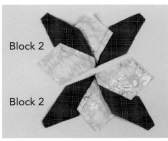

6 Fold the seam allowances in the same direction as in step 4 (block 2 complete). Make a second block 2.

7 Bring the two blocks 2 right sides together. Pin, using the same technique as in step 5 to match up junctions; sew.

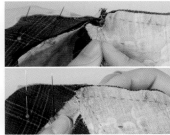

8 Sew stitch by stitch through overlapping seam allowances. Make an extra stitch at the junctions points (block 3 complete).

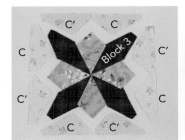

9 Prepare the pieces C and C'. Lay out all the pieces flat to check their positioning.

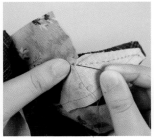

10 Pin the first edge of a piece C' and a piece A (C' and B) right sides together; sew. Do not cut the thread.

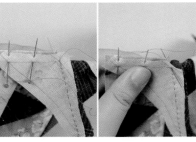

11 Pin the second edge of the piece C and to a piece B (C' and A); sew.

12 Join the other pieces C and C' to block 3 in the same way.

Heart 1

Level ✿ ✿ ✾ ✾ ✾

* *

Join pieces A and A' to form the heart shape, then add the piece B at the top, followed by pieces C and D at the corners. Match up seam lines and any marks, and make an extra stitch at the corners to avoid any gaps. Choose similar fabrics for pieces A and A'.

Folding the seam allowances

Templates

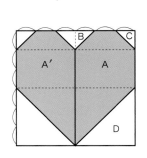

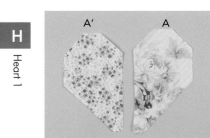

1 Prepare one piece A and one piece A'.

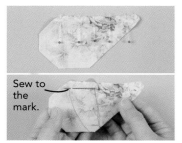

2 Pin the pieces A and A' right sides together as shown. Sew along the seam line, making an extra stitch at the start and end.

3 Trim the allowance to 6mm, then fold it towards one side (block 1 complete).

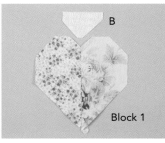

4 Prepare one block 1 and one piece B.

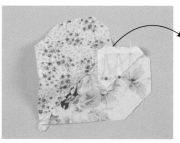

5 Bring piece B and block 1 right sides together. Pin along the first edge without piercing the allowances.

6 Sew along the seam line without piercing the allowances. Make an extra stitch; do not cut the thread.

7 Pin and sew the second edge, making an extra stitch at the end. Fold the allowances towards block 1 (block 2 complete).

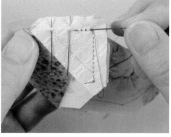

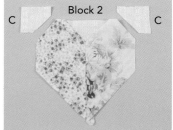

8 Join one block 2 and two pieces C, sewing along the seam line. Fold the allowances towards block 2 (block 3 complete).

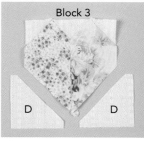

9 Prepare one block 3 and two pieces D. Sew one piece D and block 3 right sides together, then fold the allowances towards block 3.

10 Pin the second piece D and block 3 right sides together. Sew along the seam line, working stitch by stitch on overlapping allowances.

Heart 2

This block is composed of strips of fabric, made up from smaller pieces in various sizes. As well as constructing this block in the traditional pieced method, it is possible to use a sewing machine (see below). Choose dark fabrics for the pieces B and D to outline the heart shape.

Folding the seam allowances

Templates

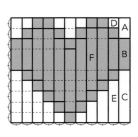

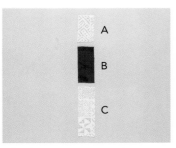

1 Prepare one piece A, one piece B and one piece C

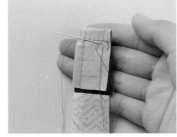

2 Pin pieces A and B right sides together as shown. Sew along the seam line, making an extra stitch at the start and end. Join on piece C in the same way.

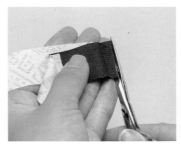

3 Trim the allowance to 6mm.

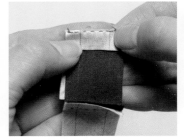

4 Fold the allowances towards piece C.

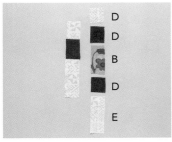

5 Lay out flat one piece B, three pieces D and one piece E as shown to check their position in the second column.

6 Join the pieces together in the order shown to make column 2.

7 Make columns 3 to 5 in the same way, the pieces arranged as shown above. Fold the allowances towards the centre pieces.

8 Pin columns 1 and 2 right sides together. Sew along the seam line, making an extra stitch at the seam junctions.

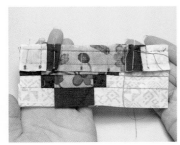

9 Continue to join on columns, following the order shown in step 5.

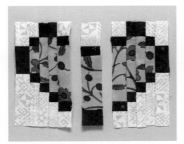

10 Follow steps 1 to 9 to make a symmetrical block. Join the pieces that form the central column. Join the three blocks together.

* Using a sewing machine

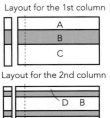

Using a sewing machine, join pieces of fabric together as indicated in the diagram and photo above. Use a rotary cutter to cut the joined fabric into strips and then piece them together as shown.

Hexagon Star

* *

Make a star composed of six A pieces, then join them with more pieces A to form a hexagon. Hexagons are then joined with pieces B to form a larger piece. Make sure the corners and points of pieces match up to get a neat finish overall. Choose contrasting fabrics for the star and the triangles.

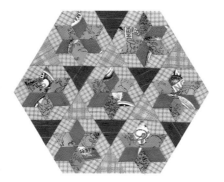

Folding the seam allowances

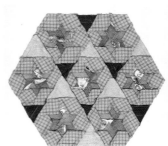

Templates

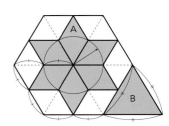

See page 87 for a hexagon template.

1 Prepare six pieces A.

2 Pin the two pieces A right sides together as shown. Sew along the seam line, making an extra stitch at the start and end. Fold the allowances to one side.

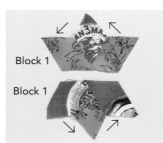

3 Join on another piece A and fold the allowances in one direction (block 1 complete). Make another block 1.

4 Bring the two blocks 1 right sides together; pin. Sew along the seam lines, making an extra stitch at the seam junctions.

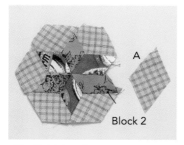

5 Fold the allowances to one side (block 2 complete). Prepare six pieces A.

6 Pin block 2 and a piece A right sides together along the first edge without piercing the allowances Sew along the seam line. Make an extra stitch; do not cut the thread.

7 Pin and sew along the second edge, making an extra stitch at the end. Fold the allowances towards block 2. Join on the other pieces A (block 3 complete).

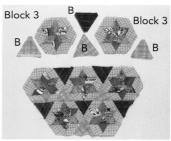

8 Assemble blocks 3 with pieces B to get strips. Then join the strips.

Variations

* *

There are many ways to create a hexagon star block. You can divide up some of the diamond shapes or replace some diamonds with triangles. Combine fabrics in three tones to create depth.

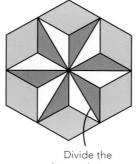

Divide the diamonds in two.

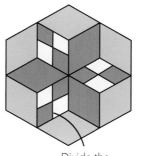

Divide the diamonds in four.

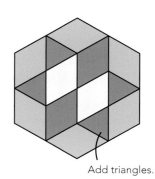

Add triangles.

Honey Bee

✳·✳

This block represents bees gathered around a flower. Join nine pieces A into one block and then add the pieces B and C as a border. The bees are appliquéd onto the border. Use floral-patterned fabrics and pick different ones for the bees.

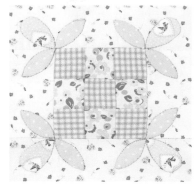

Folding the seam allowances

Templates

appliquéd

C

A

B

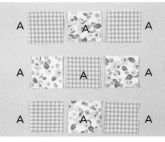

1 Prepare nine pieces A. Lay them out flat in rows of three to check their positioning.

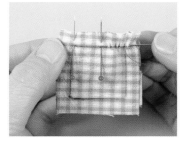

2 Pin two pieces A right sides together as shown. Sew along the seam line, making an extra stitch at the start and end.

3 Join another pieces A to make the first strip. Make two more strips. Fold the allowances in the direction of the arrows.

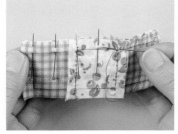

4 Pin two strips right sides together. Sew along the seam line, making an extra stitch at seam junctions.

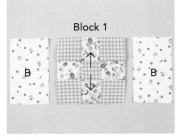

5 Fold the allowances in the direction of the arrows (block 1 complete). Prepare one block 1 and two pieces B.

6 Pin block 1 and a piece B right sides together. Sew along the seam line. Fold the allowances towards block 1. Join the other piece B in the same way (block 2 complete).

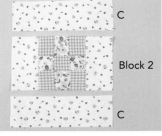

7 Join two pieces C and one block 2. Fold the allowances towards block 2.

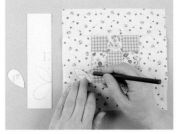

8 Draw around the bee templates on the right side of the block to mark their position. Use the template to cut out pieces, adding a 5mm allowance.

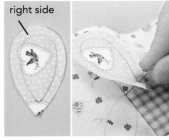

right side

9 Pin a piece to be appliquéd in position on the block, so the seam line matches up with the drawn line on the block.

10 Using the tip of the needle to turn under the edge of the piece as you go, start sewing it down with small slip stitches.

11 Where the point of the piece meets the corner of block 1, insert the needle right through the fabric and then back out again. Continue to sew with slip stitches

✳ Alternative appliqué method

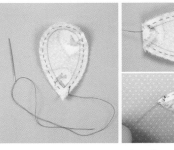

Make even stitches around the allowance of the piece to be appliquéd. Put the template on the wrong side and pull the thread to turn under the allowance. Press and remove the template.

Honeycomb

* *

This block represents a honeycomb. Make four blocks made up of two pieces A and two pieces B. Join them in pairs, with the motifs turned in different directions, before joining both pairs together. Choose two shades of two different colours for the pieces A and one fabric for the pieces B.

Folding the seam allowances

Templates

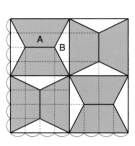

H
Honeycomb

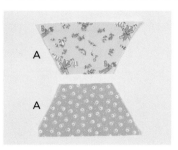

1   Prepare two pieces A.

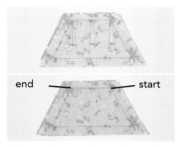

2   Pin the two pieces A right sides together as shown. Sew along the seam line, making an extra stitch at the start and end.

3   Trim the allowance to 6mm, then fold it to one side (block 1 complete).

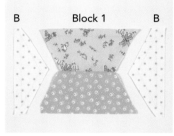

4   Prepare one block 1 and two pieces B.

5   Bring block 1 and piece B right sides together, then pin the first edge without piercing the allowances of block 1.

6   Sew along the seam line without piercing the allowances of block 1. Make an extra stitch; do not cut the thread.

7   Pin along the second edge without piercing the allowances. Sew to the end of the seam line.

8   Join on another piece B in the same way. If necessary, trim the allowances, then fold them towards block 1 (block 2 complete).

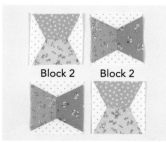

9   Prepare four blocks 2. Lay them out flat to check their positioning.

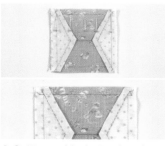

10   Pin two blocks 2 right sides together. Sew along the seam line. Repeat to join the other two blocks 2.

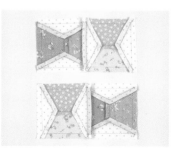

11   Fold the allowances on the strips in alternate directions.

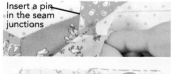

12   Bring the two strips right sides together, using a pin to match up seam junctions. Sew along the seam line, working stitch by stitch on overlapping allowances.

Hosanna

✳ ＊ ✳

Sharply pointed pieces characterise this block. With narrow pieces and angled edges, take care not to stretch edges and distort the shapes. Choose strongly coloured for B, D and F pieces and the same lighter fabric for the A, C, E and G pieces.

Folding the seam allowances

Templates

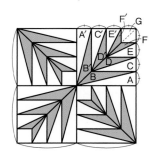

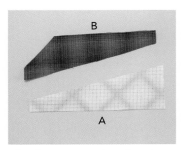

1 Prepare one piece A and one piece B.

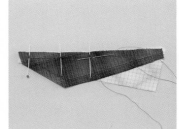

2 Pin pieces A and B right sides together as shown. Sew along the seam line, making an extra stitch at the start and end.

3 Trim the allowance to 6mm, then fold it towards B (block 1 complete).

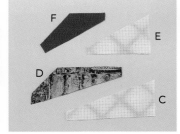

4 Join one piece C and one piece D. Fold the allowances towards the dark piece D (block 2 complete). Join one piece E and one piece F in the same way (block 3 complete).

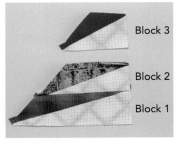

5 Join blocks 1, 2 and 3 as shown. Fold the allowances towards pieces C and E (block 4 complete).

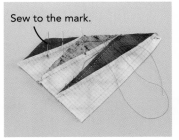

6 Join pieces A', B', C', D', E' and F' to make a symmetrical block 4 (block 4' complete). Join the blocks 4 and 4'.

7 Fold the allowances to one side (block 5 complete). Prepare one piece G.

8 Bring block 5 and piece G right sides together, then pin the first edge without piercing the allowances of the corner.

9 Sew to the corner, then make an extra stitch.

10 Pin the second edge without piercing the allowances. Sew from the corner to the end (block 6 complete).

11 Make four blocks 6, then join them in pairs to form two strips. Make extra stitches at seam junctions to prevent gaps.

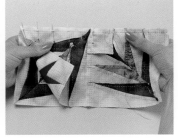

12 Pin the two strips right sides together. Sew along the seam line, making extra stitches at the seam junctions.

House

Level ★★★☆☆

* *

This block represents a house. Join the pieces together in strips before assembling the block. Check the arrangement of the different pieces and blocks at each stage of the assembly. Choose suitable fabrics for the different parts; for instance, checks for the walls.

Folding the seam allowances

Templates

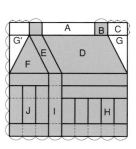

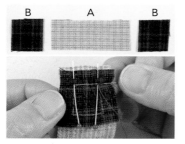

1 Prepare a piece A and two pieces B. Pin a pieces A and B right sides. Sew along the seam line, making an extra stitch at the start and end. Join on the other piece B.

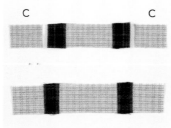

2 Fold the allowances towards the pieces B. Join two pieces C to either end of the block (block 1 complete).

3 Prepare one piece D, one piece E and one piece F. Join them together in the order shown above. Fold the allowances towards pieces D and F (block 2 complete).

4 Prepare one block 2, one piece G and one piece G'.

5 Join the block 2 and pieces G and G' right sides together. Fold the allowances towards block 2 (block 3 complete).

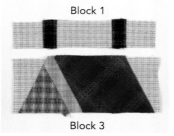

6 Prepare one block 1 and one block 3.

7 Bring blocks 1 and 3 right sides together, and pin. Sew along the seam line (block 4 complete).

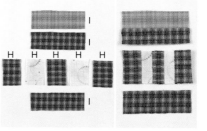

8 Prepare three pieces I and five pieces H. Join them as shown above so you have three strips.

9 Pin two strips right sides together. Sew along the seam line. Join on the other strip (block 5 complete).

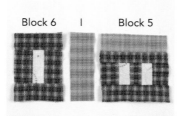

10 Join five pieces J as shown to make block 6. Join one block 5, one block 6 and one piece I. Fold the allowances outwards (block 7 complete).

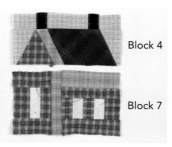

11 Lay out flat blocks 4 and 7 to check their positioning

12 Pin the two blocks right sides together. Sew along the seam line. Fold the allowance downwards.

Hunter's Star

* *

Pieces A, B and C are combined to form small triangular blocks that are then combined to form the whole. When cutting out and sewing pieces A and A', make sure to keep them symmetrical. Make extra stitches at the seam junctions to avoid any gapping.

Folding the seam allowances

Templates

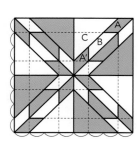

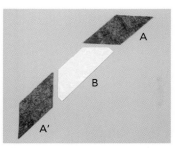

1 Prepare one piece A, one piece A' and one piece B. Lay them out flat to check their positioning.

2 Pin the pieces A and B, right sides together as shown. Sew, making an extra stitch at the start and end of the seam.

3 Trim the seam allowance to 6mm, then fold it toward piece A (block 1 complete).

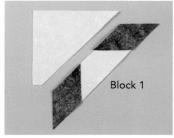

4 Prepare one block 1 and one piece C. Pin them, right sides together.

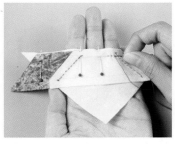

5 Sew along the seam, making extra stitches at the junctions. Fold the seam allowances towards block 1 (block 2 complete).

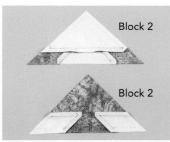

6 Make another block 2, reversing the colour combinations and folding the allowances in the opposite direction.

7 Pin the two blocks 2 right sides together along the long edges. Sew along the seam.

8 Make an extra stitch at the seam junctions. Trim the seam allowances, then fold them towards block 2 where the allowance of piece C is folded down on block 1 (block 3 complete). Make three other blocks 3.

9 Lay the four blocks 3 out flat to check their positioning and the arrangement of the colours.

10 Pin two blocks 3 right sides together; sew. Fold the seam allowances to one side (block 4 complete).

11 Pin the two blocks 4 right sides together.

12 Sew, working stitch by stitch through the overlapping seam allowances.

Ice-Cream Cone

* · *

This block represents an ice-cream cone. Pieces B, C, E, E', F and F' form the shapes. Assemble pieces A and B, D and E, D 'and E' to make small blocks, then join them with pieces C, F and F' to make the block. Make marks as shown to help sew the curves.

Folding the seam allowances

Templates

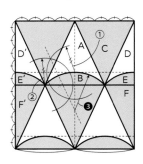

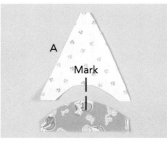

1 Make a mark in the middle of the curve on pieces A and B.

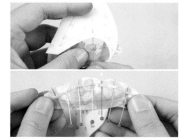

2 Bring pieces A and B right sides together, so the marked points match. Pin the ends, then pin in between.

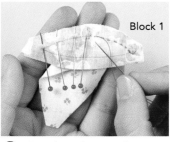

3 Sew along the curved seam. Trim the seam allowance to 6mm, then fold it towards piece B (block 1 complete).

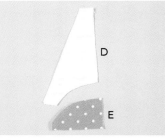

4 Join pieces D and E, and D' and E' as in steps 2 and 3. Fold back the seam allowances towards pieces E and E' (blocks 2 and 2' complete).

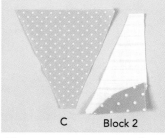

5 Lay out one piece C and one block 2 flat to check their positioning.

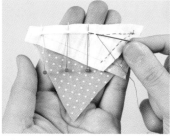

6 Pin piece C and block 2 right sides together. Stitch along the seam. Then join a block 2' and a piece C (blocks 3 and 3' complete).

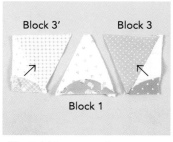

7 Fold the seam allowances of blocks 3 and 3' in the direction of the arrows. Lay out the blocks 1, 3 and 3' flat to check their positioning.

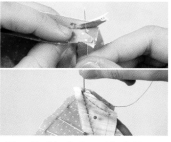

8 Pin blocks 1 and 3, right sides together. Stitch together, then join 3' to the other side. Fold the seam allowances towards 3 and 3'.

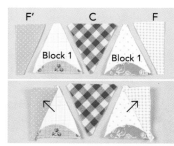

9 Join the blocks assembled to a piece C to form a strip. Join two block 1 pieces to a piece C, F and F' as shown to make second strip.

10 Fold the seam allowances on the second strip towards pieces C, F and F'.

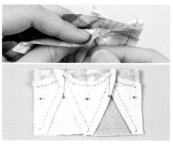

11 Pin the two strips right sides together.

12 Stitch along the seam, making an extra stitch at the junctions. Sew stitch by stitch on any overlapping edges.

Inner City

✳·✳

The three colour shades used here create a three-dimensional effect that is reminiscent of a city skyline. Make triangular blocks by assembling three pieces A, then join the blocks obtained in strips. Lay pieces and blocks out flat to check their positioning before sewing.

Folding the seam allowances

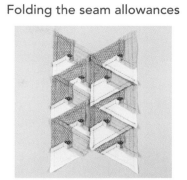

Templates

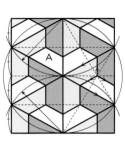

I

Inner City

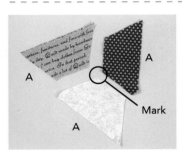

1 Prepare three pieces A.

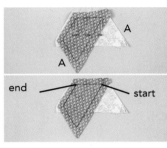

2 Pin two pieces A right sides together as shown. Sew along the seam, making an extra stitch at the start and at the end.

3 Trim the seam allowance to 6mm, then fold it towards the darker coloured piece (block 1 complete).

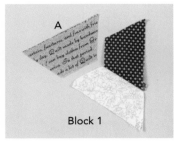

4 Join on one other piece A.

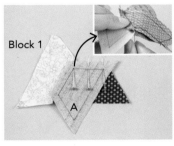

5 Bring block 1 and the piece A right sides together. Pin along the first edge as shown without piercing the seam allowances of block 1.

6 Sew along the seam, making an extra stitch at the start and at the end. Do not cut the thread.

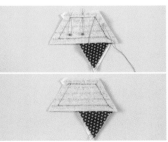

7 Pin along the next edge, then continue to sew to the end. Make an extra stitch here.

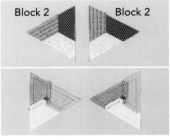

8 Fold all the seam allowances in the same direction (block 2 complete). Make another symmetrical block.

9 Make another four pairs of blocks 2 in the same way. Lay them out as shown above as a guide to positioning.

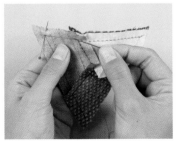

10 Join two blocks 2 right sides together, following step 9 as a guide to placement.

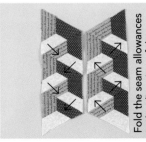

Fold the seam allowances in the direction of the arrows.

11 Join the other blocks so you have two strips as above. Fold the seam allowances in the direction of the arrows.

12 Sew the two strips together, making an extra stitch at the beginning and end of the seam, and at the junctions. Sew stitch by stitch through the overlapping allowances.

Iris

* *

Join pieces into small blocks, then assemble these to make the final block. When assembling interlocking seams, sew along seam lines edge by edge, making extra stitches at the end of each edge. Note: Some pieces are cut symmetrically.

Folding the seam allowances

Templates

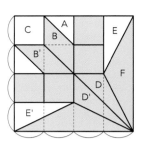

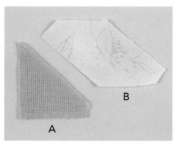

1 Lay out one piece A and one piece B (and one piece A and one piece B') flat to check their positioning.

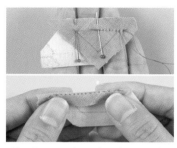

2 Pin A and B right sides together; sew. Join a piece A and B' in the same way. Fold the seam allowances towards piece B and B' (blocks 1 and 1' complete).

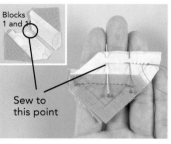

3 Pin blocks 1 and 1' right sides together. Sew along the seam line to the end.

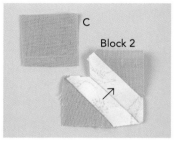

4 Fold the seam allowances to one side (block 2 complete). Prepare one piece C.

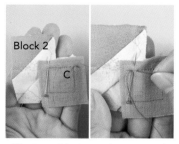

5 Bring block 2 and piece C right sides together, then pin the first edge. Sew along the edge as shown, making an extra stitch at the end.

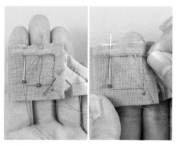

6 Do not cut the thread. Pin along the second edge, then continue to stitch along this edge (block 3 complete).

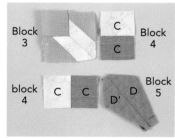

7 Join two pieces C to make block 4. Prepare two blocks 4. Join one piece D and one piece D' to make block 5.

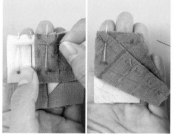

8 Join block 3 and a block 4 to form block 6. Join a block 4 and block 5 to make block 7.

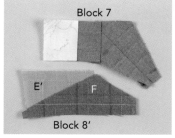

9 Join one piece E' and one piece F as shown to make block 8'. Join blocks 7 and 8' along the edges adjacent to each other as shown above. Fold the allowances towards block 7 (block 9 complete).

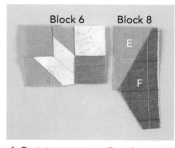

10 Join one piece E and one piece F to make block 8. Join the edges of blocks 6 and 8 as shown above. Fold the allowances towards block 6 (block 10 complete).

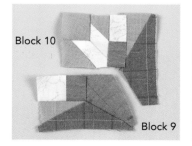

11 Bring blocks 9 and 10 right sides together so the edges that are shown adjacent to one another above match up.

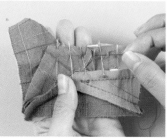

12 Pin the first part of the seam and stitch, taking an extra stitch at the end. Pin along the second part then continue stitching to the end. Fold the allowances to one side.

100

Jasmine

* *

Although this block is made up of straight-edged pieces, the way they are combined creates the impression of a ring shape. As there are quite a large number of pieces to join, pay attention to they way they are positioned and keep corners and angles neat.

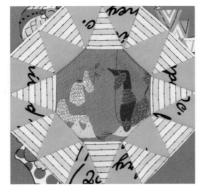

Folding the seam allowances

Templates

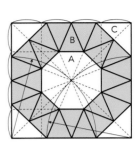

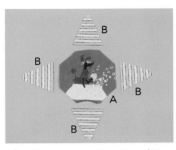

1 Prepare one piece A and 4 pieces B.

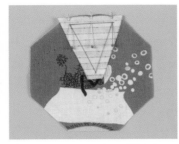

2 Bring a piece A and B right sides together as shown, then pin.

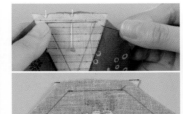

3 Sew along the seam line, starting and finishing just inside the corner points.

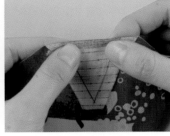

4 Trim the allowance to 6mm, then fold it towards B (block 1 complete).

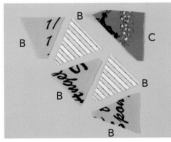

5 Prepare five pieces B and one piece C.

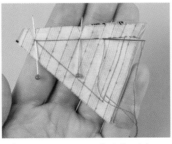

6 Pin two pieces B right sides together and sew. Join together the other pieces B in the order shown in step 5.

7 Fold the seam allowances in the same direction.

8 Pin the block from step 6 and a piece C right sides together; sew. Fold the allowance towards the block (block 2 complete).

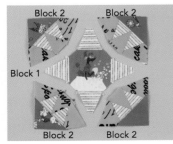

9 Make four blocks 2. Lay out the block 1 and four blocks 2 flat to check their positioning.

10 Bring block 1 and a block 2 right sides together and pin along the first edge, matching seam junctions. Sew, making an extra stitch at the end. Do not cut the thread.

11 Pin the second edge, then take out the needle in piece A and reinsert it, on the other side of the seam allowance. Make an extra stitch, then sew along the second edge.

12 Pin and sew the third edge in the same way. Join on the other blocks 2 in the same way.

Kaleidoscope

Level ✿ ✿ ✿ ✿ ✿

✳·✳

Combine two pieces A with one piece B to form a small block. Make a total of four small blocks to join together into the final block. As all the pieces have straight edges this block is a good one for beginners. Align the corners at the centre and make extra stitches at the junctions to avoid gaps.

Folding the seam allowances

Templates

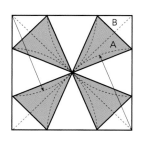

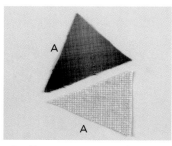

1. Prepare two pieces A. Lay them out flat to check their positioning.

2. Pin the two pieces A right sides together along one long side. Sew, making an extra stitch at the start and end of the seam.

3. Trim the seam allowance to 6mm, then fold it towards the darker coloured piece (block 1 complete).

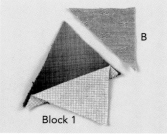

4. Prepare one block 1 and one piece B. Lay them out flat to check their positioning.

5. Pin block 1 and piece B right sides together as shown. Sew, making an extra stitch at the start and end of the seam.

6. Fold the seam allowance towards block 1 (block 2 complete).

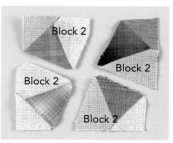

7. Prepare four blocks 2. Lay them to check their positioning.

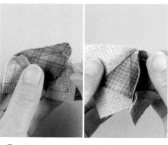

8. Bring two blocks 2 right sides together, then pin and sew (block 3 complete). Join two more blocks 2 to make another block 3.

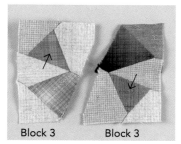

9. Fold the seam allowances on the blocks 3 in the direction of the arrows.

10. Pin the two blocks 3 right sides together. Sew, working stitch by stitch through the overlapping seam allowances.

✳ Assembling Larger Blocks

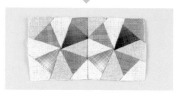

Complete two blocks, then pin them right sides together. Sew, making an extra stitch at the seam junctions.

Kansas Trouble

Use two strongly contrasting coloured fabrics to achieve this striking pattern. Make up strips of small triangles and squares (pieces A and C), then combine with squares made up of larger triangles (pieces B). Make sure the corners match up to get a neat finish.

Folding the seam allowances

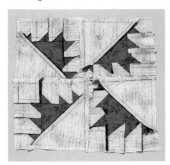

Templates

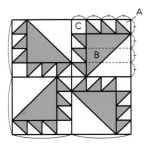

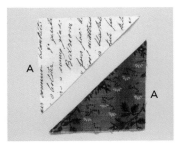

1 Prepare two pieces A. Lay them out flat to check their positioning.

2 Pin the two pieces A right sides together along the long edges. Sew, making an extra stitch at the start and end of the seam.

3 Trim the seam allowance to 6mm, then fold it towards the dark coloured piece (block 1 complete).

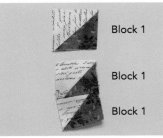

4 Assemble three blocks 1 and join together. Fold the seam allowances towards the dark coloured piece (block 2 complete).

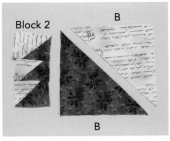

5 Prepare one block 2 and two pieces B.

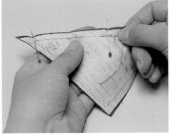

6 Pin the two pieces B right sides together along the long edges; sew. Fold the seam allowances towards the dark coloured piece.

7 Pin the block 2 and square from step 6 right sides together; sew. Fold the seam allowances towards the square block (block 3 complete).

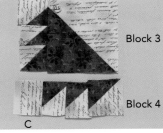

8 Assemble one block 2 and prepare one piece C; join them together. Fold the seam allowance towards a piece A (block 4 complete).

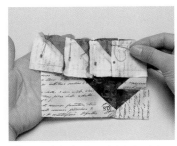

9 Pin blocks 3 and 4 right sides together, then sew. Fold the seam allowances towards block 3 (block 5 complete).

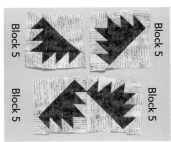

10 Make four blocks 5. Lay them out flat to check their positioning. Pin two blocks 5 right sides together; sew, making extra stitches at the junctions.

11 Join the two other blocks 5 in the same way, then join the two strips together.

12 Iron the back of the finished block to neaten the folded seam allowances.

Key West Star

Join pieces A, B, C and D to form small blocks; make four of these and join togher. The corners of eight pieces meet at the centre. It is important to match them up neatly and to make extra stitches at the corners to avoid gaps. Use contrasting colours for pieces A and D.

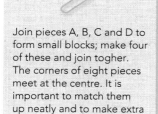

Folding the seam allowances

Templates

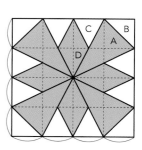

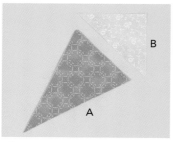

1 Prepare one piece A and one piece B. Lay them out flat to check their positioning.

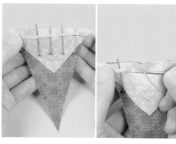

2 Pin pieces A and B, right sides together as shown. Sew along the seam line.

3 Trim the seam allowance to 6mm, then fold it towards piece A (block 1 complete).

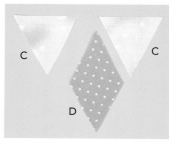

4 Prepare two pieces C and one piece D. Lay them out flat to check their positioning.

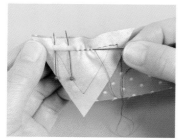

5 Pin a piece C and D, right sides together as shown. Sew along the seam line. Fold the allowances towards piece D.

6 Pin the other piece C and piece D right sides together as shown; sew. Fold the seam allowance towards piece D (block 2 complete).

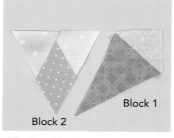

7 One block 1 and one block 2 are made. Iron block 2 to flatten the seam allowances.

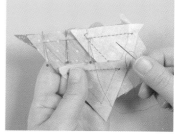

8 Pin blocks 1 and 2 right sides together, as shown; sew, making an extra stitch at the start and end of the seam (block 3 complete).

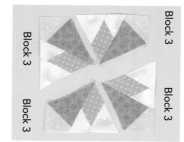

9 Fold the seam allowances towards block 1. Make three more blocks 3.

10 Pin two blocks 3 right sides together, then sew as in step 8. Iron to flatten the seam allowances (block 4 complete).

11 Make a second block 4. Pin the two blocks 4 right sides together, then sew.

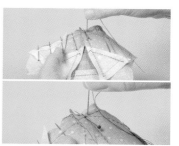

12 Sew stitch by stitch through the overlapping seam allowances. Fold the allowances to one side.

L Patch

Level ★☆☆☆☆

You just have to work from one end to the other to complete this block. First form the strips, then join them together. Make extra stitches at the junction points to avoid any gapping. Fold the seam allowances towards the dark coloured pieces.

Folding the seam allowances

Templates

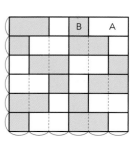

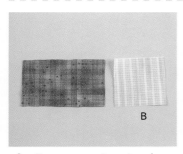

1 Prepare one piece A and one piece B.

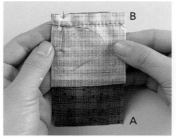

2 Pin pieces A and B right sides together as shown. Sew along the seam line, making an extra stitch at the start and end.

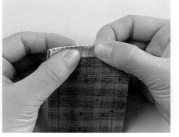

3 Trim the seam allowance to 6mm, then fold it towards piece A (block 1 complete).

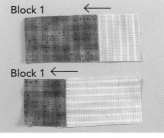

4 Prepare one other block 1 with the colours reversed. Fold the seam allowances towards piece B.

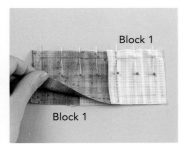

5 Bring the two blocks 1 right sides together, then pin as shown.

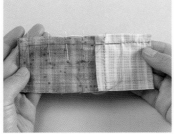

6 Sew along the seam, making an extra stitch at the start and at the end. Fold the seam allowances towards the upper block (block 2 complete).

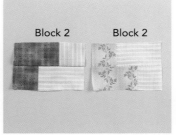

7 Assemble two adjacent blocks 1. Fold the seam allowances to one side.

8 Pin the two blocks 2 right sides together as shown. Sew along the seam.

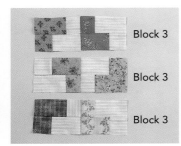

9 Make four other blocks 2, then assemble them in pairs as in step 8. Fold the seam allowances to one side (blocks 3 complete).

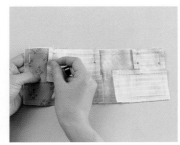

10 Bring two of the blocks 3 right sides together, then pin as shown.

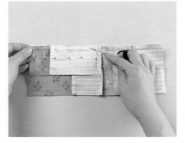

11 Sew the seam, making an extra stitch at the junctions. Fold the seam allowances to one side.

12 Join another block 3 to the first two. Iron the final block on the reverse to flatten the folded seam allowances.

L

L Patch

105

Laced Star

* · *

This complex-looking block is made up of triangle shapes in different sizes, so make sure you are using the correct one in the right place to get the finished motif just right. Use a light fabric for the background pieces A and C so the star motif stands out.

Folding the seam allowances

Templates

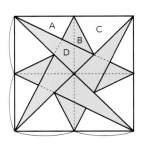

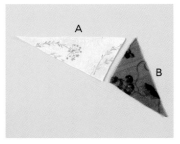

1 Prepare one piece A and one piece B.

2 Pin the pieces A and B right sides together as shown. Sew along the seam line, making an extra stitch at the start and end of the seam.

3 Trim the allowance to 6mm, then fold it towards B (block 1 complete).

4 Prepare one piece C. Pin block 1 and piece C right sides together. Sew as in step 2 (block 2 complete).

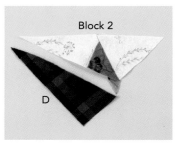

5 Prepare one block 2 and one piece D.

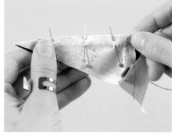

6 Pin block 2 and piece D right sides together as shown; sew (block 3 complete).

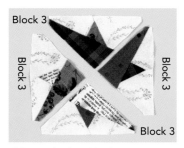

7 Make four blocks 3.

8 Pin two blocks 3 right sides together as shown, matching up seam lines and seam junctions.

9 Sew, making an extra stitch at the seam junctions.

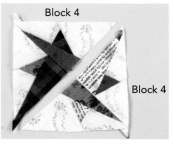

10 Assemble the two other blocks 3 in the same way (two blocks 4 complete).

11 Pin the two blocks 4 right sides together along the long edges and matching seam lines and junctions.

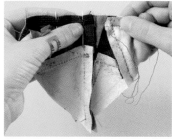

12 Sew along the seam line, making an extra stitch at the start and at the end of the seam.

Lattice

✳ · ✳

Use a combination of several fabrics in the same shade, maing the small triangle pieces A from the same fabrics as the larger pieces. Make sure the corners of the triangles match up and make extra stitches at seam junctions to prevent gaps forming.

Folding the seam allowances

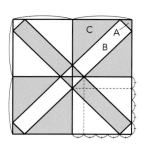

Templates

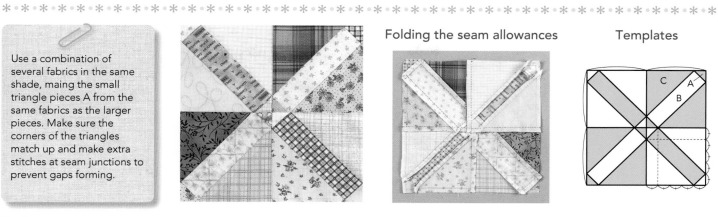

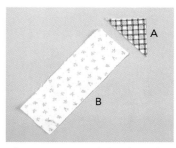

1 Prepare one dark coloured piece A and one piece B.

2 Bring pieces A and B right sides together and pin.

3 Sew along the seam line, making an extra stitch at the start and end.

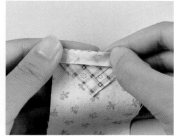

4 Trim the allowance to 6mm, then fold it towards piece A.

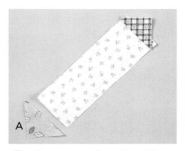

5 Prepare another piece A in a light colour.

6 Pin the piece A right sides together at the other end of the piece B; sew. Fold the allowances towards piece A (block 1 complete).

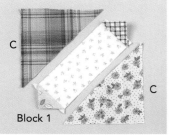

7 Prepare one light and one dark coloured piece C and one block 1.

8 Pin a block 1 and piece C right sides together. Sew along the seam line. Fold the allowances towards the dark coloured piece. Join on the other piece C (block 2 complete).

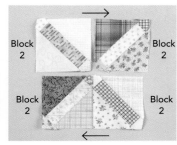

9 Prepare four blocks 2.

10 Pin two blocks 2 right sides together, matching seam junctions. Sew along the seam line. Make an extra stitch at the seam junctions. Join the other two blocks.

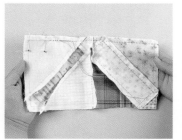

11 Bring the two pieces right sides together then pin at the ends, the junctions and in between. Sew along the seam line. Make an extra stitch at the seam junctions.

12 Fold back the allowances and iron on the wrong side.

L
Lattice

Lemoyne Star

Level

* *

Diamond-shaped pieces A are joined together to form the central star. Square and triangular pieces B and C are joined to the star. Sew interlocking seams edge by edge and make extra stitches at seam junctions to avoid gaps and mismatching.

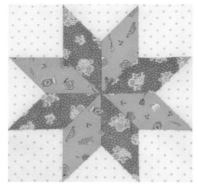

Folding the seam allowances

Templates

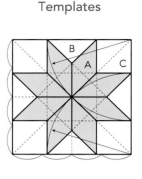

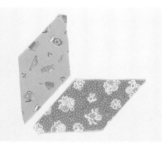

1 Prepare two pieces A.

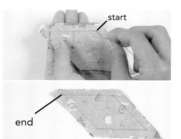

2 Pin the two pieces A right sides together as shown. Sew along the seam line, making an extra stitch at the start and end.

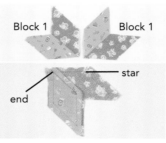

3 Trim the allowance to 6mm, then fold it to the right (block 1 complete). Make four blocks 1, then assemble them in pairs, sewing along the seam line.

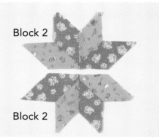

4 Fold the allowances in the same direction as in step 3 (two blocks 2 complete).

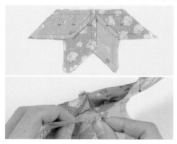

5 Pin the two blocks 2 right sides together and matching the central seam junction.

6 Sew along the seam line, making an extra stitch at the central seam junction (block 3 complete).

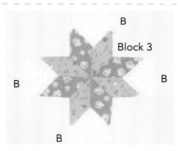

7 Prepare one block 3 and four pieces B.

8 Pin block 3 and a piece B right sides together along the first edge without piercing the allowances.

9 Sew to the end of the seam line without piercing the allowances. Make an extra stitch; do not cut the thread

10 Pin and sew the second edge in the same way. Join on the other pieces B in the same way (block 4 complete).

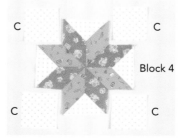

11 Join block 4 and four pieces C in the same way as steps 8 to 10.

* Centre Allowances

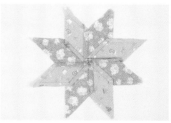

Fold the allowances at the centre in a spiral.

108

Light and Dark

✽ ✻ ✽

Join one piece A and two pieces B to form a central strip. Assemble pieces B, C and D to create two triangular blocks then join them to the central strip. Made up of simple squares and triangles, this is a good beginners' block. Match up any marks to avoid gaps.

Folding the seam allowances

Templates

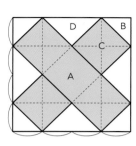

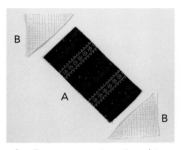

1 Prepare one piece A and two pieces B. Lay them out flat to check their positioning.

2 Pin piece A and a piece B, right sides together as shown; sew. Fold the allowance towards piece A. Join on the other piece B (block 1 complete).

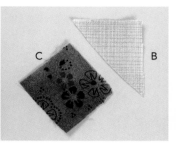

3 Bring one piece B and one piece C right sides together, then pin along the seam line.

4 Sew, making an extra stitch at the start and end of the seam. Fold the seam allowance towards piece C (block 2 complete).

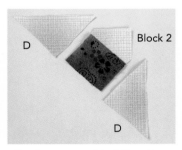

5 Prepare one block 2 and two pieces D.

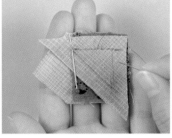

6 Pin block 2 and a piece D right sides together; sew. Fold the seam allowance towards piece C. Join on the other piece D (block 3 complete).

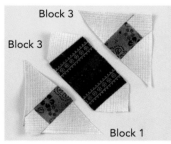

7 Prepare one block 1 and two blocks 3. Bring block 1 and a block 3 right sides together, then pin along the long edges.

8 Sew, making an extra stitch at the start, end and seam junctions. Fold the seam allowances towards block 1. Join on the other block 3.

✷ Assembling Blocks

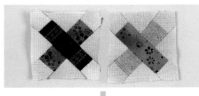

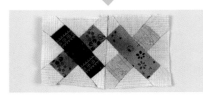

Make sure corners match up when joining together finished blocks. Make extra stitches at the seam junctions so the are more secure.

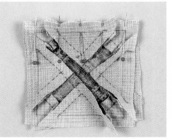

1 Bring two blocks right sides together, then pin along the seam line.

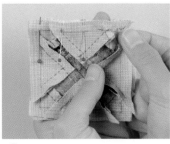

2 Sew, making an extra stitch at the start, end and at the seam junctions.

Log Cabin

* *

Strips of fabric are joined around a central square to represent a log cabin on this block. Start by cutting out the central square, then simply cut the remaining fabrics into strips, trimming them as they are joined. The centre square is traditionally cut from red fabric to represent a fire.

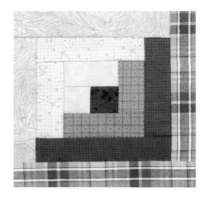

Folding the seam allowances

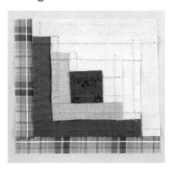

Templates

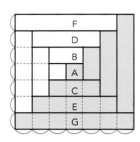

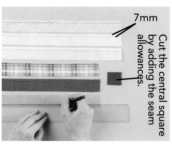

1 Cut out the central square with 7mm seam allowances. Cut out strips of your chosen fabric, the same width as the centre square. Draw the seam line along one edge of each strip.

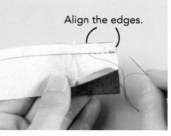

2 Bring the centre piece and first strip right sides together, aligning the edges; pin.

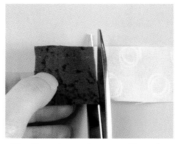

3 Sew along the seam line of the central piece. Cut off the excess strip.

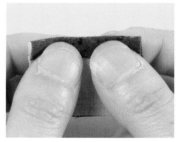

4 Fold the allowance outwards.

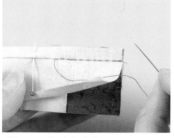

5 Pin the block from step 4 and the remaining strip from step 3 right sides together. Sew along the seam line.

6 Cut off the excess strip.

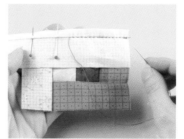

7 Continue to add strips around the centre block in the same way.

8 Iron the back to fold down the allowances.

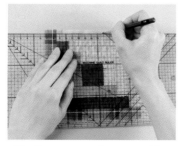

9 Draw a seam line around the finished block to facilitate the joining of this block to others.

* Tip

Using a rotary cutter is an easy way to cut out strips.

If you are making a small block and there are not many pieces, cut them out using templates.

London Bridge

* *

One piece A is joined to two pieces B to make a small block. Four of these are made and then joined. Mark curved edges and match these up; sew the curves with small stitches and make extra stitches at the junctions to avoid mismatch. Choose contrasting fabrics for the background pieces B.

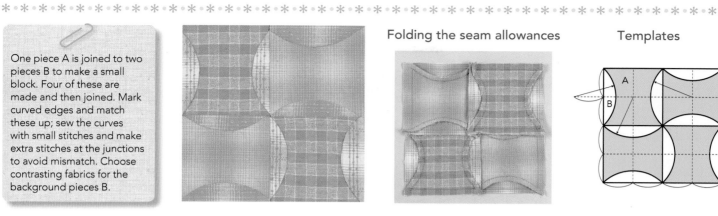

Folding the seam allowances

Templates

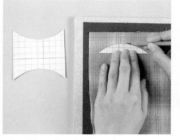

1 Transfer the templates to the wrong side of the fabric. Add seam allowances and mark the curved seam lines as shown on the template diagram. Cut out the pieces.

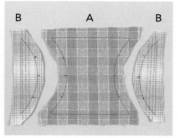

2 Prepare one piece A and two pieces B.

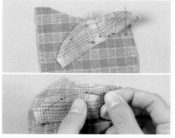

3 Pin one piece B one piece A right sides together up to the centre point, matching points. Sew to the centre point. Make an extra stitch; do not cut the thread.

4 Pin along the other half of the edge, then sew to the end. Make an extra stitch.

5 Trim the allowance to 6mm, then fold it towards piece B.

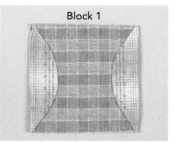

6 Join on the other piece B in the same way (block 1 complete). Make four blocks 1.

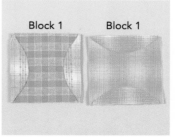

7 Prepare two blocks 1.

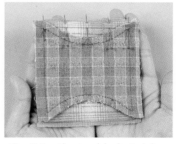

8 Bring the two blocks 1 right sides together, then pin.

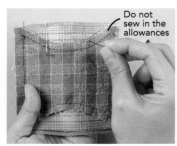

9 Sew along the seam line, making an extra stitch at the start and end and without stitching in the allowances of block 1 (block 2 complete). Make two blocks 2.

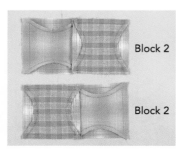

10 Prepare two blocks 2. Fold back the allowances in the opposite direction for the two blocks.

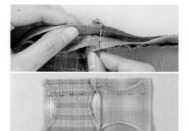

11 Bring the two blocks 2 right sides together, then pin without piercing the central allowances.

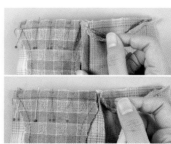

12 Sew along the seam line. Make an extra stitch at the centre without piercing the allowances.

Lost Ship

* *

This block represents a boat sinking. Choose dark coloured fabric pieces for the boat shapes. All the pieces are joined together along straight edges, so it's a simple block to make. Join pieces into diagonal strips before joining them.

Folding the seam allowances

Templates

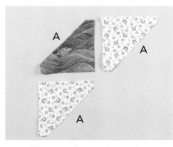

1   Prepare three pieces A.

2   Pin two pieces A right sides together as shown. Sew along the seam line, making an extra stitch at the start.

3   Sew to the end, making an extra stitch.

4   Trim the allowance to 6mm, then fold it towards the dark coloured piece. Join on the other piece A in the same way (block 1 complete).

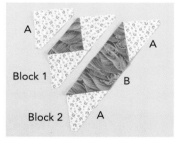

5   Assemble two pieces A and one piece B in the same way. Fold back the allowances towards piece B (block 2 complete). Prepare one block A, one block 1 and one block 2.

6   Pin blocks 1 and 2 right sides together. Sew along the seam line. Fold the allowances towards the dark colour piece. Join on piece A (block 3 complete).

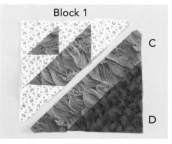

7   Pin one piece C and one piece D right sides together. Sew along the seam line. Fold the allowances towards piece C (block 4 complete).

8   Bring blocks 3 and 4 right sides together and pin. Sew along the seam line. Fold the allowances towards block 4.

Variations of the Lost Ship Block

* *

There are several ways to join the pieces. Join the small triangles to form strips, then join them to the other pieces.

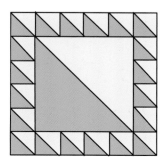

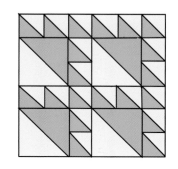

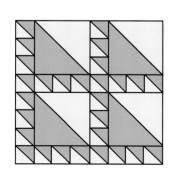

Magnolia Bud

＊・＊

A combination of small blocks make up the bud and leaves of this block. Some pieces are cut symmetrically so check their positioning before assembly. And take care not to stretch those edges cut on the diagonal. Use suitable coloured fabrics to represent the flowers and leaves.

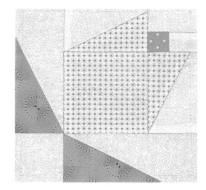

Folding the seam allowances

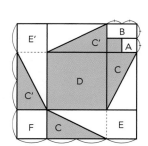

Templates

1. Prepare two pieces A and one piece B.

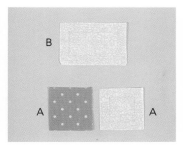

2. Pin the two pieces A right sides together. Sew along the seam line. Fold the allowances towards the dark coloured piece (block 1 complete).

3. Pin block 1 and piece B right sides together. Sew along the seam line. Fold the allowances towards block 1 (block 2 complete).

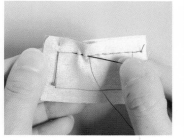

4. Prepare two pieces C and two pieces C'.

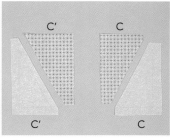

5. Pin and sew the two pieces C right sides together. Fold the allowances towards the dark coloured piece. Join the two pieces C' (blocks 3 and 3' complete).

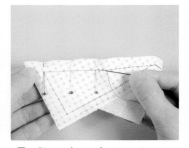

6. Join one piece C and one piece E as in step 5; repeat with one piece C' and one piece E'. Fold the allowances towards pieces C and C' (blocks 4 and 4' complete).

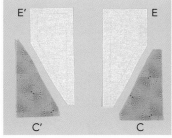

7. Prepare blocks 2, 3, 3' and 4 and one piece D. Lay them out flat to check their positioning.

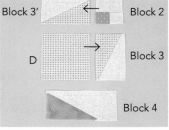

8. Pin blocks 2 and 3' right sides together. Sew along the seam line. Join block 3 and piece D in the same way.

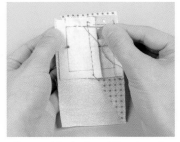

9. Pin the top and centre strips right sides together. Sew, making an extra stitch at the junctions. Join the lower strip in the same way (block 5 complete).

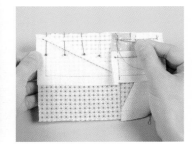

10. Join block 4' and one piece B. Fold the allowances towards block 4' (block 6 complete).

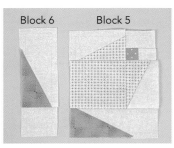

11. Pin blocks 5 and 6 right sides together at the ends, at the seam junctions and in between.

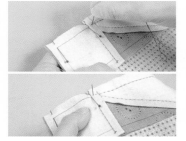

12. Sew along the seam line. Sew stitch by stitch on the overlapping allowances. Fold the allowances towards block 5.

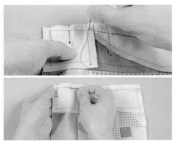

Maple Leaf 1

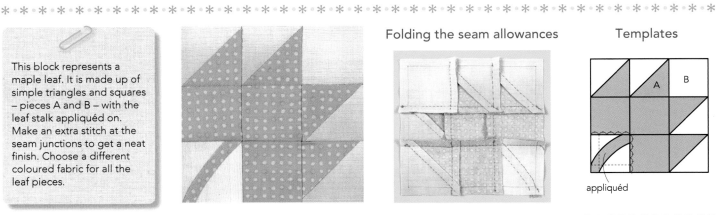

This block represents a maple leaf. It is made up of simple triangles and squares – pieces A and B – with the leaf stalk appliquéd on. Make an extra stitch at the seam junctions to get a neat finish. Choose a different coloured fabric for all the leaf pieces.

Folding the seam allowances

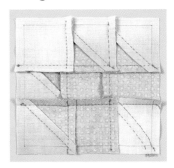

Templates

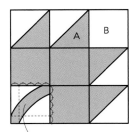

appliquéd

M

Maple Leaf

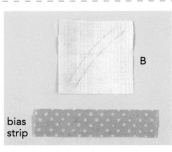

bias strip

1 Cut a bias strip three times the width of the stem and mark with seam lines. Prepare one piece B and draw around the stem template on the right side of the piece.

2 Pin the bias strip on piece B, right sides together and matching one seam line on the strip with the inner curve of the stem on piece B; sew. Fold the strip over and turning the edge under as you go, slip stitch it in place.

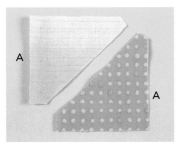

3 Prepare two pieces A in different fabrics.

4 Pin the two pieces A right sides together as shown. Sew along the seam line, making an extra stitch at the start and end (block 1 ocmplete).

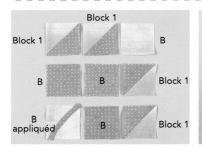

5 Fold the allowances of block 1 towards the dark piece. Prepare four pieces B, one appliquéd piece B and four blocks 1. Lay them out flat to check their positioning.

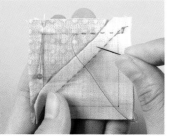

6 Bring two adjacent blocks right sides together, then pin. Sew along the seam line.

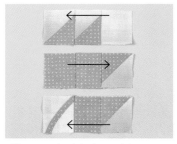

7 Join the blocks and the pieces to get three strips. Fold the allowances in the direction of the arrows.

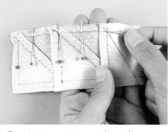

8 Pin two strips right sides together, then sew, making an extra stitch at the seam junctions. Join on the other strip. Fold the allowances towards the central strip.

Variation of the Maple Leaf Block Maple Leaf 2 ✳✳✳✳✳✳✳✳✳✳✳✳✳✳✳✳✳✳✳✳✳✳✳✳

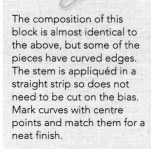

The composition of this block is almost identical to the above, but some of the pieces have curved edges. The stem is appliquéd in a straight strip so does not need to be cut on the bias. Mark curves with centre points and match them for a neat finish.

Folding the seam allowances

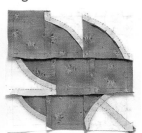

Templates

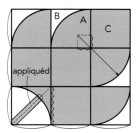

appliquéd

Mariner's Compass

* · *

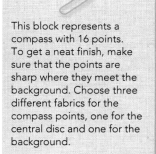

This block represents a compass with 16 points. To get a neat finish, make sure that the points are sharp where they meet the background. Choose three different fabrics for the compass points, one for the central disc and one for the background.

Folding the seam allowances

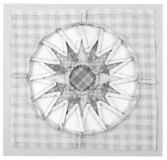

Templates

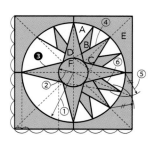

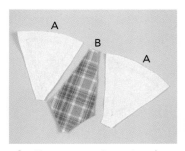

1 Prepare two pieces A and one piece B.

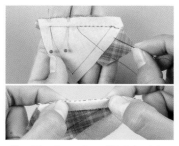

2 Pin pieces A and B right sides together as shown. Sew along the seam line, making an extra stitch at the start and end. Trim the allowance and fold towards piece B.

3 Join on the other piece A in the same way (block 1 complete).

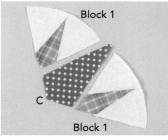

4 Prepare two blocks 1 and one piece C.

5 Pin block 1 and piece C right sides together. Sew along the seam line. Fold the allowances towards piece C. Join on the other block 1 (block 2 complete).

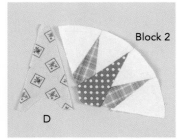

6 Join block 2 and one piece D right sides together as in step 5. Fold the allowance towards piece D (block 3 complete).

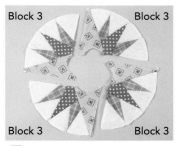

7 Make four blocks 3. Assemble them to form a circle (block 4 complete)

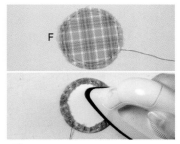

8 Make even stitches around the allowance of piece F. Put the template on the wrong side and pull the thread to turn under the allowance. Press and remove the template.

9 Pin the piece F to the centre of block 4 and sew in place, using slip stitches.

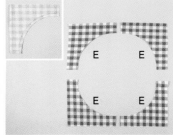

10 Prepare four pieces E. Make marks along the curved edges that match up with the points on block 4. Join the four pieces E (block 5 complete).

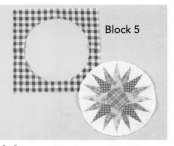

11 Bring blocks 4 and 5 right sides together and pin, matching the marks on block 5 with the points on block 4.

12 Sew, using small stitches. Fold the allowances inwards.

Mariner's Delight

Pieces A and B are joined to form diamond shapes, that are, in turn, joined together to form the central star. The bottom edges of pieces A and B are curved, so take care to match these edges during construction. Match up seam lines and corners to get a crisp result.

Folding the seam allowances

Templates

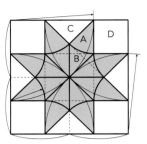

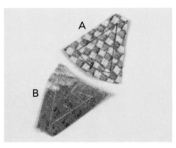

1 Prepare one piece A and one piece B. Mark on the seam lines.

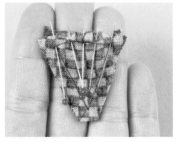

2 Pin pieces A and B right sides together along their curved edges, as shown.

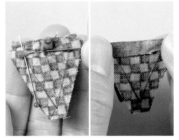

3 Sew, making an extra stitch at the start and end of the seam line. Trim the allowance to 6mm, then fold it towards piece A (block 1 complete).

4 Make eight blocks 1. Join them in pairs right sides together. Fold the allowances to one side (block 2 complete).

5 Make four blocks 2. Join them in pairs, right sides together. Fold the allowances to one side (two blocks 3 complete).

6 Pin the blocks 3 right sides together. Sew along the seam line, making an extra stitch at the start and end. Fold the allowances towards the upper block (block 4 complete).

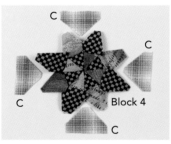

7 Prepare one block 4 and four pieces C. Lay them out flat to check their positioning.

8 Bring the block 4 and one piece C right sides together and pin along the first edge; sew.

9 Make an extra stitch at the end. Do not cut the thread. Pin the second edge without piercing the seam allowances.

10 Sew, without stitching in the allowances. Fold the allowances towards block 4. Join on the three other pieces C in the same way (block 5 complete).

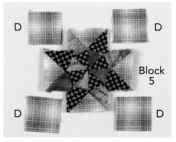

11 Prepare one block 5 and four pieces D.

12 Join the pieces D to block 5 in the same way as described in steps 8 and 9. Fold the allowances towards block 5.

May Flower

* *

Pieces A, B and C are joined to make four small blocks, that are then joined together. When joining the small blocks take care to sew the seams one by one, making extra stitches at the junctions. Choose a different fabric for the pieces A so these shapes stand out.

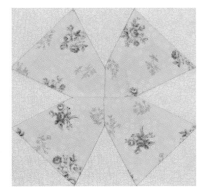

Folding the seam allowances

Templates

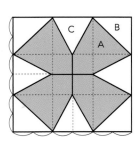

1 Prepare one piece A, one piece B and one piece C.

2 Pin pieces A and B right sides together as shown. Sew along the seam line, making an extra stitch at the start and end.

3 Trim the allowance to 6mm, then fold it towards piece A

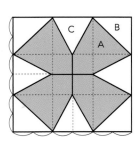

4 Pin the block from step 3 and piece C right sides together. Sew along the seam. Fold the allowances towards piece A (block 1 complete).

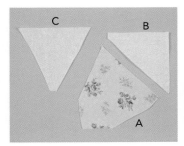

5 Make four blocks 1.

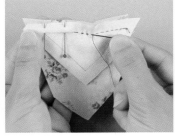

6 Bring two blocks 1 right sides together, then pin along the first edge.

7 Sew along the seam line. Make an extra stitch; do not cut the thread.

8 Pin the next edge without piercing the allowances. Sew along this seam line. Make an extra stitch.

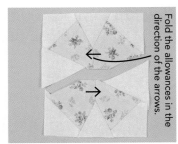

Fold the allowances in the direction of the arrows.

9 Join the other two blocks 1. Fold the allowances in the direction of the arrows.

10 Pin two strips right sides together along the first edge. Sew along the seam line. Make an extra stitch; do not cut the thread.

11 Pin the second edge. Sew along the seam line without piercing the allowances. Make an extra stitch; do not cut the thread.

12 Pin and sew the third edge in the same way. Fold the allowances towards piece A.

Merry-Go-Round

✻ ✻

Start by joining one piece A to three pieces B, then join three more pieces B to pairs of pieces C. Assemble these blocks to make the whole. Choose strongly coloured fabrics for the square pieces B so the pattern they form stands out.

Folding the seam allowances

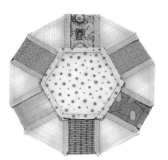

Templates

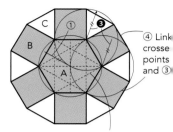

④ Link crosse points and ③

② Draw the hexagon in the circle ①. Connect the angles and extend these

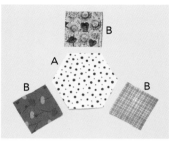

1 Prepare one piece A and three pieces B.

2 Pin pieces A and B right sides together as shown. Sew along the seam line, making an extra stitch at the start and end. Join the other pieces B. Fold the allowances towards the pieces B (block 1 complete).

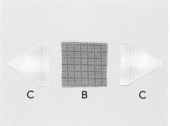

3 Prepare one piece B and two pieces C.

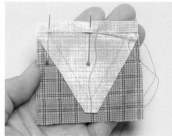

4 Pin pieces B and C right sides together. Sew along the seam line, making an extra stitch at the start and end. Join the other pieces C. Fold the allowances towards the piece B (block 2 complete).

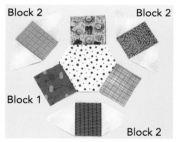

5 Prepare one block 1 and three blocks 2. Lay them out to check their positioning.

6 Pin a block 1 and 2 right sides together along the first edge without piercing the allowances. Sew along the seam line. Make an extra stitch; do not cut the thread.

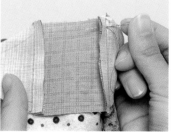

7 Pin the second edge. Insert the needle in the corner of the first piece and bring it out at the corner of the second piece without piercing the allowances.

8 Sew along the seam line. Pin and sew the third edge in the same way. Join on the remaining blocks 2.

✱Assembling several blocks

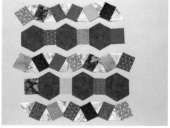

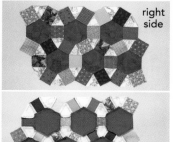

right side

wrong side

Join the pieces in strips as shown above. Sew strips together as in steps 6 to 8. Fold the allowances of pieces A outwards and those of pieces C towards pieces C.

Variation of the Merry-Go-Round Block Morning Glory 1

Folding the seam allowances

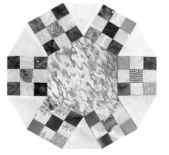

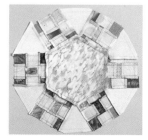

Use nine small squares to make the pieces B of the Merry-Go-Round block. Use light and dark colours for this nine-patch block, folding allowances towards the dark coloured pieces.

M
Merry-Go-Round

118

Midnight Summer

* *

The design of this block features two crosses that meet at the centre. Pieces A and B are joined to form the first cross; pieces C, D and E are joined in blocks to form the second cross and background. Piece A is not a regular octagon so check its position.

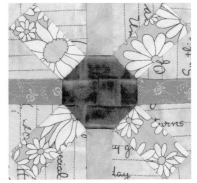

Folding the seam allowances

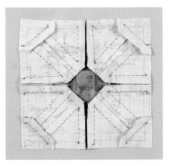

Templates

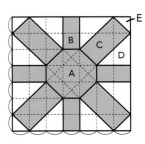

1 Prepare one piece A and four pieces B. Lay them out flat to check their positioning: the short ends of the B pieces should meet the shorter sides of A.

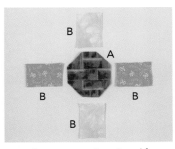

2 Pin pieces A and B right sides together as shown. Sew along the seam line, making an extra stitch at the start and end.

3 Trim the allowance to 6mm, then fold it towards piece B. Join the three other pieces B in the same way (block 1 complete).

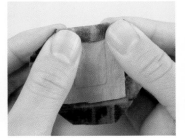

4 Prepare one piece C , two pieces D and one piece E. Lay them out flat to check their positioning.

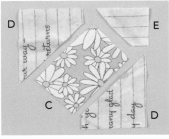

5 Pin the pieces C and D right sides together as shown. Sew along the seam line, making an extra stitch at the start and end.

6 Join the other piece D to the opposite side of the piece C. Trim the allowances, then fold them towards piece C.

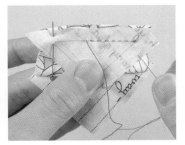

7 Pin the block made in step 6 and the piece E right sides together as shown. Sew along the seam line. Fold the allowances towards piece C (block 2 complete). Make three more blocks 2.

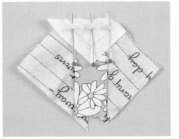

8 Prepare one block 1 and four blocks 2. Lay them out flat to check their positioning.

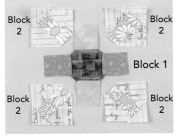

9 Bring block 1 and a block 2 right sides together, then pin along the first edge without piercing the allowances; sew.

10 Make one extra stitch at the first corner: do not cut the thread.

11 Pin the second edge without piercing the allowances. Take the needle out through the corner of piece D and in through the corner of piece C.

12 Pin and sew the second edge; pin and sew the third edge. Join on the other blocks 2 in the same way.

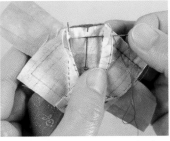

M
Midnight Summer

Mill & Star

Level ★ ★ ☆ ☆ ☆

* · *

By combining triangles and kite-shaped pieces, this block features a star and windmill motifs. Choose four different fabrics – two light and two dark. Alternate between light and dark as you assemble the pieces to get the maximum effect. This is a good block to make using larger pieces of fabric.

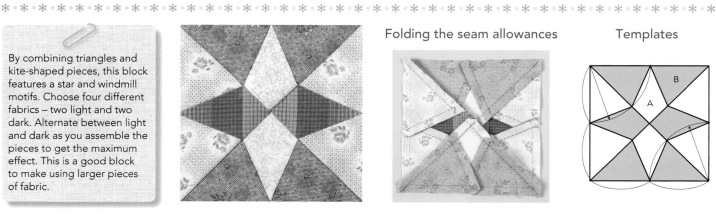

Folding the seam allowances

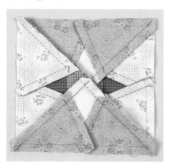

Templates

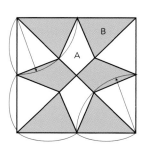

1 Prepare one piece A and two pieces B.

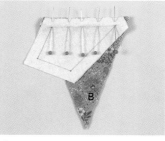

2 Pin pieces A and B right sides together as shown.

3 Sew along the seam line, making an extra stitch at the start and end.

4 Trim the allowance to 6mm, then fold it towards piece A.

5 Join on the other piece B in the same way (block 1 complete).

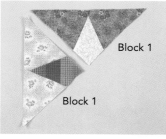

6 Make two blocks 1, reversing the colour combination for the second block.

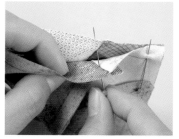

7 Bring the two blocks 1 right sides together, then pin at the ends, at the seam junctions and in between.

8 Sew along the seam line, making an extra stitch at the seam junctions. Sew stitch by stitch on overlapping allowances (block 2 complete).

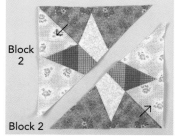

9 Make two blocks 2. Fold the allowances in the direction of the arrows.

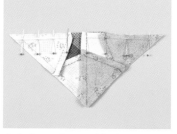

10 Bring the two blocks 2 right sides together, then pin at the ends, at the seam junctions and in between.

11 Sew along the seam line, making an extra stitch at the start, end and seam junctions. Sew stitch by stitch on overlapping allowances.

*Assembling four blocks

By changing the direction of the blocks when combining blocks, a pinwheel appears in the centre.

Mixed T

✳ ✳

Pieces A and C are joined to form the letter T on four small blocks that are combined into a whole. Choose similar but different coloured fabrics for these pieces to highlight the letters. Make sure corners match up and make extra stitches at seam junctions to avoid gapping.

Folding the seam allowances

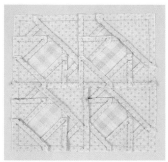

Templates

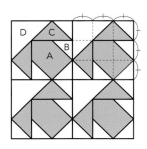

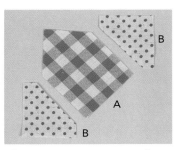

1 Prepare one piece A and two pieces B.

2 Pin pieces A and B right sides together as shown. Sew along the seam line, making an extra stitch at the start and end.

3 Trim the allowance to 6mm, then fold it towards piece A. Join on the other piece B in the same way (block 1 complete).

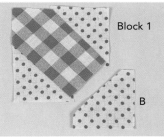

4 Join one block 1 and one piece B. Fold the allowances towards piece A (block 2 complete).

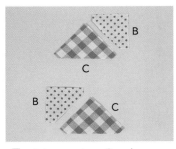

5 Join one piece C and one piece B. Fold the allowances towards piece C (block 3 complete). Make two blocks 3.

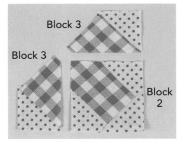

6 Join one block 2 and two blocks 3, sewing along the seam lines. Fold the allowances towards the blocks 3 (block 4 complete).

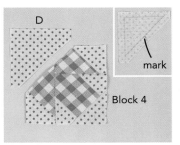

7 Prepare one block 4 and one piece D. Mark the centre point on the long edge of piece D.

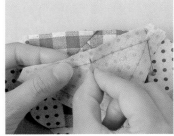

8 Pin block 4 and piece D right sides together, matching the mark on piece D to the tip of the point on piece A of block 4; sew.

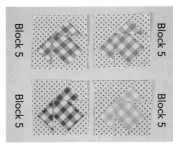

9 Fold the allowances towards block 4 (block 5 complete). Make four blocks 5.

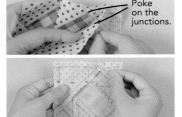

10 Bring two blocks 5 right sides together, then pin the ends, the seam junctions and in between. Sew along the seam line, making an extra stitch at the start, end and seam junctions.

11 Join the two other blocks 5 in the same way. Fold back the allowances in alternate directions.

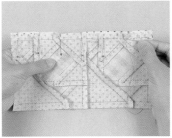

12 Pin the two strips right sides together. Sew along the seam line, making an extra stitch at the start, end and seam junctions. Fold the allowances to one side.

Morning Glory 2

✳＊✳

Make a mark in the middle of the curve on pieces A and B. When pinning the curved edges, use pins closely spaced and then sew using small stitches to avoid any gapping. Alternate pieces of fabric in dark and light colours.

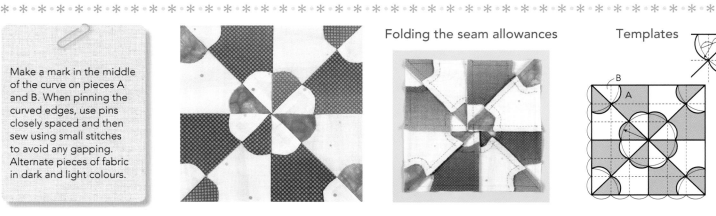

Folding the seam allowances

Templates

1   Prepare one piece A and two pieces B. Mark the centre points of the curved edges.

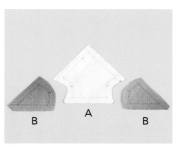

2   Bring a piece B and a piece A right sides together, matching the centre points on the curves, and pin.

3   Sew using small stitches. Make an extra stitch at the start and end of the seam.

4   Trim the allowances if necessary, then fold towards piece B. Join on the other piece B in the same way (block 1 complete).

5   Make seven more blocks 1. Lay them out flat to check their positioning.

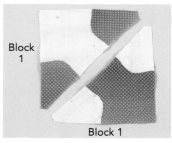

6   Bring two blocks 1 right sides together, then pin along the seam as shown.

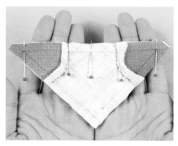

7   Sew along the seam, working stitch by stitch on overlapping allowances. Make an extra stitch at the seam junction (block 2 complete). Make three more blocks 2.

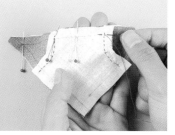

8   Lay out the four blocks 2 flat to check their positioning.

9   Bring two blocks 2 right sides together, then pin along the seams as shown. Sew along the seam.

10   Join the two other blocks 2 in the same way. Fold the seam allowances in the opposite direction for the two strips just made.

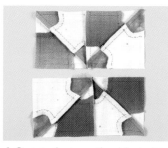

11   Bring the two strips right sides together, then pin the seam as shown. Sew the seam, making an extra stitch at each junction point to avoid any gapping. Fold the seam allowances to one side.

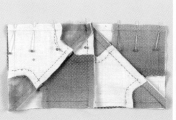

Mosaic 1

* *

Pieces A, B and C are joined into diagonal strips that are then joined. Match up seam junctions and corners to avoid a mismatch. Fold the allowances towards dark coloured pieces. Choose fabrics that highlight the cross motif.

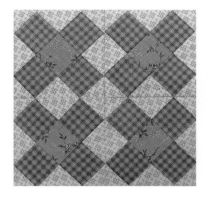

Folding the seam allowances

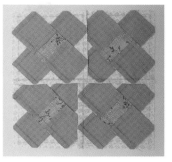

Templates

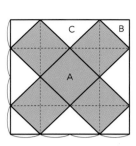

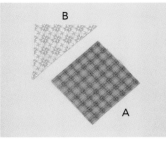

1 Prepare one piece A and one piece B.

2 Bring the pieces A and B right sides together and pin.

3 Sew along the seam line, making an extra stitch at the start and end of the seam.

4 Trim the allowance to 6mm, then fold it towards piece B (block 1 complete).

M
Mosaic 1

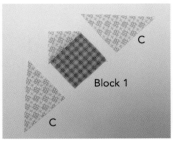

5 Prepare one block 1 and two pieces C.

6 Pin block 1 and a piece C right sides together. Sew along the seam line. Fold the allowances towards piece C. Join on the other piece C (block 2 complete).

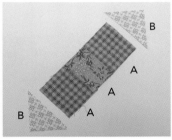

7 Join three pieces A. Fold the allowances towards the centre. Join on one piece B on either side (block 3 complete).

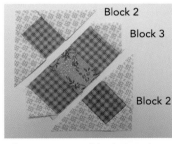

8 Prepare two blocks 2 and one block 3.

9 Pin a block 2 and 3 right sides together. Sew along the seam line. Join the other block 2 in the same way (block 4 complete).

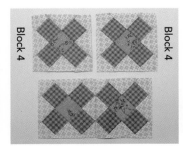

10 Prepare four blocks 4. Join them in pairs to form two strips. Fold back the allowances, alternating the direction for the two strips.

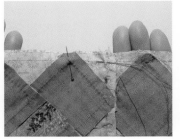

11 Pin the two strips right sides together. Sew along the seam line, making an extra stitch at the seam junctions.

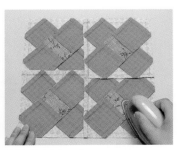

12 Fold the allowances to one side; press.

Mosaic 2

✳ ✳

As all the pieces are joined along straight edges, this block is good for beginners. Blocks are formed into diagonal strips and then joined. Be careful not to stretch any edges cut on the diagonal. Make extra stitches at seam junctions. Choose two different fabrics for the square pieces.

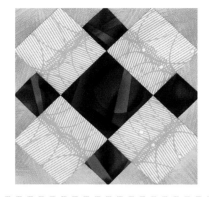

Folding the seam allowances

Templates

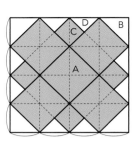

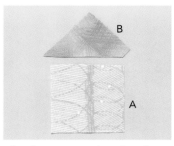

1 Prepare one piece A and one piece B.

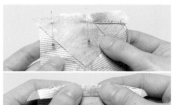

2 Pin pieces A and B right sides together. Sew along the seam line, making an extra stitch at the start and end. Fold the allowances towards piece B (block 1 complete).

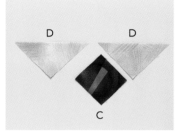

3 Prepare one piece C and two pieces D.

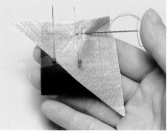

4 Pin the pieces C and D right sides together. Sew along the seam line. Fold the allowances towards piece C. Join on the other piece D in the same way (block 2 complete).

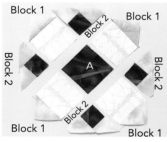

5 Prepare four blocks 1, four blocks 2 and one piece A. Lay them out flat to check their positioning.

6 Pin a block 1 and 2 right sides together. Sew along the seam line. Fold the allowances towards block 2. Join on another block 2 (block 3 complete).

7 Pin a block 1 and piece A right sides together. Sew along the seam line. Fold the allowances towards piece A. Join on the other block 1 (block 4 complete).

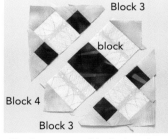

8 Prepare two blocks 3 and one block 4.

9 Pin a block 3 and 4 right sides together. Sew along the seam line. Make an extra stitch at the seam junctions. Fold the allowances outwards. Join on the other block 3.

✳ Assembling several blocks

Make sure you match the corners of each pieces to get a neat finish.

Pin 2 blocks right sides together. Sew stitch by stitch on overlapping allowances and make extra stitches at the seam junctions.

Mother's Choice

* *

Choose two different fabrics for the strips (pieces A and C) that cross in this pattern. Use one lighter-coloured fabric for the pieces B that form the background. As all the pieces being join along straight lines, this block is easy for beginners.

Folding the seam allowances

Templates

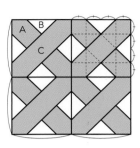

1. Prepare one piece A and two pieces B.

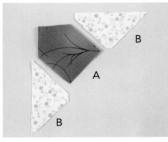

2. Pin pieces A and B right sides together as shown. Sew along the seam line, making an extra stitch at the start and end.

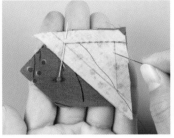

3. Trim the allowance to 6mm, then fold it towards piece A.

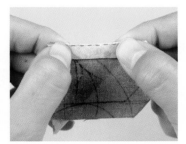

4. Join on the other piece B in the same way. Fold the allowances in the direction of the arrows (block 1 complete). Make eight blocks 1.

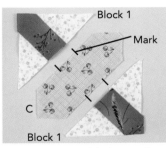

5. Prepare two blocks 1 and one piece C. Mark the long edges of piece C with the positions of the seam junctions on the blocks 1.

6. Bring a block 1 and piece C right sides together, matching up the marks and seam junctions; pin.

7. Sew along the seam line, making an extra stitch at the start and end. Join on the other block 1 in the same way. Fold the allowances towards piece C (block 2 complete).

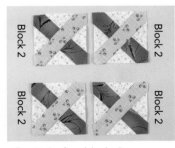

8. Make four blocks 2.

9. Bring two blocks 2 right sides together, matching up the seam junctions, then pin.

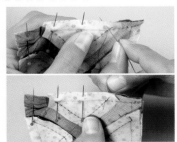

10. Sew along the seam line, making an extra stitch at the seam junctions. Sew stitch by stitch on overlapping allowances.

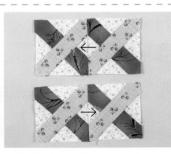

11. The two strips are made. Fold the allowances in the direction of the arrows.

12. Join the two strips together as described in steps 9 and 10. Fold the allowances to one side.

M

Mother's Choice

Nine Patch

* • * •

This block is made up of nine equal squares. Choose two different coloured fabrics and alternate between them. Pieces are joined in threes to form three strips, that are then joined together. Match up corners for a neat finish. This is the basic block of traditional patchwork.

Folding the seam allowances

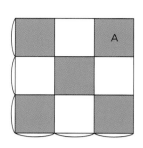

Templates

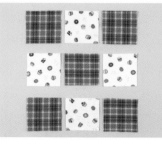

1 Prepare nine pieces A, using light and dark coloured fabrics.

2 Pin two pieces A right sides together as shown. Sew along the seam line, making an extra stitch at the start and end.

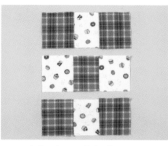

3 Join pieces A in threes as shown to make three strips. Fold the allowances towards the dark coloured pieces.

4 Pin two strips right sides together. Sew along the seam line making an extra stitch at the seam junctions. Fold the allowances towards the top and bottom strips.

Variations on the Nine Patch

Calicot Puzzle

* • * • * • * • * • * • * • * • * • * • * • * • * • * • * • * • * • * • * • *

This block is similar to the nine patch – it varies in that the outer squares are made up out of two triangles (pieces A). Join the pieces A and then follow the steps above. Choose two different fabrics for the four pieces B forming the cross and two other contrasting colours for the triangles.

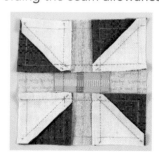

Folding the seam allowances

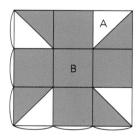

Templates

Hourglass

* • * • * • * • * • * • * • * • * • * • * • * • * • * • * • * • * • * • * • *

In this block, only two of the outer squares are divided into triangles – they are positioned opposite each other. Use four different fabrics and arrange them as shown to create the hourglass shape.

Folding the seam allowances

Templates

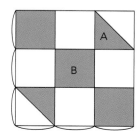

Nocturne

✳ · ✳

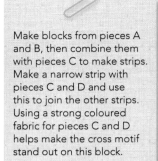

Make blocks from pieces A and B, then combine them with pieces C to make strips. Make a narrow strip with pieces C and D and use this to join the other strips. Using a strong coloured fabric for pieces C and D helps make the cross motif stand out on this block.

Folding the seam allowances

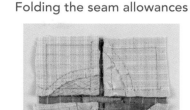

Templates

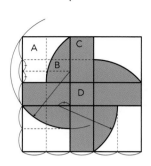

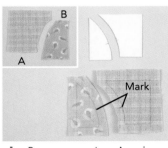

1   Prepare one piece A and one piece B. Mark the seam lines, marking the centre point on the curved edges.

2   Pin pieces A and B right sides together along their curved edges, matching up the centre points.

3   Sew along the seam line, using small stitches and making an extra stitch at the start and end.

4   Trim the allowance to 6mm, then fold it towards piece B (block 1 complete). Make four blocks 1.

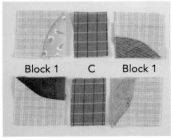

5   Prepare four blocks 1 and two pieces C. Lay them out flat to check their positioning.

6   Pin a block 1 and piece C right sides together; sew. Fold the allowances towards piece C. Join on another block 1 (block 2 complete). Assemble another block 2.

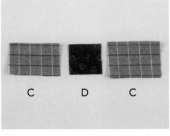

7   Prepare two pieces C and one piece D.

8   Pin a piece C and D right sides together. Sew along the seam line. Fold the allowances towards piece C. Join on the other piece C (block 3 complete).

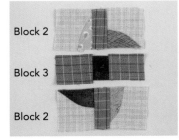

9   Lay the blocks out flat to check their positioning.

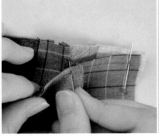

10   Bring blocks 2 and 3 right sides together. Use a pin to help match up the seam junctions; pin. Sew along the seam line making an extra stitch at the seam junctions. Join the other block 2 on the opposite side of block 3 in the same way.

✳ Tip

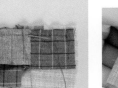
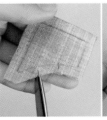

Snipping into the curved edges of pieces A will make it easier to fold the allowances.

Ocean Wave

* *

Take care with how you combine colours for this block. Alternate between light and dark colours for the pieces A. Join small triangles around piece B to form a larger square. Then join on more small blocks around the square.

Folding the seam allowances

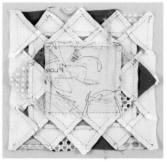

Templates

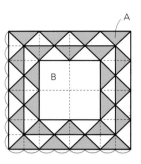

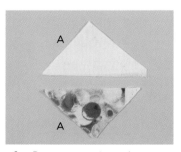

1 Prepare two pieces A.

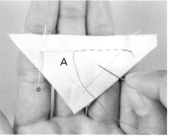

2 Pin the two pieces A right sides together. Sew along the seam as shown, making an extra stitch at the start and the end.

3 Trim the seam allowance to 6mm, then fold it towards the darker coloured piece (block 1 complete).

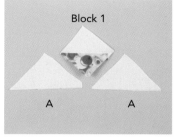

4 Prepare two other pieces A, position them on either side of block 1.

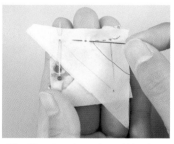

5 Pin one piece A and block 1 right sides together. Sew along the seam as shown. Join the other piece A to block 1 (block 2 complete).

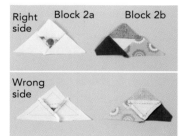

6 Assemble six blocks 2a with a dark colour in the centre and six blocks 2b with a light colour in the centre. Fold seam allowances towards dark coloured pieces.

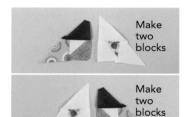

7 Assemble eight blocks 2a and 2b in pairs to make four blocks 3.

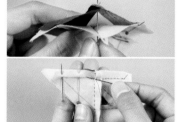

8 Pin together as shown, matching the junctions. Sew along the seam as shown. Fold the allowances towards block 2b.

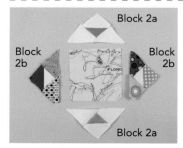

9 Position the remaining blocks 2a on either side of piece B, and the remaining blocks 2b on the other sides

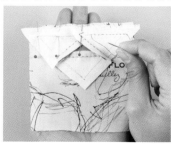

10 Pin piece B and a block 2a right sides together. Sew the seam as shown. Join on the other 2a and 2b pieces (block 4 complete).

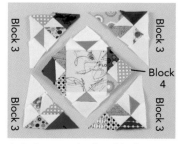

11 Position the four blocks 3 around the block 4. Pin the blocks 3 and 4 right sides together, then pin the ends and junctions and between the pins.

12 Sew the blocks together, working stitch by stitch where the seam allowances overlap.

Octagon

Level ✿✿✿✿✿

* • *

Join pieces A horizontally to form strips. Combine pieces B so that they interlock with the strips. It is important to make an extra stitch at junction points between pieces to avoid any gapping.

Folding the seam allowances

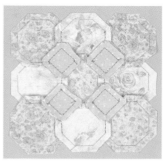

Templates

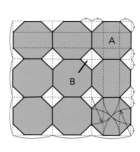

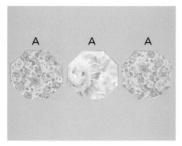
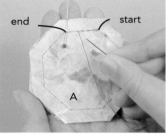

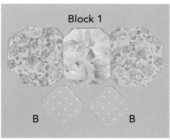

1 Prepare three pieces A.

2 Bring two pieces A right sides together and pin at the start and end of one seam. Sew, making an extra stitch at the start and at the end.

3 Trim the seam allowance to 6mm then fold it to one side.

4 Join on the other piece A in the same way (block 1 complete). Prepare two pieces B.

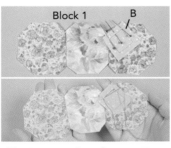
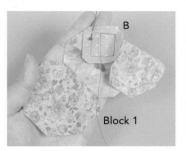
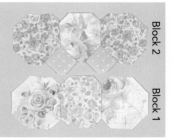

5 Pin one edge of a piece B to block 1 right sides together as shown. Sew the seam without piercing the seam allowances of piece A. Make an extra stitch at the end.

6 Do not cut the thread. Pin the next edge of the piece B as shown. Sew the seam, making an extra stitch at the end. Trim the allowances to 6mm.

7 Join the other piece B to the block 1 in the same way. Fold the seam allowances towards the pieces A (block 2 complete). Prepare another block 1.

8 Pin blocks 1 and 2 right sides together. Sew along the top edges of the pieces A first, then join the edges of the pieces B to the diagonal edges of the pieces A (block 3 complete).

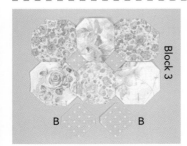
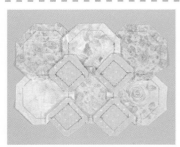
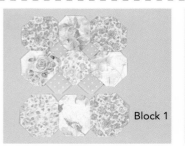
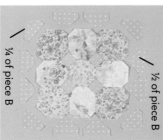

9 Join two pieces B to block 3 as in steps 5 and 6.

10 Fold the seam allowances of pieces B towards pieces A. Fold the allowances of pieces A in alternating directions.

11 Assemble another block 1 then join it on in the same way as described in step 8.

12 To make a square block, prepare triangular pieces (piece B divided into two or four) and join them to the edges of the block.

Octagon

129

Ohio Star

* · *

This block is made up of triangular and square pieces, so all the elements have straight edges. Choose contrasting colours to make the star stand out from the background. Make an extra stitch at each junction point to reinforce it and to obtain neat points.

Folding the seam allowances

Templates

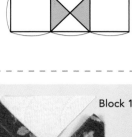

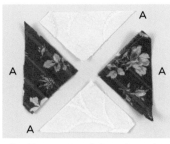

1 Prepare two light coloured and two dark coloured A pieces. Lay them out flat to check the colour arrangement.

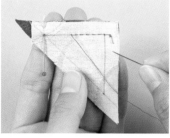

2 Pin a light and dark coloured piece A right sides together. Sew along the seam, making an extra stitch at the start and end of the seam.

3 Trim the seam allowance to 6mm, then fold it towards the dark coloured piece (block 1 complete).

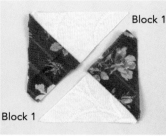

4 Make another block 1.

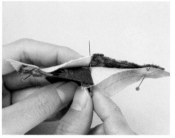

5 Bring the two blocks 1 right sides together and pin along the seam, making sure you match up the junction points.

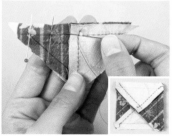

6 Sew along the seam, making an extra stitch at either end. Fold the seam allowances towards the lower block (block 2 complete). Make four blocks 2.

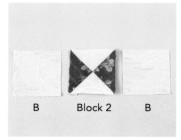

7 Prepare one block 2 and two pieces B. Lay them out flat to check the colour arrangement.

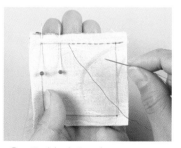

8 Pin block 2 and one piece B right sides together. Sew along the seam. Fold the allowance towards block 2. Join on the other piece B (block 3 complete).

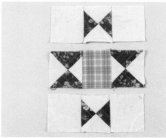

9 Make another block 3. Assemble two more blocks 2 and join them to either side of a piece B to make block 4.

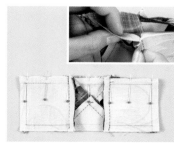

10 Bring a block 3 and block 4 right sides together and pin along the long edge, making sure you match up the junction points.

11 Sew along the seam, making an extra stitch at the junction points. Sew stitch by stitch through the overlapping seam allowances. Join the remaining block 3 to the other side of the block 4. Fold the seam allowances towards the block 4.

Ohio Star

Orange Peel

✳ ✳

Assemble A and B pieces to make disc-shaped blocks, then add combine with other pieces to form strips that are joined together to form this block. With all the pieces having curved edges, it is important to match up any marks. Make extra stitches at junction points to strengthen joins.

Folding the seam allowances

Templates

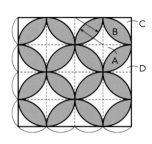

1 Make the template for piece A in card to avoid distortion. Place on the wrong side of the fabric and draw round, adding a 7mm allowance and any marks. Cut out.

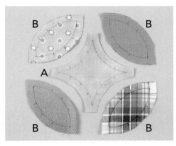

2 Prepare one piece A and four pieces B, marking the curved edges as shown.

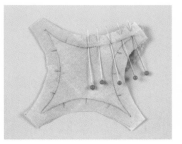

3 Bring piece A and a piece B right sides together, and pin along the curved edge to the centre.

4 Sew along the seam to the middle. Pin and then sew along other half of the curve. Fold the seam allowance towards piece B.

5 Add one piece B to the opposite edge of piece A.

6 Pin a third piece B to piece A right sides together, matching up seam lines and marks.

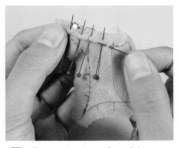

7 Sew as in steps 3 and 4.

8 Join on the fourth piece B in the same way (block 1 complete). Fold the seam allowances towards pieces B.

✳ Assembling of several blocks

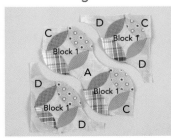

1 Prepare several blocks 1. Combine them with pieces A, C and D to form diagonal strips.

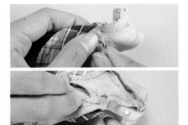

2 Pin the strips together, piece by piece, matching up seam lines and junction points.

3 Sew along the first seam line, making an extra stitch at the junction point.

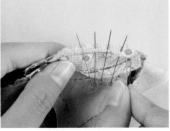

4 Pin along the next seam line, then sew, making an extra stitch at the junction. Continue in this way to join the strips together.

O

Orange Peel

Painted Daisies

* *

Assemble pieces A, A', B and C, then add piece D to make one block. Repeat so you have four small blocks. When pinning curved edges, use plenty of pins to make sure they keep together while sewing. The central disc is appliquéd in place.

Folding the seam allowances

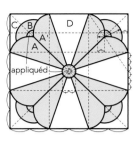

Templates

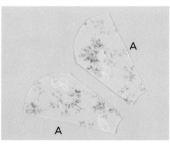

1 Prepare one piece A and one piece A'. Lay them out flat to check their proportion.

2 Pin the pieces A and A' right sides together as shown. Sew along the seam indicated. Fold the allowances towards piece A' (block 1 complete).

3 Cut out the piece to be appliquéd onto B, adding an allowance of 3mm. Make a few stitches along the curved allowance. Pull the thread slightly to fold the allowance.

4 Prepare a piece B. Pin on the piece to be appliqued to piece B, so the seam lines match up. Appliqué in place with slip stitches.

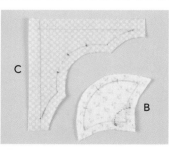

5 Prepare a piece C. Make the marks on the curved edges of pieces B and C as shown above.

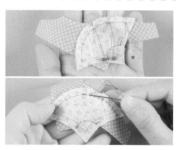

6 Pin piece B to piece C right sides together, up to the centre point. Sew along the seam to this point, then repeat to join the other side of the seam.

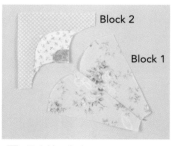

7 Fold back the seam allowances towards piece B (block 2 complete).

8 Bring block 1 to block 2 right sides together. Pin along the first curved edge at the top of the block 1.

9 Sew along the pinned seam, making an extra stitch through the junction between A and A'. Pin and sew along the second curved edge.

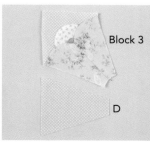

10 Fold back the seam allowances towards block 1 (block 3 complete). Join block 3 and a piece D (block 4 complete).

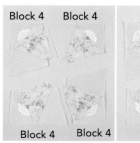

11 Make four blocks 4. Join them in pairs to get two strips as shown above. Pin these two strips right sides together, then sew along the seam. Fold the seam allowances towards pieces A.

12 Cut out the disc for the centre. Using the same technique as in step 3, turn under the edges then appliqué to the centre.

Pansy

* ✳ * ✳

This block represents a pansy flower. Choose a suitable colour scheme for the pieces that make up the flower; shades of purple work well. Use two different fabrics in light and dark tones. And use a small piece of yellow fabric for the centre of the flower.

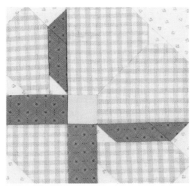

Folding the seam allowances

Templates

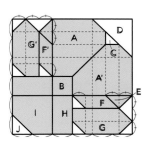

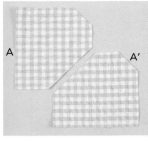

1 Prepare one piece A and one piece A'.

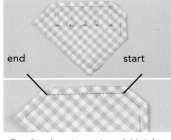

2 Pin the pieces A and A' right sides together as shown. Sew along the seam line, making an extra stitch at the start and end.(block 1 complete).

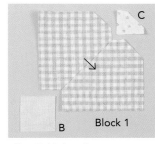

3 Fold the allowances in the direction of the arrow Prepare one piece B and one piece C.

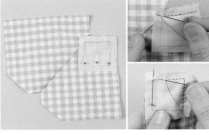

4 Pin block 1 and piece B right sides together along the first edge as shown. Sew, making an extra stitch, then pin and sew the second edge. Join on piece C in the same way (block 2 complete).

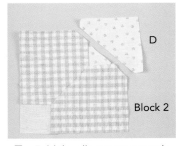

5 Fold the allowances towards block 1. Join block 2 and one piece D, sewing along the seam line. Fold the allowances towards block 2 (block 3 complete).

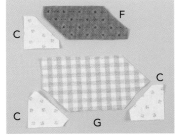

6 Join one piece C and one piece F (block 4 complete). Join two pieces C and one piece G (block 5 complete). Fold the allowances as shown in step 7.

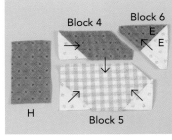

7 Join two pieces E (block 6 complete). Prepare one block 4, one block 5, one block 6 and one piece H.

8 Join blocks 4, 5 and 6, then join on piece H. Make extra stitches at the seam junctions (block 7 complete). Make another symmetrical block 7 (block 7').

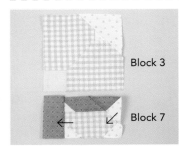

9 Fold the allowances in the direction of the arrows. Prepare one block 3 and one block 7.

10 Pin blocks 3 and 7 right sides together. Sew along the seam line, making an extra stitch at the seam junctions (block 8 complete).

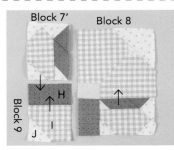

11 Join one piece H, one piece I and one piece J (block 9 complete). Join the blocks 7' and 9 (block 10 complete).

12 Pin blocks 8 and 10 right sides together. Sew along the seam line, making an extra stitch at the junctions and working stitch by stitch on overlapping allowances.

P

Pansy

Peeled Orange

* *

Match the seam lines of the curves during the construction of this block. Sew half of a curved edge, then the other half for smoother assembly. Fold all the allowances towards the pieces A and arrange the allowances where they meet in the centre in a spiral shape.

Folding the seam allowances

Templates

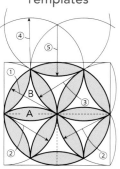

1 When making the template for piece B leave margins at the tips (see page 7). Draw around the template, then use the curved edge of template A to fill in the missing section.

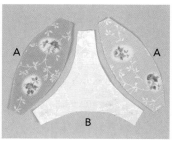

2 Prepare two pieces A and one piece B.

3 Bring pieces A and B right sides together, pinning from the start of the seam line to the centre.

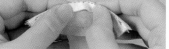

4 Sew to the centre, making an extra stitch. Pin the other half and continue sewing to the end. Fold the allowances towards piece A.

5 Join the other piece A to the piece B in the same way (block 1 complete). Make six blocks 1.

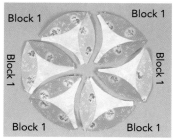

6 Lay out the six blocks 1 flat to check their positioning.

7 Bring two blocks 1 right sides together and pin as in step 3, without piercing the allowances.

8 Sew as in step 4. Fold the allowances towards piece A (block 2 complete).

9 Join the other blocks 2 in pairs in the same way as steps 7 and 8. Join two blocks 2 (block 3 complete).

10 Bring the remaining block 2 and block 3 right sides together and pin along one curved edge. Sew as in steps 4 and 5 up to the centre point, making an extra stitch.

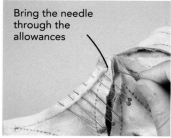

11 Pin along the remaining curved edge. Bring the needle through the allowances and sew.

Peony

* *

This block is a variation of the Lemoyne star block. When joining the background pieces to the diamond shapes, make sure to sew the seams one edge at a time, and with neat corners to get a good finish. Choose pastel shades for the 'petals' and greens for the leaves and stem.

Folding the seam allowances

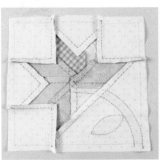

Templates

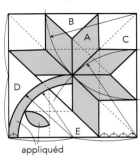

appliquéd

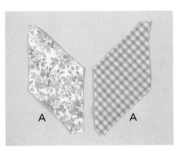

1 Prepare two pieces A.

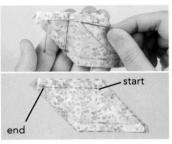

2 Pin the two pieces A right sides together as shown. Sew along the seam line, making an extra stitch at the start and end.

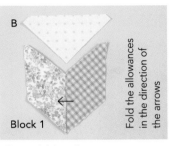

3 Fold the allowances to one side (block 1 complete). Prepare one piece B.

4 Pin the block 1 and piece B right sides together along the first edge. Sew, without stitching through the allowances and making an extra stitch at the junctions.

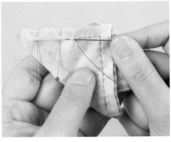

5 Pin and sew the second edge as in step 4. Fold the allowances towards piece A (block 2 complete).

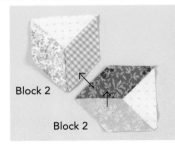

6 Make another block 2.

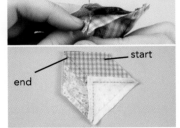

7 Pin the two blocks 2 right sides together as shown, matching up seams. Sew, then fold the allowances in the direction of the arrows indicated in step 6 (block 3 complete).

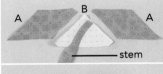

8 Prepare two pieces A, one piece B and the stem piece. Appliqué the stem to piece B without sewing in the seam allowance. Join the two pieces A to piece B. Fold the alllowances as indicated (block 4 complete).

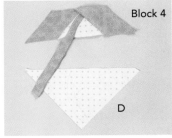

9 Join block 4 and a piece D. Appliqué the rest of the stem and the leaf onto D (block 5 complete).

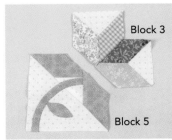

10 Pin blocks 3 and 5 right sides together as indicated above.

11 Sew along the seam line, working stitch by stitch through overlapping allowances.

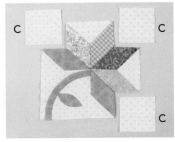

12 Prepare three pieces C and join to the block just made as in steps 4 and 5.

P

Peony

135

Pete's Paintbox

If you select fabrics carefully you can create a great effect; position the patterns of the fabrics so that they fall in the centre of, or along the length of your pieces and you can form borders and frames for the motif. Many of the edges of the pieces are cut at an angle so take care not to stretch them along the bias. Match up corners and make extra stitches at the seam junctions to avoid gapping.

Folding the seam allowances

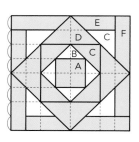

Templates

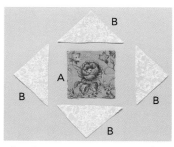

1 Prepare one piece A and four pieces B.

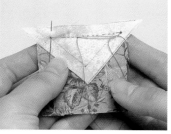

2 Pin pieces A and B right sides together as shown. Sew along the seam line, making an extra stitch at the start and end.

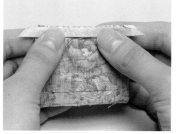

3 Trim the allowance to 6mm, then fold it towards piece A

4 Join on the other three pieces B in the same way (block 1 complete).

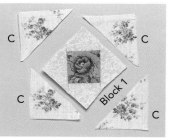

5 Prepare one block 1 and four pieces C. Mark the centre points of the long edges on the pieces C and on the edges of block 1. Join them, matching the marks. Fold the allowances towards block 1 (block 2 complete).

6 Join one block 2 and four pieces D in the same way as in step 5.

7 Fold the allowances towards pieces D (block 3 complete).

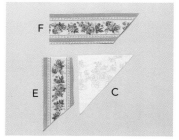

8 Prepare one piece C, one piece E and one piece F.

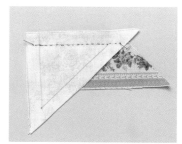

9 Pin the pieces C and E right sides together. Sew along the seam line. Fold the allowances towards piece E (block 4 complete).

10 Pin block 4 and piece F right sides together. Sew along the seam line. Fold the allowances towards piece F (block 5 complete). Make four blocks 5.

11 Lay one block 3 and four blocks 5 out flat to check their positioning.

12 Pin blocks 3 and 5 right sides together. Sew along the seam line, working stitch by stitch on overlapping allowances.

Picket Fence

* *

This is similar to the Chevron block in look, but here a square and rectangle have been combined to make V shapes that interlock. The blocks are assembled in strips before being joined. Choose different colour schemes for the strips to highlight the direction of the V shapes.

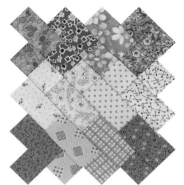

Folding the seam allowances

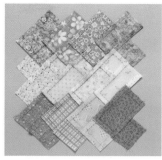

Templates

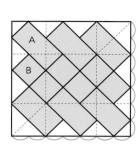

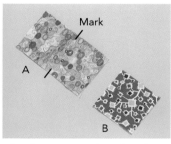

1 Prepare one piece A and one piece B. Mark the centre point of the seam line on both long edges.

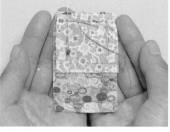

2 Pin pieces A and B right sides together as shown. Sew along the seam line, making an extra stitch at the start and end.

3 Trim the allowance to 6mm, then fold it towards B (block 1 complete).

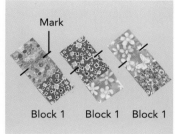

4 Make three blocks 1.

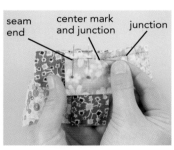

5 Pin two blocks 1 right sides together, lining up seam ends, centre marks and junctions as shown in step 4; sew. Join on another block in the same way.

6 The three blocks 1 are assembled (wrong side shown). Fold the allowances in one direction (block 2 complete).

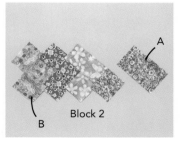

7 Join one piece B at the bottom left of block 2 (when right side up) and one piece A at the top right (first row complete).

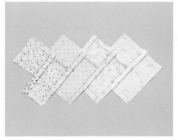

8 Join more pieces A and B in the same way to make the second row. Fold the allowances in the opposite direction to that shown in step 6.

9 Make the third row in the same way, folding the allowances in the same way as step 6.

10 Pin rows 1 and 2 right sides together along the first edge. Sew, making an extra stitch without piercing the allowances. Pin and sew the second edge in the same way.

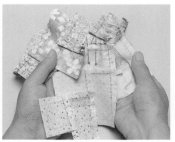

11 Pin and sew the remaining edges in the same way.

12 Make extra stitches at each corner without sewing through the allowances. Repeat steps 10 and 11 to join the remaining strip.

Pin Cushion

* ＊ * ＊

This block is made up of only two different shaped pieces, but most are joined along curved edges. It is important to mark the curved edges as indicated on the template diagram to help join them. A careful choice of colours can help give this block a 3D effect.

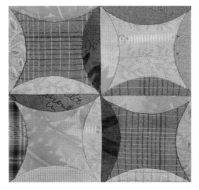

Folding the seam allowances

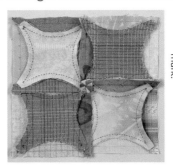

Templates

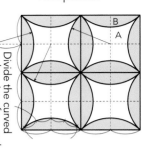

Divide the curved edges into four and mark.

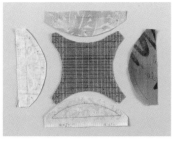

1 Prepare one piece A and four pieces B. Make the marks on the curved edges as shown on the template diagram.

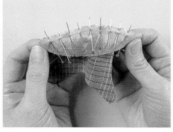

2 Pin piece B and piece A right sides together, matching up the marks.

3 Sew along the seam line, making an extra stitch at the start and end, and making sure the marks are matched up.

4 Trim the allowance to 6mm, then fold it towards piece B.

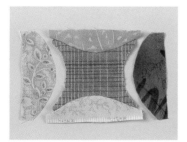

5 Join another piece B to the opposite edge.

6 Pin a third piece B to piece A right sides together, matching up the marks.

7 Sew to the first mark without piercing the allowances of piece A.

8 Continue to sew to the other end of the seam. Join on the last piece B in the same way.

---

* Blocks assembly

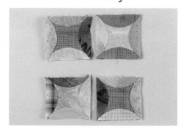

1 Prepare 4 blocks.

2 Pin two blocks right sides together. Sew along the seam line without piercing the seam allowances at either end. Join the other two blocks to make a second strip.

3 Pin the two strips right sides together. Sew along the seam line without piercing any of the seam allowances.

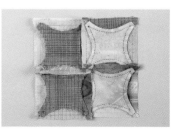

4 Where the allowances meet at the centre, fold them in a spiral shape.

Pine Tree

✳ ✳

This figurative block represents a pine tree. The triangular pieces form the canopy of the tree so use fabrics in shades of green for some of these. Make strips of pieces A and B, then a block of pieces C, C', D, E and F the block, and combine them to finish.

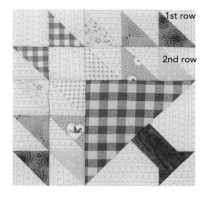

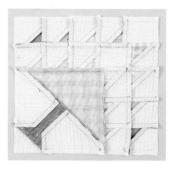
Folding the seam allowances

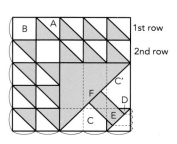
Templates

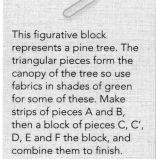

1 Prepare two pieces A.

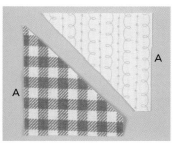 (step 2 photo)

2 Pin the two pieces A right sides together along the long edges. Sew along the seam line, making an extra stitch at the start and end.

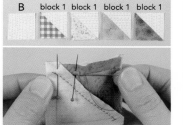 (step 3 photo)

3 Fold the allowances towards the dark coloured piece (block 1 complete). Make four blocks 1 and join them to one piece B to make the first row.

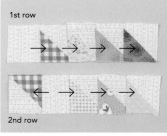 (step 4 photo)

4 Join four blocks 1 and one piece B as shown above to make the second row. Fold the allowances in the direction of the arrows.

 (step 5 photo)

5 Pin rows 1 and 2 right sides together. Sew along the seam line.

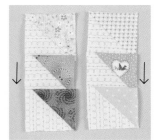 (step 6 photo)

6 Join three blocks 1 to make a strip. Join another two to make another strip. Join them, folding the allowances towards the left block (block 2 complete).

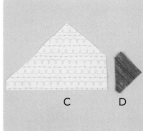 (step 7 photo)

7 Join one piece C and one piece D. Fold the allowances towards piece D (block 3 complete).

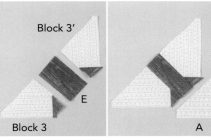 (step 8 photo)

8 Make another symmetrical block 3 (block 3' complete). Join piece E, the block 3 and the block 3'. Fold the allowances towards piece E. Join on one piece A as shown. Fold the allowances towards piece A (block 4 complete).

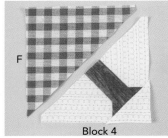

9 Join block 4 and one piece F. Fold the allowances towards piece F.

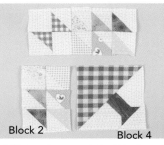

10 Lay the completed blocks out flat to check their positioning.

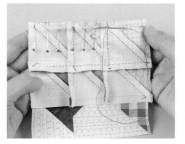

11 Pin block 2 and block 4 right sides together. Sew along the seam line. Fold the allowance to the block 2 (block 5 complete).

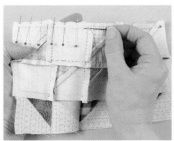

12 Pin block 5 and the two strips joined in step 5 right sides together. Sew along the seam line. Fold the allowance upwards.

P
Pine Tree

139

Pineapple

Start with the joining the pieces B to the centre piece A, then work outwards to join on the pieces C to G in order. Choose two different fabrics for the pieces radiating outwards, and another fabric for the centre.

Folding the seam allowances

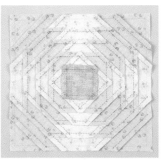

Templates

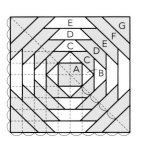

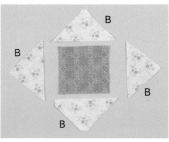

1 Prepare one piece A and four pieces B.

2 Pin pieces A and B right sides together as shown. Sew along the seam line, making an extra stitch at the start and end. Join on a piece B opposite.

3 Fold the allowances towards piece B. Join on the other two pieces B in the same way (block 1 complete).

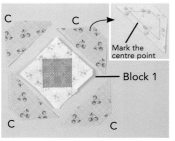

4 Prepare one block 1 and four pieces C. Mark the centre points of the long edges of pieces C as shown.

5 Pin block 1 and a piece C right sides together, matching the centre point to the tip of piece A. Sew along the seam line.

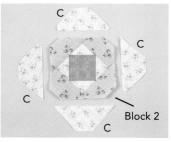

6 Join the other pieces C to the block 1 (block 2 complete). Join four more pieces C to block 2. Fold the allowances outwards (block 3 complete).

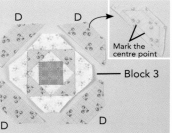

7 Join the block 3 and four pieces D. Fold the allowances outwards (block 4 complete).

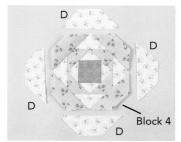

8 Join the block 4 and four more pieces D. Fold the allowances outwards (block 5 complete).

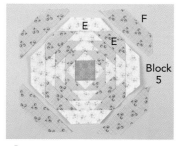

9 Join the block 5 and four pieces E, then join on four more pieces E as in steps 7 and 8. Fold the allowances outwards (block 6 complete).

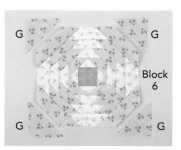

10 Prepare the block 6 and four pieces G.

11 Pin block 6 and piece G right sides together. Sew along the seam line. Fold the allowances outward. Assemble the three other pieces G in the same way.

P

Pineapple

Pinwheel 1

* *

Four pieces A are joined to create the pinwheel shape. Several seam allowances overlap at the centre, so when the allowances are folded in a spiral, a small hole may form at the centre. When sewing, avoid stitching into seam allowances so you can fold them neatly.

Folding the seam allowances

Templates

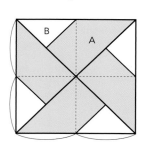

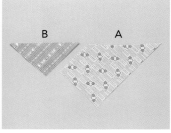

1 Prepare one piece A and one piece B. Lay them out flat to check their positioning.

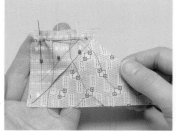

2 Pin the pieces A and B right sides together as shown. Sew along the seam line, making an extra stitch at the start and end.

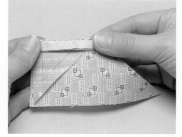

3 Trim the seam allowance to 6mm, then fold it back to B (block 1 complete).

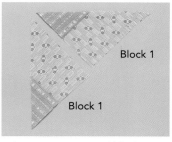

4 Prepare a second block 1.

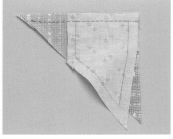

5 Pin the two blocks 1 right sides together as shown. Sew along the seam line, making an extra stitch at the start and end.

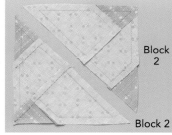

6 Fold the seam allowance to one side (block 2 complete). Make another block 2. Fold back the seam allowances in the opposite direction.

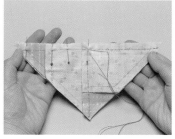

7 Pin the two blocks 2 right sides together along the long edges. Sew along the seam, making an extra stitch at the junctions. Fold the allowances to one side (block 3 complete).

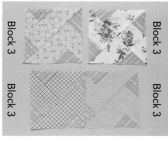

8 Prepare four blocks 3.

9 Bring two blocks 3 right sides together, then pin, matching up the seam junctions. Sew, making an extra stitch at the junctions. Join the other two blocks 3.

10 Fold back the seam allowances, alternating the direction for the two strips. Bring the two strips right sides together, then pin, matching up the seam junctions; sew.

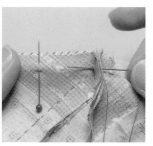

11 Do not stitch down the seam allowances at the corners of the blocks 3.

12 Above shows the wrong and right sides of the centre of the final block. Fold down the central seam allowances in a spiral shape.

Pinwheel 2

* · *

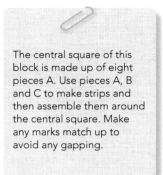

The central square of this block is made up of eight pieces A. Use pieces A, B and C to make strips and then assemble them around the central square. Make any marks match up to avoid any gapping.

Folding the seam allowances

Templates

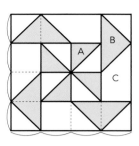

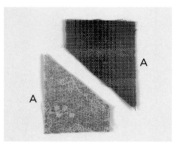

1 Prepare two pieces A.

2 Pin the two pieces A right sides together as shown. Sew along the seam line. Fold back the seam allowances towards the dark coloured piece A (block 1 complete).

3 Make four blocks 1. Pin two blocks 1 right sides together as shown. Sew along the seam line (block 2 complete). Make another block 2.

4 Fold back the seam allowances of blocks 2 in alternative directions. Pin the two blocks 2 right sides together.

5 Sew along the seams as shown. Sew stitch by stitch through the overlapping seam allowances. Fold the allowances towards the right-hand block.

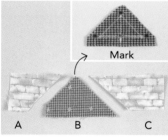

6 Prepare pieces A, B and C. Mark piece B as shown. Join pieces A and B as in step 2, then piece C. Fold the allowances towards piece B (block 3 complete).

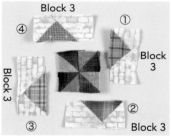

7 Make four blocks 3. Join them them to the central block in order ① to ④ as shown. Start by pinning block 3-① to the central block.

8 Sew from the end of the seam to the mark on the centre of the long edge of the piece B (see step 6). Make an extra stitch at the junctions.

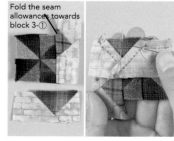

9 Pin the central block and block 3-② right sides together. Sew from the end of the seam to the mark on the centre of the long edge of the piece B (see step 6). Join on block 3-③ the same way.

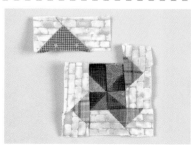

10 Pin the short edge of blocks 3-④ and blocks 3-① right sides together. Sew from the end to the mark. Do not cut the thread.

11 Pin the next edge, then sew from the mark to the end. Fold the seam allowances towards blocks 3.

P

Pinwheel 2

142

Pinwheel 3

* · *

Make four squares by joining pieces A, B and C, then assemble these to finish the block. Make sure you match the edges of the same length when joining pieces A and B. Do not sew down the seam allowances in the centre of the block so you can fold them into a spiral. Choose contrasting colours for the pattern of the pinwheel.

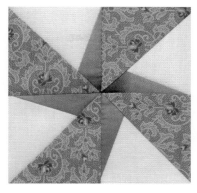

Folding the seam allowances

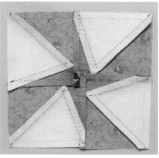

Templates

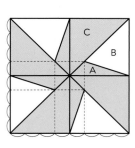

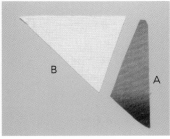

1 Prepare one piece A and one pieces B. Lay them out flat to check their positioning.

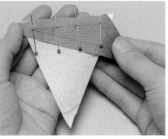

2 Bring pieces A and B right sides together, then pin along the seam line.

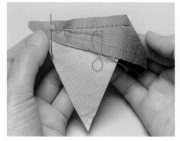

3 Sew along the seam, making an extra stitch at the start and end.

4 Trim the seam allowance to 6mm, then fold it towards piece A (block 1 complete).

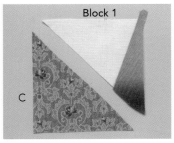

5 Prepare one block 1 and one piece C.

6 Pin a block 1 and a piece C, right sides together along the long edges; sew.

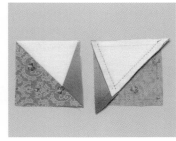

7 Fold the seam allowances towards piece C (block 2 complete). Make three more blocks 2.

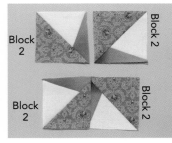

8 Lay the four blocks 2 out flat to check their positioning.

9 Bring two blocks 2 right sides together, and pin. Sew along the seam, making an extra stitch at the start and end (block 3 complete). Make another block 3.

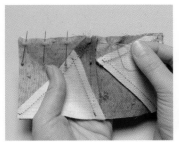

10 Fold back the seam allowances in alternate directions. Bring them right sides together as shown and pin.

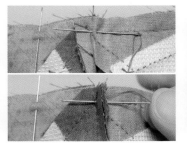

11 Sew along the seam to the centre junction. Do not sew through the seam allowances. Make an extra stitch and pull the thread taut to avoid forming a hole. Continue to sew to the end.

12 Fold down the seam allowances in the centre to form a spiral.

Pinwheel 4

Four pieces B are joined around a piece A to make a square. This square is repeated three more times and then all four are assembled into the final block. You can combine more squares if liked to make a larger final block.

Folding the seam allowances

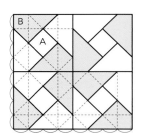

Templates

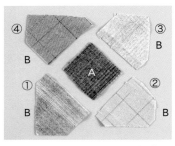

1 Prepare one piece A and four pieces B. Lay them out flat to check their positioning. Assemble them in the order shown, ① to ④.

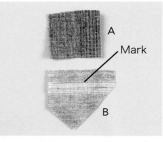

2 Mark the piece A and pieces B as shown. Bring the piece A and piece B-① right sides together, aligning the marks.

3 Pin as shown, then sew from one end to the mark. Make an extra stitch at the start and end of the seam.

4 Trim the seam allowance to 6mm, then fold it towards piece B.

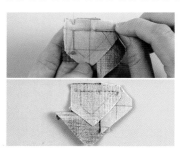

5 Open up piece B-①. Pin piece A and piece B-②, right sides together as shown; sew. Join on piece B-③.

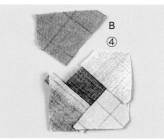

6 Three pieces B are assembled. Fold the seam allowances towards the pieces B.

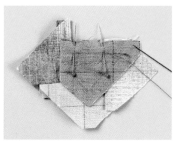

7 Pin the long edge of piece B-④ and piece A right sides together. Sew from the end to the mark, making an extra stitch at the start, at the junction and at the corner.

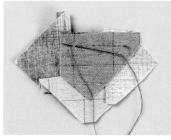

8 Do not cut the thread. Pin the short edge of piece B-④. Do not sew through the seam allowances of piece A.

9 Insert the needle in the corner and take it out through piece B. Make an extra stitch then continue sewing to the end (block 1 complete).

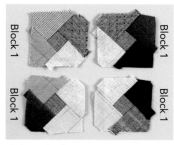

10 Make four blocks 1. Lay them to check their positioning.

11 Bring two blocks 1 right sides together and pin at the marks. Sew along the seam (block 2 complete). Join two other blocks 1. Fold back the seam allowances of both blocks 2 in alternate directions.

12 Pin the two strips of blocks 2 right sides together. Sew along the seam, making an extra stitch at the start and end.

Pinwheel 4

Pinwheel 5

✻ · ✻

This block is composed of just one shaped piece. Pieces are combined in pairs to make four smaller blocks that are then assembled to make the finished pinwheel motif. The simplicity of the design makes this a good block for beginners.

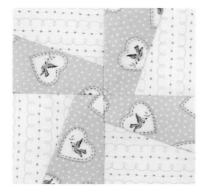

Folding the seam allowances

Templates

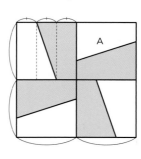

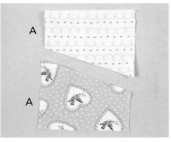

1 Prepare two pieces A. Lay them out flat to check their positioning.

2 Bring the two pieces A right sides together, then pin along the seam line.

3 Sew along the seam, making an extra stitch at the start and end.

4 Trim the seam allowance to 6mm, then fold it towards the patterned fabric piece (block 1 complete).

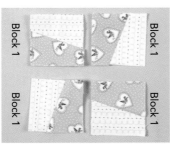

5 Make four blocks 1.

6 Bring two blocks 1 right sides together, as shown, and pin. Sew along the seam (block 2 complete). Make a second block 2.

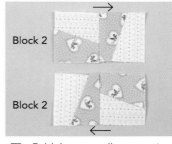

7 Fold the seam allowances in the direction of the arrows.

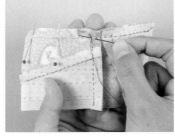

8 Pin the two blocks 2 right sides together as shown. Sew, making an extra stitch at the junctions to secure.

Variation Pinwheel 6 with Triangular Pieces

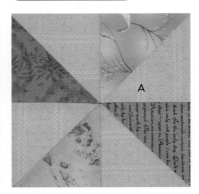

Fold back the seam allowances

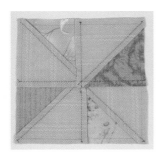

First prepare eight triangular pieces. Assemble the pieces in pairs, then join to form squares. Arrange light and dark colours side by side.

✱ Tip

When you pin, make sure the corners at the centre match up. As you sew seams, make extra stitches at the seam junctions.

Plane

* *

This figurative block represents a plane. Assemble the pieces in diagonal strips and then join these together. All the pieces have straight edges, so this is an easy block to make. Choose a light blue fabric for the background of this block to suggest the sky.

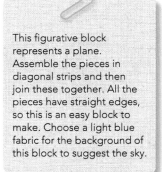

Folding the seam allowances

Templates

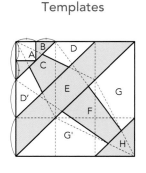

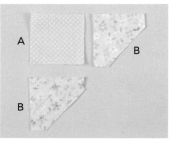

1 Prepare one piece A and two pieces B.

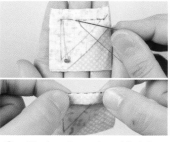

2 Pin the pieces A and B right sides together. Sew along the seam line. Fold the allowances towards piece B (block 1 complete).

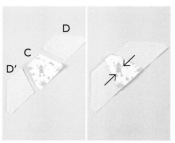

3 Join one piece C, one piece D and one piece D', sewing along the seam lines. Fold the allowances towards piece C (block 2 complete).

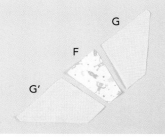

4 Join one piece F, one piece G and one piece G' as in step 3. Fold the allowances towards piece F (block 3 complete).

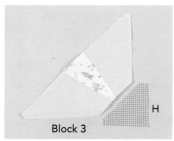

5 Prepare one block 3 and one piece H.

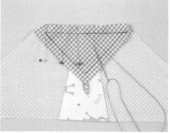

6 Pin block 3 and piece H right sides together as shown. Sew along the seam line. Fold the allowances towards piece H. (block 4 complete).

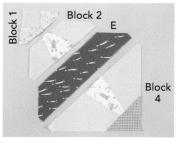

7 Lay out flat blocks 1, 2, 4. and one piece E. Mark the edges of block E with the positions of the seam junctions on the adjacent blocks. Mark the centre point of the top edge of block 2.

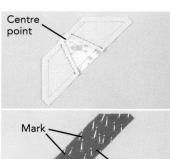

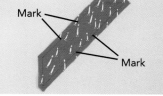

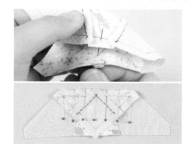

8 Join the blocks, working from top to bottom. Pin blocks 1 and 2 right sides together, matching the mark on block 2 with the point of piece A.

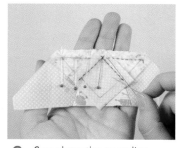

9 Sew along the seam line, making an extra stitch at the start and end. Fold the allowances towards block 2.

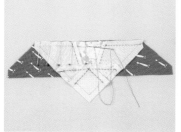

10 Join the block from step 9 and piece E, matching the marks on piece E with the seam junctions on the block. Fold the allowances towards piece E. Join block 4 in the same way.

P
Plane

Pointed Star

✳ ✳

Simple triangles and hexagons form the motifs of this block; a combination of many pieces will create a star-covered finish. The pieces are sewn together in strips that are then joined. Choose contrasting colours for pieces A and B so the star shapes stand out.

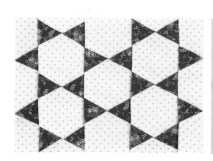

Folding the seam allowances

Templates

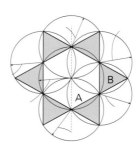

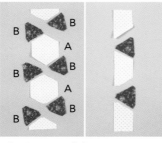

1 Prepare all the necessary pieces.

2 Pin pieces A and B right sides together as shown. Sew along the seam line, making an extra stitch at the start and end.

3 Trim the allowance to 6mm, then fold it towards piece B (block 1 complete).

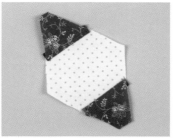

4 Make another block 1. Join one other piece B to the opposite edge of the piece A (block 2 complete).

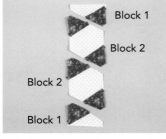

5 Make the number of blocks 2 required for your strip. Make two blocks 1. Place the blocks flat to check their positioning.

6 Join the blocks 2 right sides together, making extra stitches at seam junctions. Join a block 1 at either end of the strip. Fold the allowances to one side.

7 Cut out half A pieces, plus allowances; cut out two quarter A pieces, plus allowances. Join them together with pieces B. Fold allowances towards pieces B.

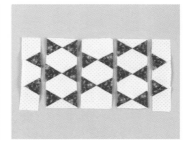

8 Make as many strips as required, to be joined into the finished block.

9 Pin two strips right sides together. Sew along the seam line. Make an extra stitch at corners to avoid gapping.

✳ To make a rectangular block

Template for the finished rectangle

Join together pieces to create an assembled piece bigger than required. Create a template for the finished size of rectangle. Place it on the pieced patchwork and draw around it.

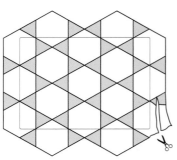

Remove the template. Adding a 1cm seam allowance all round, cut out your rectangular block.

P

Pointed Star

Polka Dot

* *

This block is a variation of the Daisy Path block (page 68). It is composed of only two different pieces. Match up any marks and sew in small stitches to get a neat finish. Choose two different fabrics for the background B pieces, and four different fabrics for the quarter-circle A pieces.

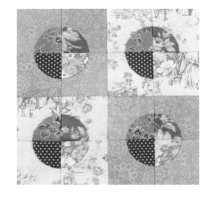

Folding the seam allowances

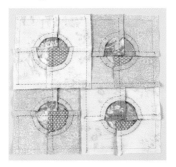

Templates

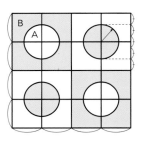

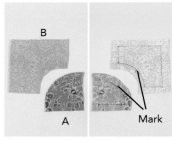

1 Prepare one piece A and one piece B. Mark the centre points on the curved edges.

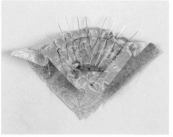

2 Bring piece A and piece B right sides together, then pin the ends, at the mark and in between.

3 Sew in small stitches along the seam line, making an extra stitch at the start and end.

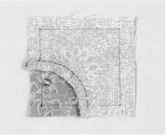

4 Fold the allowance towards piece A (block 1 complete).

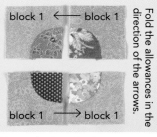

Fold the allowances in the direction of the arrows.

5 Make four blocks 1.

6 Bring two blocks 1 right sides together, then pin the ends, at the seam junctins and in between.

7 Sew along the seam line, making an extra stitch at the start and end.

8 Sew stitch by stitch on overlapping allowances (block 2 complete). Join the two other blocks 1 in the same way.

9 Pin the two blocks 2 right sides together, then sew as in steps 6 to 8 (block 3 complete).

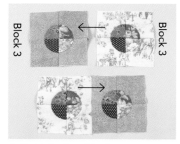

10 Make four blocks 3.

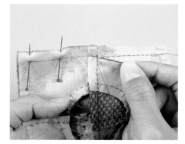

11 Pin two blocks 3 right sides together, then sew along the seam line. Join the two other blocks 3 in the same way. Fold back the allowances, alternating the direction for the two strips.

12 Pin the two strips right sides together then sew along the seam line. Make an extra stitch at the seam junctions. Fold the allowances towards the lower strip.

Pot

* · *

This block represents a tea pot. Choose one fabric for the pieces that make up the pot; choose a lighter coloured fabric for the pieces for the background. Make a template for the handle and cut out the fabric, adding a 5mm allowance; the handle is appliquéd in place.

Folding the seam allowances

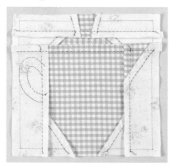

Templates

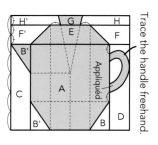

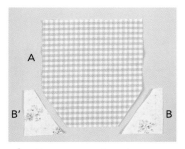

1 Prepare one piece A, one piece B and one piece B'.

2 Pin pieces A and B right sides together as shown. Sew along the seam line, making an extra stitch at the start and end.

3 Join on the peice B'. Fold the allowance towards piece A (block 1 complete).

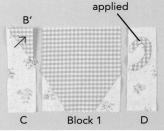

4 Join one piece B' and one piece C. Fold the allowances towards piece B' (block 2 complete). Appliqué the handle to piece D (see below).

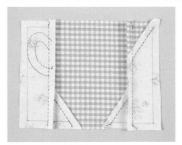

5 Join the blocks 1 and 2. Join on the piece D. Fold the allowances towards block 1 (block 3 complete).

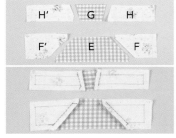

6 Join pieces E, F and F ', and pieces G, H and H' to make two strips, as above. Fold the allowances towards pieces E and G.

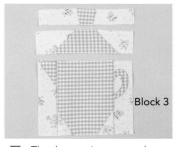

7 The three strips are made.

8 Bring the lower and central strips right sides together, then pin the ends, at the junctions and in between.

9 Sew along the seam line, making an extra stitch at the start, end and at the seam junctions. Sew stitch by stitch on overlapping allowances.

10 Pin the upper strip to the top edge, right sides together. Sew along the seam line. Fold the allowances towards the central strip.

* Appliquéing the handle

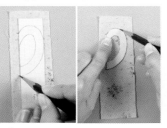

1 Place the handle template on the right side of piece D and draw around it.

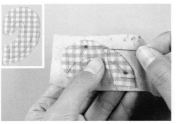

2 Snip into the inner curved edge of the handle. Pin the handle on piece D. Turning the edges under as you go, slip stitch them in place.

P
Pot

149

Puzzle

* · *

This simple block is made up of four identical pieces. As you join the pieces together, match them up along the edges that are the same size when completed. As all the edges being joined are cut on a slant, do not stretch the pieces during construction. Choose two light and two dark fabrics for this block.

Folding the seam allowances

Templates

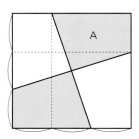

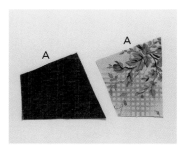

1 Prepare two pieces A.

2 Bring the two pieces A right sides together as shown; pin.

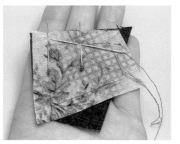

3 Sew along the seam line, making an extra stitch at the start and end.

4 Trim the allowance to 6mm, then fold it towards the dark coloured piece (block 1 complete).

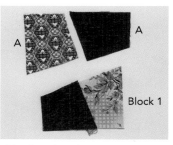

5 Join the other two pieces A to make another block 1.

6 Lay out the two blocks 1 flat to check their positioning. Fold their allowances in opposite directions.

7 Bring the two blocks 1 right sides together and pin.

8 Sew along the seam line, making an extra stitch at the start and end, and at the seam junctions. Fold the allowances to one side.

* Assembling several blocks

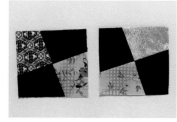

1 Prepare two blocks. Lay them out flat to check their positioning.

2 Pin the two blocks right sides together and sew along the seam line. Join other blocks in pairs in the same way.

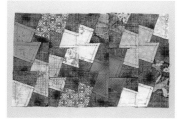

3 Join pairs into strips, then join strips together. Alternate the direction the allowances fold between each strip.

4 View of the right side. By carefully combining colours and shapes, pinwheel motifs appear.

Rail Fence

* *

Rectangular pieces are joined to form a stepped pattern. With only one piece to use and straight edges to join, this is an ideal beginner's block. The clever combination of colours achieves the effect – pick three different fabrics to use.

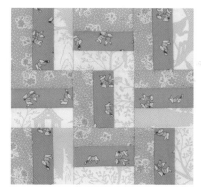

Folding the seam allowances

Templates

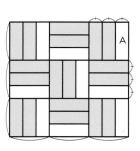

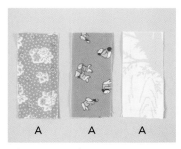

1 Prepare three pieces A in different fabrics.

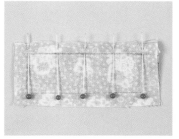

2 Bring two pieces A right sides together and pin.

3 Sew along the seam line, making an extra stitch at the start and end.

4 Trim the allowance to 6mm, then fold it to the left.

5 Join on the other piece A in the same way. Fold the allowance in the same direction (block 1 complete).

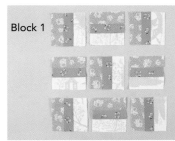

6 Make nine blocks 1. Arrange them in sets of three as shown to form 3 strips.

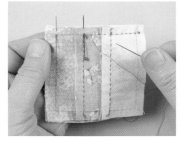

7 Bring two blocks 1 right sides together and pin. Sew along the seam line. Join on the other block 1.

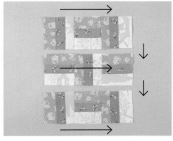

8 Join the other sets of three blocks 1 to make the other two strips. Fold the allowances in the direction of the arrows.

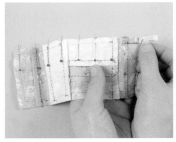

9 Bring two strips right sides together, then pin .

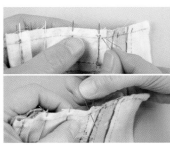

10 Sew along the seam line, working stitch by stitch on the overlapping allowances.

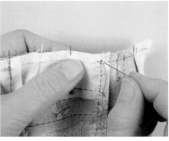

11 Make extra stitches at the seam junctions.

R

Rail Fence

Railroad Crossing

✳ ✳

This block is composed of only pieces of two different shapes. Join three rectangular pieces A to make a small square, then add four triangular pieces B around these. Different colour combinations of fabric can create different visual effects.

Folding the seam allowances

Templates

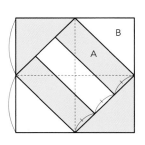

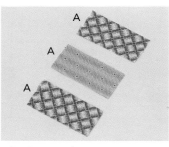

1 Prepare three pieces A.

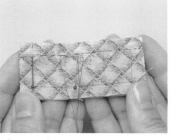

2 Pin the two pieces A right sides together as shown. Sew along the seam line, making an extra stitch at the start and end.

3 Trim the allowance to 6mm, then fold it towards the outer piece. Join the other piece A in the same way (block 1 complete).

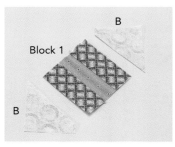

4 Prepare one block 1 and two pieces B.

5 Pin block 1 and piece B right sides together. Sew along the seam line. Fold the allowances towards block 1. Join on another piece B (block 2 complete).

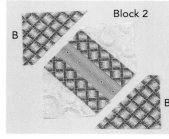

6 Join one block 2 and two pieces B, sewing along the seam lines. Fold the allowances towards pieces B (block 3 complete).

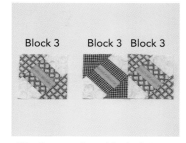

7 Prepare three blocks 3. Lay them out flat to check their positioning.

8 Bring two blocks 3 right sides together, then pin. Sew along the seam line, making an extra stitch at the start, end and seam junctions. Join on the other block 3.

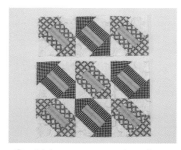

9 Make two more strips of three blocks 3. Fold back the allowances in alternate directions.

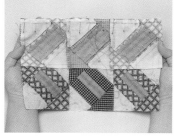

10 Pin two strips right sides together. Sew along the seam line. Fold the allowances in one direction. Join on the other strip.

Cracker ✳ ✳ ✳ ✳ ✳ ✳ ✳ ✳ ✳ ✳ ✳ ✳ ✳

Folding the seam allowances

The design of this block is the same as the Railroad Crossing block but here, the central piece A is divided into three squares.

Ribbon 1

Level ★✿✿✿✿

This block resembles a ribbon tied in a bow. Join the upper section first, then the bottom and then join together. Match up seam lines when joining on piece C for neat seams. Choose the same fabric for the pieces A, B and B', and for two of the E and E' pieces.

Folding the seam allowances

Templates

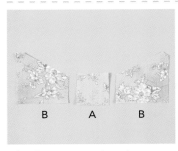

1 Prepare one piece A, one piece B and one piece B'.

2 Bring the pieces A and B right sides together, then pin along the seam line.

3 Sew along the seam line, make an extra stitch at the start and end. Fold the allowances towards piece A. Join on piece B' in the same way (block 1 complete).

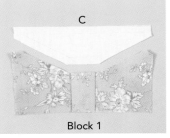

4 Prepare one block 1 and one pieces C.

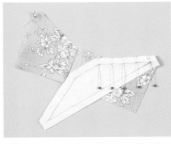

5 Pin block 1 and piece C right sides together along the first edge.

6 Sew to the end of the seam line. Make an extra stitch; do not cut the thread.

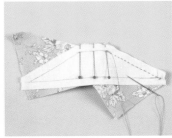

7 Pin the second edge without piercing the allowances at the corner.

8 Sew along the seam line. Make an extra stitch. Pin and sew the third edge in the same way. Fold the allowances towards the dark coloured piece (block 2 complete).

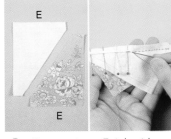

9 Pin two pieces E right sides together. Sew along the seam line (block 3 complete). Join two pieces E' in the same way (block 3' complete).

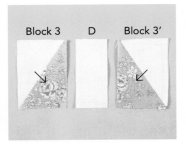

10 Fold the allowances in the direction of the arrows. Join one block 3, one block 3' and one piece D. Fold the allowances towards blocks 3 and 3' (block 4 complete).

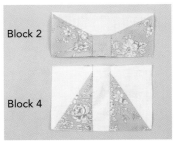

11 Prepare one block 2 and one block 4.

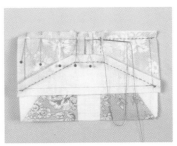

12 Pin blocks 2 and 4 right sides together. Sew along the seam line. Make an extra stitch at the seam junctions.

R

Ribbon 1

153

Ribbon 2

* *

By using the same fabric for the pieces that cross at the centre of this block and the triangles above, a flowing ribbon shape is formed. Matching up seam allowances will help keep seams neat when joining pieces with interlocking edges.

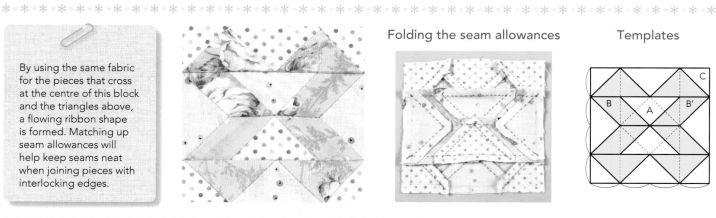

Folding the seam allowances

Templates

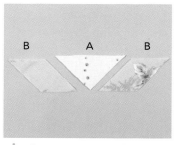

1 Prepare one piece A, one piece B and one piece B'.

2 Pin pieces A and B right sides together. Sew along the seam line, making an extra stitch at the start and end. Fold the allowances towards piece B.

3 Join on piece B' as in step 2. Fold the allowances towards the dark piece B' (block 1 complete). Make two blocks 1.

4 Join one block 1 and two pieces A, matching seam lines. Fold the allowances towards pieces B and B' (block 2 complete).

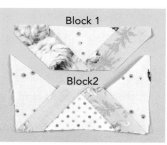

5 Prepare one block 1 and one block 2.

6 Pin the blocks 1 and 2 right sides together along the first edge. Sew to the end of the seam line. Make an extra stitch; do not cut the thread.

7 Pin the second edge without piercing the corner allowances.

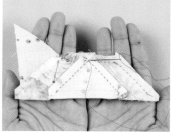

8 Sew to the seam junction at the centre. Make an extra stitch, then continue sewing to the end of the seam line. Pin the third edge and sew to the end (block 3 complete).

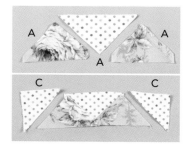

9 Join three pieces A to form a trapezoid block. Prepare two pieces C.

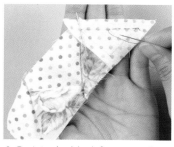

10 Join the block from step 9 and a piece C together. Join on the other piece C (block 4 complete). Make another block 4.

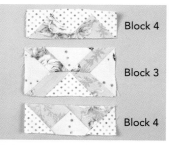

11 Prepare one block 3 and two blocks 4.

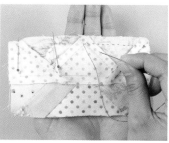

12 Pin a block 3 and 4 right sides together. Sew along the seam line, making an extra stitch at the start and end.

Ribbon 3

This block represents waving ribbons. There are several pieces and many are joined in interlocking seams. Pieces A, A' and B are combined to make small blocks that look like cubes; this can be enhanced by your choice of fabric.

Folding the seam allowances

Templates

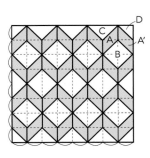

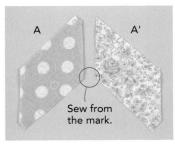

1 Prepare one piece A and one piece A'.

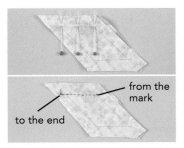

2 Pin the two pieces A right sides along the short edge. Sew along the seam line, making an extra stitch at the start and end.

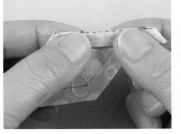

3 Trim the allowance to 6mm, then fold it towards piece A (block 1 complete).

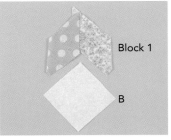

4 Prepare one block 1 and one piece B.

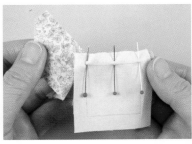

5 Pin the block 1 and piece B right sides together along the first edge without piercing the allowance. Sew along the seam line. Pin and sew the second edge.

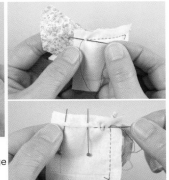

6 Fold the allowances towards Block 1 (block 2 complete). Make 11 blocks 2 (see step 7 to see the direction for folding the allowance).

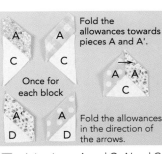

7 Join pieces A and C, A'and C, A and D, and A' and D. Join one piece A, one piece A' and one piece C as in steps 2 to 5; repeat twice more.

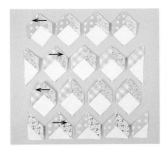

8 Lay out the blocks flat as shown.

9 Join the blocks as shown in step 8, making extra stitches at the start and end of seams. Fold allowances in the direction of the arrows in step 8.

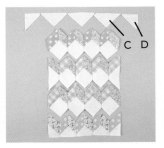

10 Four strips are made. Join four pieces C and two pieces D as shown to create the upper strip.

11 Join two strips right sides together along the first edge. Continue to sew, edge by edge, without stitching in the allowances, until all strips are joined.

155

Ribbon Bow

This block represents a bow tied in thin ribbon. If you use two colours for the bow and ribbon you can suggest shade and depth. Although there are many pieces they are all joined along straight edges so this block is not difficult to make.

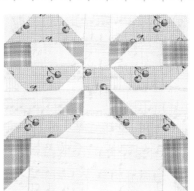

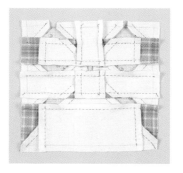

Folding the seam allowances

Templates

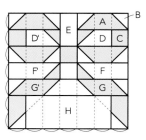

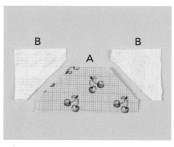

1 Prepare one piece A and two pieces B.

2 Pin pieces A and B right sides together as shown. Sew along the seam line, making an extra stitch at the start and end.

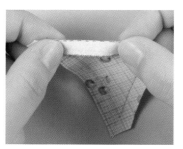

3 Trim the allowance to 6mm, then fold it towards piece A. Join the other piece B in the same way (block 1 complete). Make four blocks 1.

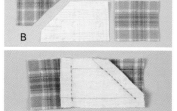

4 Join one piece B, one piece C and one piece D in the same way (block 2 complete). Make another symmetrical block (block 2' complete).

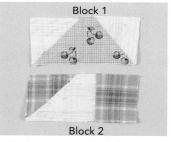

5 Prepare one block 1 and one blocks 2. Lay them out flat to check their positioning.

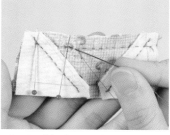

6 Pin blocks 1 and 2 right sides together. Sew along the seam line, making an extra stitch at the start and end. Fold the allowances towards block 1 (block 3 complete).

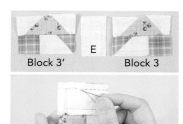

7 Join a block 1 and block 2' to make block 3'. Join this to the block 3 and a piece E. Fold the allowances towards blocks 3 and 3' (strip 1 complete).

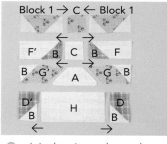

8 Join the pieces shown above to form strips 2 to 5. Fold the allowances in the direction of the arrows.

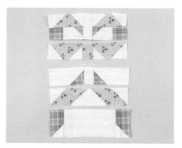

9 Lay all the strips out flat to check their positioning.

10 Pin two strips right sides together.

11 Sew along the seam line, working stitch by stitch on the overlapping allowances.

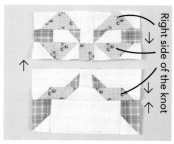

12 Continue to join on the strips 3 to 5. Fold the allowances in the direction of the arrows.

Rock Garden

❋＊

The kite-shaped pieces A are joined in fours to to make small star blocks. These are connected by being joined by pieces B and C. Make neat tight stitches at seam junctions to avoid any gaps forming. Choose fabrics that highlight the stars' shapes.

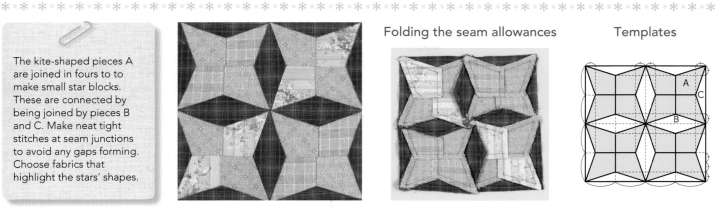

Folding the seam allowances

Templates

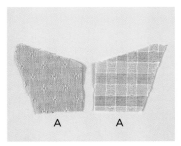

1 Prepare two pieces A.

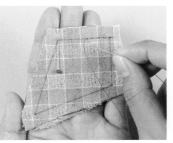

2 Pin the two pieces A right sides together as shown. Sew along the seam line, making an extra stitch at the start and end.

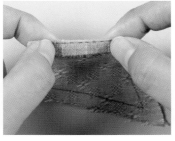

3 Trim the allowance to 6mm, then fold it to one side (block 1 complete). Make another block 1.

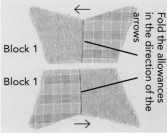

Fold the allowances in the direction of the arrows

Block 1

Block 1

4 Bring two blocks 1 right sides together, then pin.

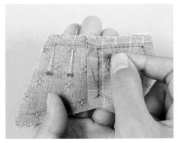

5 Sew along the seam line. Make an extra stitch at the seam junction in the centre. Fold the allowances towards the lower block (block 2 complete).

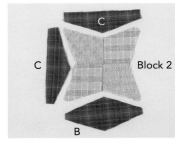

C

C   Block 2

B

6 Prepare one block 2, one piece B and two pieces C.

7 Pin block 2 and a piece C right sides together along the first edge. Sew along the seam line. Make an extra stitch; do not cut the thread.

8 Pin along the second edge without piercing the allowances, then sew to the end of the seam line.

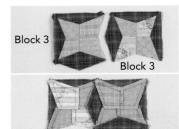

Block 3

Block 3

9 Join on the piece B and other piece C in the same way (block 3 complete). Make four blocks 3. Join them in pairs in as steps 7 and 8.

10 The two strips are made.

11 Pin the two pieces right sides together along the first edge without piercing the allowances. Sew along the seam line. Make an extra stitch; do not cut the thread.

12 Pin the second edge, then sew along the seam. Continue to sew along the seam in the same way, edge by edge.

R

Rock Garden

Rolling Star

An eight-pointed star is surrounded by eight squares in the centre of this block. Although all the pieces have straight edges, there are a lot of corners and points to match up neatly, so take care during construction. Choose a dark colour for the eight squares so the star stands out.

Folding the seam allowances

Templates

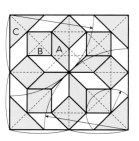

1 Prepare two pieces A.

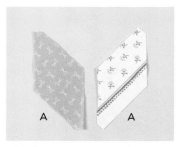

2 Pin the pieces A right sides together as shown. Sew along the seam, making an extra stitch at the start and end .

3 Fold the seam allowance. towards the darker colour (block 1 complete). Prepare one piece B.

4 Pin the block 1 and piece B right sides together along the first edge. Sew along the seam line, making an extra stitch at the end. Don't cut off the thread.

5 Pin the second edge without piercing the allowance, then continue sewing. Fold the allowances towards the dark piece B (block 2 complete).

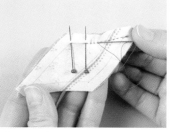

6 Make four blocks 2. Pin two blocks 2 right sides together as shown; sew (block 3 complete). Assemble a second block 3.

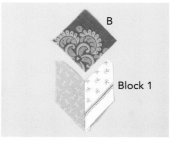

7 Pin the two blocks 3 right sides together as shown, matching up seam junctions. Sew, making an extra stitch at the seam junctions (block 4 complete).

8 Prepare two pieces A and one piece B. Join together as shown. Fold the allowances towards piece B (block 5 complete). Make four blocks 5.

9 Lay out flat the block 4 and four blocks 5 to check their positioning.

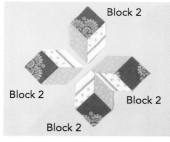

10 Pin the first edge of a block 5 to block 4 right sides together as shown, without piercing the seam allowances.

11 Sew, then make an extra stitch. Pin and sew the remaining edges in the same way, one after the other, making sure not to sew through the allowances. Fold allowences towards the centre of the block.

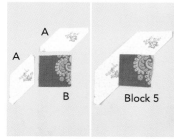

12 Prepare four pieces C and join them to the corners of the central block as shown. Fold the allowances towards the pieces C.

Rolling Stone

✳·✳

Assemble pieces A and B to make small squares. Make other squares by joining pieces C. Then join them around a square D in the same way as making the nine patch block. Make sure the corners of the the squares match up so you get a neat finish with no gaps.

Folding the seam allowances

Templates

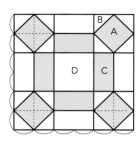

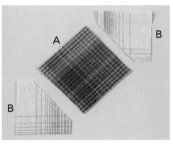

1 Prepare one piece A and two pieces B. Lay them out flat to check their positioning.

2 Pin the pieces A and a piece B right sides together as shown and sew along the seam line. Fold the seam allowances towards piece B.

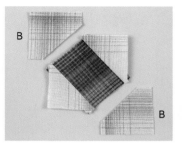

3 Join on the other piece B in the same way. Prepare two other pieces B.

4 Pin the pieces A and a piece B right sides together as shown; sew. Fold the allowances towards piece B. Join on the other piece B (block 1 complete). Make four blocks 1.

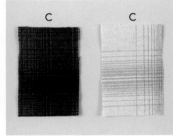

5 Prepare two pieces C. Bring the two pieces C right sides together and pin along one long edge.

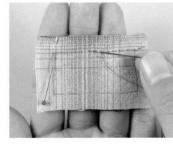

6 Sew along the seam line, making an extra stitch at the start and end. Fold the allowances to one side (block 2 complete). Make four blocks 2.

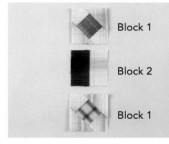

7 Lay out flat two blocks 1 and one block 2 to check their positioning.

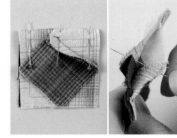

8 Pin a block 1 and block 2 right sides together, matching up seam junctions and making sure not to pierce any seam allowances.

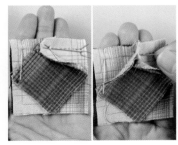

9 Sew to the seam junction. Make an extra stitch, then continue, avoiding working through the allowances (block 3 complete). Join on the other block 2.

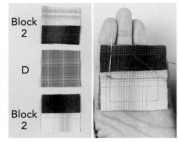

10 Join one piece D and two blocks 2. Fold the allowances towards the blocks 2 (block 4 complete).

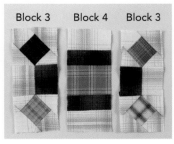

11 Prepare two blocks 3 and one block 4. Lay them out flat to check their positioning.

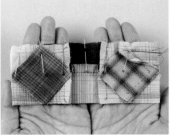

12 Join a block 3 to one side of block 4, then join on the other block 3 on the opposite side. Match up seam junctions and don't stitch through allowances.

Rose

* • *

Although the pieces for this block are straight edged, there are lots of them and their construction is complex, so check the positioning of each piece before assembly. Make extra stitches at the corners and at seam junctions to avoid gapping. The stem is appliquéd in place.

Folding the seam allowances

Templates

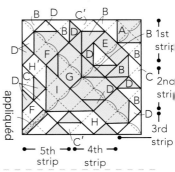

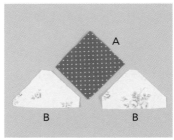
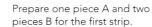

1 Prepare one piece A and two pieces B for the first strip.

2 Pin pieces A and B right sides together as shown. Sew along the seam line, making an extra stitch at the start and end. Join on the other piece B.

3 Trim the allowances to 6mm, then fold them towards piece A. The first strip is made.

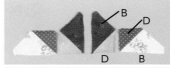
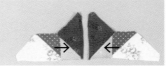

4 Join one piece B and one piece D. Fold the allowances towards the dark coloured piece (block 1 complete). Make two blocks 1 in two different colours as shown. Join them in pairs (two blocks 2 complete).

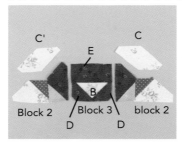

5 Join one piece B and two pieces D, then one piece E (block 3 complete). Join two blocks 2 on either side of block 3. Fold the allowances towards the blocks 2 (block 4 complete). Prepare one piece C and one piece C'.

6 Pin block 4 and piece C right sides together along the first edge; sew. Make an extra stitch, then pin and sew the second edge. Join on the piece C' in the same way. The second strip is made.

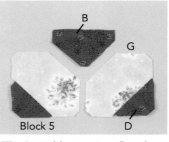

7 Assemble one piece D and one piece G (block 5 complete). Make two blocks 5 and join them together. Join on one piece B in the same way as described in step 6. Fold the allowances towards piece G (block 6 complete).

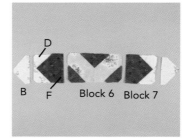

8 Join two blocks D and one block F (block 7 made). Make another block 7. Join the blocks 7 to block 6; join on a piece B at either end. Fold the allowances towards block 7. The third strip is made.

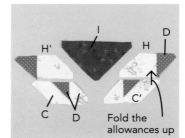

9 Join a piece C, two pieces D and piece H'; join piece C', two pieces D and piece H as shown. Join them together, then join piece I as in step 6. Fold the allowances towards piece I. The fourth strip is made.

10 Use the template to mark the position of the stem on piece F. Appliqué the stem in that position.

11 Join a piece D on either side of piece F. The 5th strip is made.

12 Pin two strips right sides together, matching seam junctions. Sew along the seam line. Join the other strips in the same way.

Rose Dream

Level ★ ★ ☆ ☆ ☆

* *

Make four small blocks, each one composed of one piece A, two pieces B and two pieces C, then join them together. The pieces A and C form diagonal motifs that cross at the centre; use two different fabrics, one for each diagonal. Choose two different colours for the background B pieces.

Folding the seam allowances

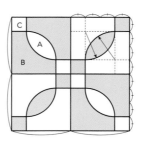

Templates

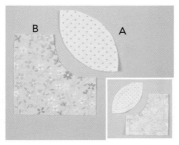

1 Prepare one piece A and one piece B. Mark the centre points of the curved edges.

2 Bring pieces A and B right sides together, and pin, matching the centre points.

3 Sew along the seam line to the centre point. Make an extra stitch, then continue sewing. Fold the allowances towards piece A (block 1 complete).

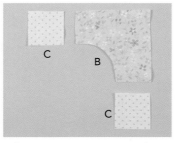

4 Prepare one piece B and two pieces C.

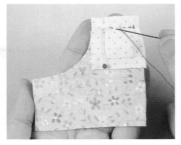

5 Pin a piece B and C right sides together as shown. Sew along the seam line, making an extra stitch at the start and end. Join on the other piece B (block 2 complete).

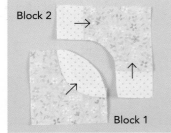

6 Prepare one block 1 and one block 2. Fold the allowances in the direction of the arrows.

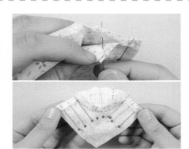

7 Pin blocks 1 and 2 right sides together, matching the centre points.

8 Sew along the seam line, making an extra stitch on the seam junctions.

9 Sew stitch by stitch on the overlapping allowances. Fold the allowances towards block 1 (block 3 complete). Make four blocks 3.

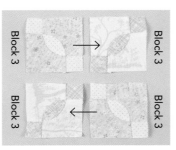

10 Join the four blocks 3 in pairs to make two strips. Fold the allowances in the direction of the arrows.

11 Bring two strips right sides together and pin. Sew along the seam line, making an extra stitch at the seam junctions.

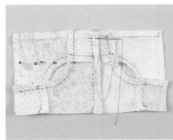

12 Pin the two strips right sides together, then sew along the seam line. Make an extra stitch at the seam junctions.

161

Rose of Sharon

* *

The centre of this block is made up of eight shapes that are assembled to form four joined hearts. The flower motif is then appliquéd to the background fabric. This is cut away behind the flower motif so the design comes into contact with any padding when quilted.

Folding the seam allowances

Templates

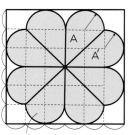

appliquéd

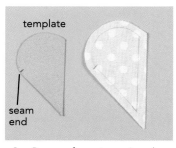

1 Prepare four pieces A and four pieces A'. Mark the ends of the seam lines as shown.

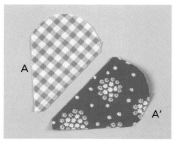

2 Prepare one piece A and one piece A'.

3 Bring pieces A and A' right sides together and pin. Sew along the straight edges.

4 Trim the allowance to 6mm, then fold it to one side (block 1 complete).

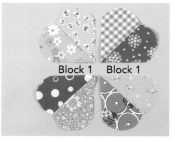

5 Make four blocks 1.

6 Pin two blocks 1 right sides together. Sew along the seam line to the marked end. Make an extra stitch at the start and at the end of the seam (block 2 complete).

7 Join the other two blocks in the same way. Fold the allowances in the opposite direction for the two blocks 2.

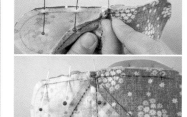

8 Pin the two blocks 2 right sides together. Sew along the seam line to the marked end. Sew stitch by stitch on overlapping allowances. Make an extra stitch at the seam junctions (block 3 complete).

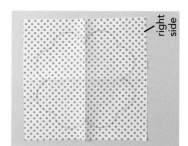

9 Fold the base fabric in four and press to mark the folds and find the centre point. Use the template to draw the outline of the flower motif on the right side.

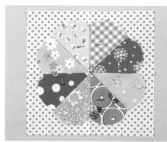

10 Snip into the seam allowances of block 3. Pin it on the background fabric so the centre point matches the centre of the fabric.

11 Using the tip of the needle to turn under the seam allowance as you go, slip stitch the edge in place.

12 Turn the block over and cut away the background fabric behind the flower shape, leaving a 6mm allowance.

Scrap Windmill

* *

This block is a variation on the Grace's Windmill (see page 88), with triangles arranged around the square. Use light colours for the pieces that form a background. Make sure corners match up and make extra stitches at the seam junctions to obtain a neat finish.

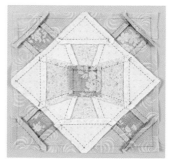
Folding the seam allowances

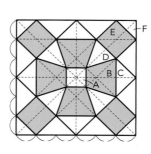
Templates

1 Prepare one piece A and two pieces B.

2 Pin the pieces A and B right sides together as shown. Sew along the seam line, making an extra stitch at the start and end. Join on the other piece B in the same way.

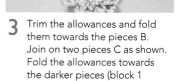

3 Trim the allowances and fold them towards the pieces B. Join on two pieces C as shown. Fold the allowances towards the darker pieces (block 1 complete).

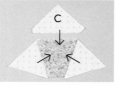

Fold the allowances in the direction of the arrows.

4 Join one piece B and two pieces D, then join on one piece C as shown. Fold the allowances in the direction of the arrows above (block 2 complete).

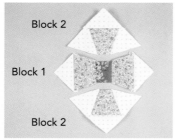

5 Make another block 2. Prepare one block 1 and two blocks 2 and lay them out flat to check their positioning.

6 Bring blocks 1 and 2 right sides together, then pin along the first edge without piercing the allowances.

7 Sew, making an extra stitch at the end. Do not cut the thread. Pin along the second edge without piercing the allowances.

8 Insert the needle in the corner at the end of the first edge, then take it out through the corner of the next piece.

9 Pin and sew along the second edge, making an extra stitch at the corner. Pin and sew the third edge in the same way. Fold the allowances towards block 2 (block 3 complete).

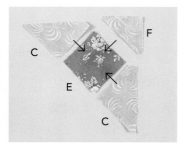

10 Join one piece E and two pieces C, then join on one piece F. Fold the allowances towards piece E (block 4 complete). Make three more blocks 4.

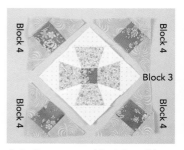

11 Prepare one block 3 and four blocks 4 and lay them out flat to check their positioning.

12 Pin a block 3 and 4 right sides togethe; sew, making an extra stitch on the junctions. Join a block 4 on the opposite side, then join on the other blocks 4 in the same way.

Scrap Basket

✳ ‧ ✳

Begin by joining the diamond-shaped pieces A, then combine these with the background pieces, before adding on the shapes that make the 'basket' and remaining background. Use the same fabric for the two 'basket' pieces and strong colours for the 'scraps'; set them on a light background.

Folding the seam allowances

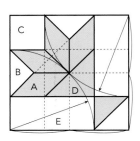

Templates

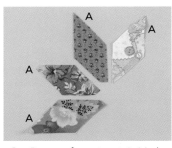

1 Prepare four pieces A. Mark each one with seam lines.

2 Pin two pieces A right sides together, as shown. Sew along the seam line, making an extra stitch at the start and end.

3 Trim the seam allowance to 6mm, then fold it to one side. Join another two pieces A in the same way.

4 Join the two combined pieces A. Fold all the allowances in the same direction (block 1 complete).

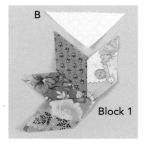

5 Prepare one block 1 and one piece B.

6 Pin block 1 and piece B right sides together as shown. Sew along the first edge, making an extra stitch at the end. Do not cut the thread.

7 Pin the next edge of piece B, then sew to the end of the seam. Fold the allowances towards block 1.

8 Join one piece C and one piece B to block 1 in the same way. Fold the allowances towards block 1 (block 2 complete).

9 Prepare one block 2 and one piece D.

10 Pin block 2 and piece D right sides together along the long edge of piece D; sew. Fold the allowances towards piece D (block 3 complete).

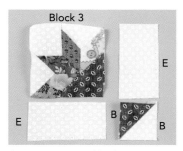

11 Lay out one block 3, two pieces B and two pieces E to check their positioning. Join the two pieces B and then one piece E to make a strip.

12 Pin the piece E to block 3, right sides together; sew. Fold the allowance towards block 3. Join on the other strip.

S
Scrap Basket

Season

* ✳ *

With only nine pieces, all with straight edges, this block is ideal for beginners to tackle. Start by joining three pieces to create the central diagonal strip, then form the other pieces into large triangles to add to either side. Use one colour and pattern for the C pieces to form a background.

Folding the seam allowances

Templates

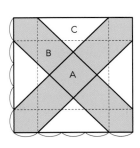

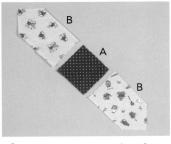

1 Prepare one piece A and two pieces B. Lay them out flat to check their positioning.

2 Bring pieces A and B right sides together, then pin along the seam as shown.

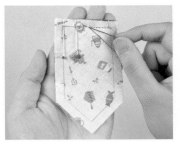

3 Sew along the seam, making an extra stitch at the start and end.

4 Trim the seam allowance to 6mm.

5 Fold the seam allowance towards piece B. Join on the other piece B in the same way (block 1 complete).

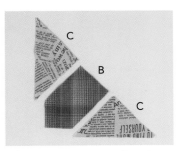

6 Prepare one piece B and two pieces C. Lay them out flat to check their positioning.

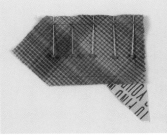

7 Bring pieces B and C right sides together as shown and pin along the seam line.

8 Sew along the seam. Fold the allowance towards piece B. Join on the other piece C in the same way (block 2 complete).

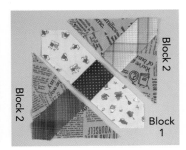

9 Prepare one block 1 and two blocks 2. Lay them out flat to check their positioning.

10 Pin the block 1 and and one block 2 right sides together along the long edges.

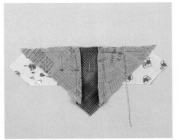

11 Sew along the seam, making an extra stitch at the start, the end, and at the seam junctions.

12 Trim the seam allowances, then fold them back to block 1. Join on the other block 2 in the same way.

Sawtooth

* · * ·

This block is based on a nine-patch pattern, with the nine patches composed from triangles or combinations of squares and small triangles. Make sure corners match up to avoid any gapping. Check the proportion and positioning of small blocks before assembly.

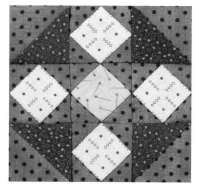

Folding the seam allowances

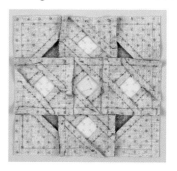

Templates

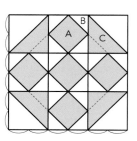

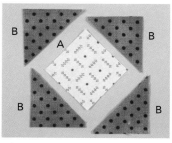

1 Prepare one piece A and four pieces B.

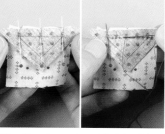

2 Pin pieces A and B right sides together as shown. Sew along the seam line, making an extra stitch at the start and end.

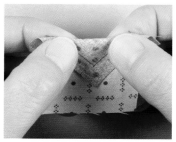

3 Trim the allowance to 6mm, then fold it towards piece A

4 Join the second piece B on the opposite edge of piece A.

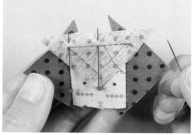

5 Pin the third piece B and piece A right sides together. Sew along the seam line. Join on the fourth piece B in the same way. Fold the allowances towards piece A (block 1 complete). Make five blocks 1.

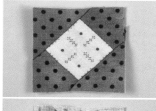
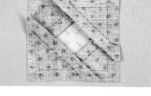

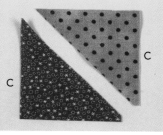

6 Prepare two pieces C.

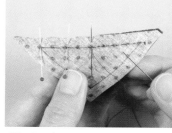

7 Pin the two pieces C right sides together. Sew along the seam line, then fold the allowances towards the dark coloured piece (block 2 complete).

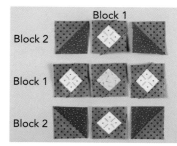

8 Prepare five blocks 1 and four blocks 2. Lay them out flat as shown above to check positioning.

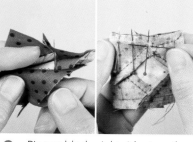

9 Pin two blocks right sides together. Sew along the seam line.

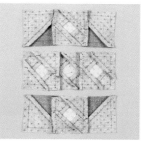

10 Assemble the blocks in threes as laid out in step 8 to make three strips.

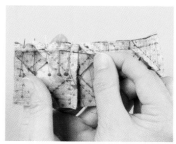

11 Pin two strips right sides together. Sew along the seam line. Join on the other strip in the same way. Fold the allowances towards the outer strips.

S
Sawtooth

166

Shoo Fly

* *

This block is made up of square and triangular pieces. Assemble pieces to into three strips, then join these together. Make sure corners match up and use extra stitches at seam junctions to avoid gaps. Choose a light colour for the background pieces.

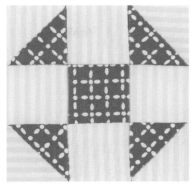

Folding the seam allowances

Templates

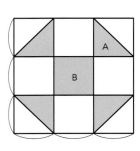

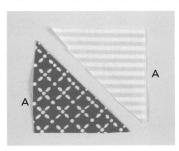

1 Prepare two pieces A.

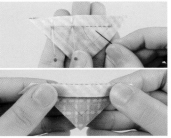

2 Pin the two pieces A right sides together as shown and sew. Fold the allowances towards the dark coloured piece (block 1 complete).

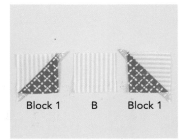

3 Prepare two blocks 1 and one piece B.

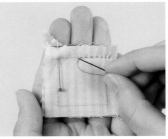

4 Pin the block 1 and piece B right sides together as shown; sew. Fold the allowances towards block 1 (block 2 complete). Make another block 2.

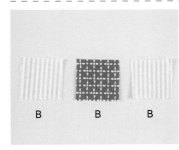

5 Prepare three pieces B and join together (block 3 complete). Fold the allowances towards the dark coloured pieces.

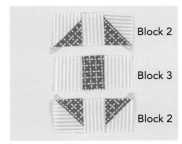

6 Lay out the block 3 and two blocks 2 flat to check their positioning.

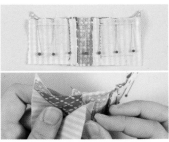

7 Pin a blocks 2 and block 3 right sides together as shown.

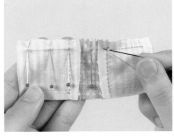

8 Sew along the seam line. Join on the other block 2 to the opposite side of bloack 3. Fold the allowances towards blocks 2.

Variation of the Shoo Fly block

Monkey Wrench

* *

This block is a variation of the Shoo Fly block above. With the exception of the centre, the squares are composed of two rectangles or two triangles. Use strongly coloured and patterned fabric for the central design so it stands out.

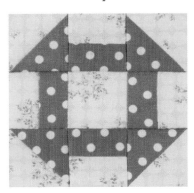

Folding the seam allowances

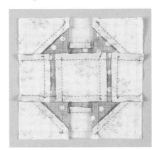

Templates

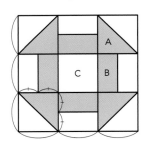

Single Wedding Ring

A combination of squares and triangles at the centre of this block form a ring shape. Use a dark and light coloured fabric to make the design stand out. The triangular shapes are assembled first, then joined with squares to form strips that are sewn together.

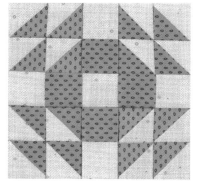

Folding the seam allowances

Templates

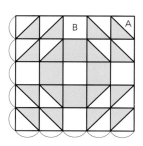

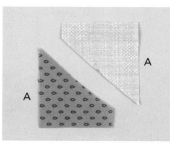

1 Prepare one dark A piece and one light A piece.

2 Pin the two pieces A right sides together as shown. Sew, making an extra stitch at the start and end of the seam line.

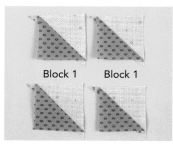

3 Trim the seam allowance to 6mm, then fold it towards the dark coloured piece (block 1 complete). Make four blocks 1.

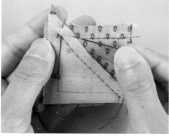

4 Pin two blocks 1 right sides together as shown. Sew, making an extra stitch at the start and end of the seam line.

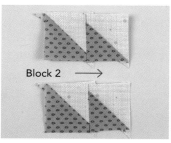

5 Trim the allowance to 6mm, then fold it in the direction of the arrow shown above (block 2 complete). Make two blocks 2.

6 Pin two blocks 2 right sides together as shown and sew as in step 4. Fold the allowances upwards (block 3 complete).

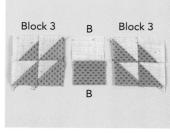

7 Make two blocks 3. Join two pieces B together. Lay out the blocks 3 and two pieces B flat to check positioning.

8 Pin a block 3 and the pieces B right sides together. Sew, making an extra stitch at the start and end of the seam. Join on the other block 3.

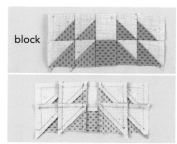

9 Fold the allowances towards the centre block (block 4 complete).

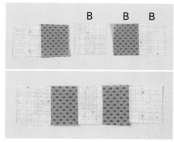

10 Join two pieces B. Repeat, then join these to another piece B. Fold the allowances towards the dark coloured pieces (block 5 complete).

11 Prepare two blocks 4 and one block 5.

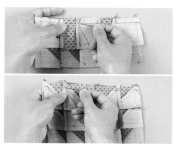

12 Pin a block 4 and 5 right sides together, matching seam junctions. Join on the other block 4.

Snail's Trail

* ✳ *

Choose a combination of two fabrics to accentuate the spiral shape on this block. Start at the centre, joining on larger and larger pieces until the block is complete. Although it looks complex, the simple, straight-sided square and triangular pieces make it an easy block to complete.

Folding the seam allowances

Templates

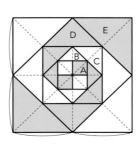

1   Prepare two pieces A.

2   Pin the pieces A right sides together as shown. Sew, making an extra stitch at the start and end of the seam line. Fold the allowances to one side (block 1 complete).

3   Make another block 1. Lay them out flat to check their positioning, inverting the colours.

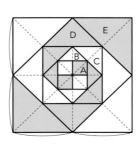

4   Pin two blocks 1 right sides together and sew. Fold the allowances to one side (block 2 complete).

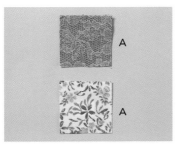

5   Prepare one block 2 and four pieces B.

6   Pin block 2 and a piece B right sides together. Sew, making an extra stitch at the start and end of the seam line.

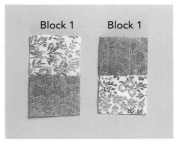

7   Trim the allowance to 6mm, then fold it towards piece B. Join on the other pieces B in the same way (block 3 complete).

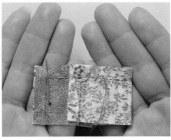

8   Prepare one piece B and four pieces C. Join them to block 3 as in steps 6 and 7 (block 4 complete).

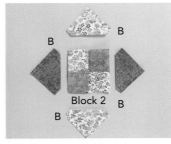

9   Fold the allowances towards the outside of the block.

10   Prepare one block 4 and four pieces D. Join them to block 4 as in steps 6 and 7 (block 5 complete).

11   Fold the allowances towards the outside of the block. Prepare one block 5 and four pieces E. Assemble them as in step 6 and 7.

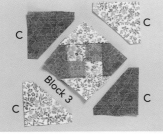

12   Fold the allowances towards the outside of the block.

S

Snail's Trail

169

Snow Ball 1

❋·❋

This block is composed of four squares, each with a quarter-circle in two corners. Matching up the corners forms a whole circle. Choose two contrasting colours and alternate them for a dramatic effect. Be accurate when matching up and sewing curves for a good finish.

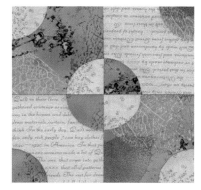

Folding the seam allowances

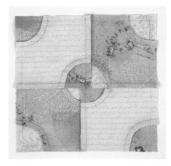

Templates

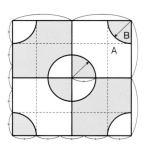

1 Transfer the templates to the wrong side of the fabric.

2 Add 7mm seam allowances and mark on the seam lines and centre points of curved edges, then cut out.

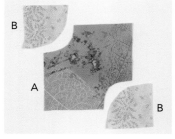

3 Prepare one piece A and two pieces B.

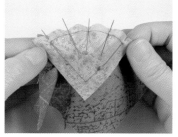

4 Bring a piece A and B right sides together, and pin, matching the marks.

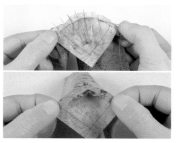

5 Sew along the seam line. Fold the allowances towards piece B. Join on the other piece B in the same way (block 1 complete).

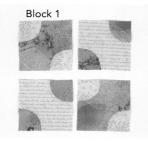

6 Make another block 1 in the same colour way. Then make two blocks 1 in the opposite colour way.

7 Bring two blocks 1 in different colour ways right sides together. Pin, matching the seam lines.

8 Make sure the pins are close together.

9 Sew along the seam line, working stitch by stitch through overlapping seam allowances.

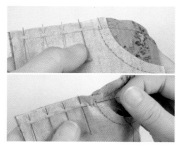

10 Make an extra stitch at seam junctions.

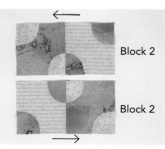

11 Fold the allowances in the direction of the arrows shown above (block 2 complete). Make a second block 2.

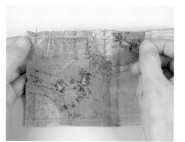

12 Pin the two blocks 2 right sides together matching the seam junctions; sew.

Snow Ball 2

* *

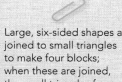

Large, six-sided shapes are joined to small triangles to make four blocks; when these are joined, the small triangles form a small square at the centre. Use two different fabrics; make two blocks in one combination, then reverse this for the other two blocks.

Folding the seam allowances

Templates

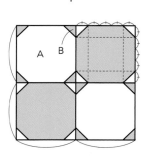

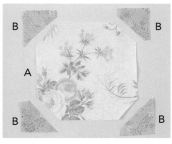

1 Prepare one piece A and four pieces B.

2 Bring the pieces A and B right sides together and pin.

3 Sew along the seam line, making an extra stitch at the start and end.

4 Trim the allowance to 6mm, then fold it towards piece A

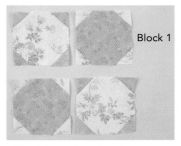

Block 1

5 Join on the other three pieces B in the same way (block 1 complete). Make four blocks 1 in two different colour combinations.

6 Bring two blocks 1 right sides together and pin.

7 Sew along the seam line, making an extra stitch at the start and end, working stitch by stitch on the overlapping allowances.

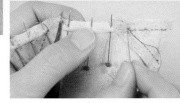

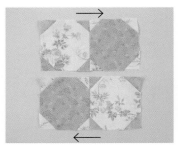

8 Two strips are made. Fold the allowances in the directions of the arrows.

9 Bring the two strips right sides together and pin.

10 Sew along the seam line, making an extra stitch at the seam junctions. Fold the allowances to one side.

* Folding the allowances

Fold the allowances towards the dark coloured pieces in alternating directions.

Spinning Machine

* · *

This simple block is made up of three shapes; one rectangle and two different triangles. Be careful not to stretch the slanted edges of the triangles as you join them together. Choose a dark coloured fabric for pieces A and C, with a lighter one for the B pieces

Folding the seam allowances

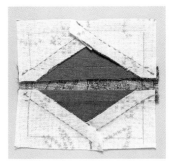

Templates

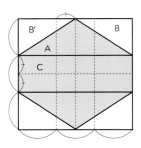

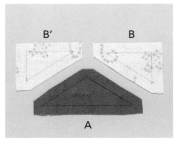

1 Prepare one piece A, one piece B and one piece B'.

2 Pin pieces A and B right sides together as shown. Sew along the seam line, making an extra stitch at the start and end.

3 Trim the allowance to 6mm, then fold it towards piece A.

4 Pin piece B' and the block from step 3 right sides together, matching the tip of piece A and the corner of piece B. Sew along the seam line.

5 Fold back the allowances towards piece A (block 1 complete). Make two blocks 1.

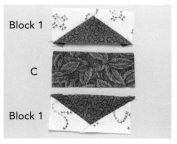

6 Prepare two blocks 1 and one piece C.

7 Bring block 1 and piece C right sides together and pin. Sew along the seam line.

8 Fold back the allowances towards piece C. Join on the other block 1 in the same way.

---

* Assembling several blocks

1 Bring two blocks right sides together and pin. Start sewing along the seam line.

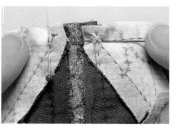

2 Make an extra stitch at the seam junctions. Sew stitch by stitch through overlapping allowances.

3 Two blocks are assembled. Continue to join blocks to the length of strip required. Make other strips as needed. Join the strips, folding allowances in alternate directions.

Spool 1

* *

This figurative block represents a reel of sewing thread. Match up any marks and snip into the seam allowances to help assemble curved edges. Choose a stripy pattern for the centre to suggest the thread on the reel. Fold seam allowances towards the centre.

Folding the seam allowances

Templates

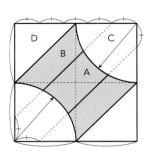

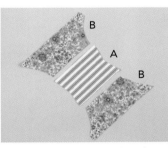

1 Prepare one piece A and two pieces B.

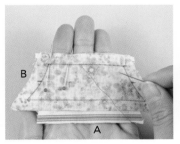

2 Pin pieces A and B right sides together as shown. Sew along the seam line, making an extra stitch at the start and end.

3 Trim the seam allowance to 6mm, then fold it towards piece A.

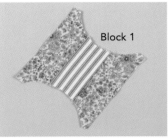

4 Join the other piece B to piece A in the same way (block 1 complete).

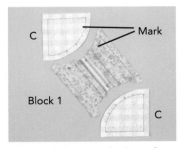

5 Mark the curved edges of block 1 and two pieces C as shown.

6 Snip into any curved edges to within 1mm of a seam line; this will help when joining the curves.

7 Pin a piece C to block 1.

8 Sew along the seam. Do not sew into the seam allowances of pieces A and B.

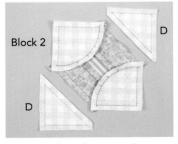

9 Join the other piece C to block 1 in the same way. Fold the seam allowances towards block 1 (block 2 complete). Prepare two pieces D.

10 Pin piece D and block 2 right sides together. Sew the seam as shown. Fold the allowances towards piece B. Join on the other piece D in the same way.

✱ Another way to fold the seam allowances

It is possible to fold the seam allowances towards pieces C at step 9. In this case, it is not necessary to snip into the seam allowances in step 6 but you must sew the seam allowances of pieces A and B in step 8.

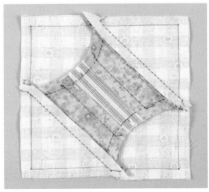

Spool 2

* *

This simpler block also represents a reel of thread. Assemble one piece A and two pieces B to make the shape, then join on two more pieces B. Choose the same fabric for the top and bottom of the reel, and a striped one for the centre. Use lighter coloured fabrics on either side.

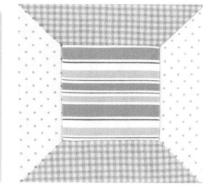

Folding the seam allowances

Templates
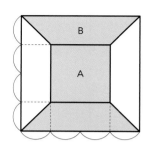

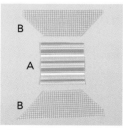

1 Prepare one piece A and two pieces B.

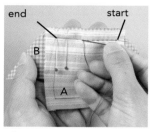

2 Pin pieces A and B right sides together as shown. Sew along the seam line, making an extra stitch at the start and end.

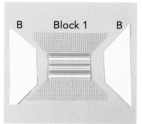

3 Join on the other piece B in the same way. Fold the seam allowances towards piece A (block 1 complete). Prepare two pieces B.

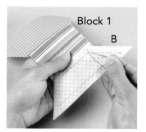

4 Join one piece B and block 1 right sides together along the first edge stitching in the seams of piece A. Make an extra stitch but do not cut off the thread.

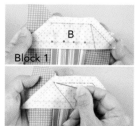

5 Pin and sew along the second edge. Repeat along the third edge. Join the other piece B to block 1 in the same way.

Variation of the Spool Block Spool 3 Variation

* *

The long pieces C are the main characteristics here. By rotating blocks, you get a rhythmic pattern. Join pieces A, B and B' to form a band, then join on piece C. With all the pieces having straight eges, this block is good for beginners. Choose strong colours for pieces A and C.

Folding the seam allowances
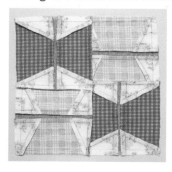

Templates
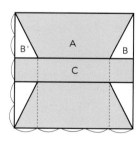

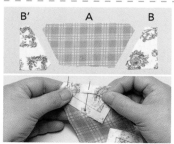

1 Pin one piece A and one piece B right sides together, as shown; sew. Make an extra stitch at the beginning and end of the seam.

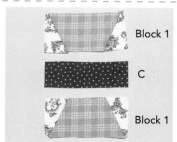

2 Join another piece B in the same way. Trim the seam allowances to 6mm and fold them towards piece A (block 1 complete). Make another block 1.

3 Pin one block 1 and one piece C right sides together. Sew along the seam as shown. Fold the allowance towards piece C. Join on the other block 1 in the same way (block 2 complete).

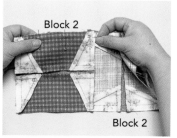

4 Make four blocks 2. Join them in pairs as shown to get two strips. Then join the two strips.

S

Spool 2

174

Spool 4

✳ ⋆ ✳

Combine light and dark to get the best effect with this block. Made up of just one shape of piece, this block makes the most of the curving shapes. Make sure you match up the centre marks on the curved edges to help the seam junctions meet neatly.

Folding the seam allowances

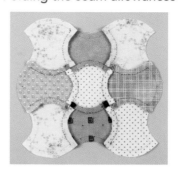

Templates

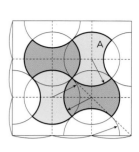

1 Draw around the template on the wrong side of the fabric. Divide each curved edge in half and mark this on each piece.

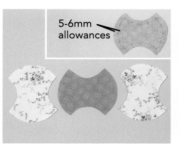

2 Add 5–6mm seam allowances and cut out the pieces.

5-6mm allowances

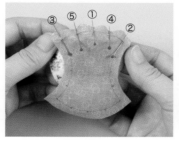

3 Bring two pieces right sides together and pin along the edge in the order shown.

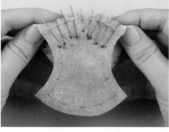

4 Add more pins between the pins placed in step 3 to avoid any mismatch.

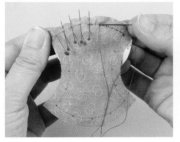

5 Sew, making an extra stitch at the start and end of the seam line.

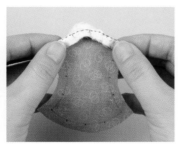

6 Fold the allowance towards the darker fabric

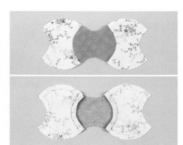

7 Join on the other piece A in the same way (block 1 complete). Make two more blocks 1.

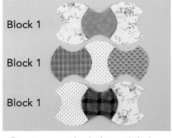

Block 1
Block 1
Block 1

8 Arrange the light and dark colours alternately as shown in the three strips above.

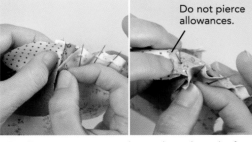

Do not pierce allowances.

9 Bring two strips together and pin along the first curved edge and to the centre of the second curved edge, matching up marks and seam junctions.

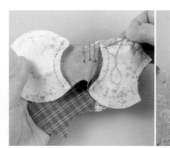

10 Sew, making an extra stitch at the start and at the seam the junction, without pierceing the allowance. Sew to the centre of the second curved edge.

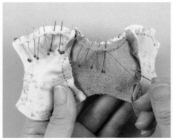

11 Pin and sew to the end of the strip. Join on the other strip in the same way. Fold the allowances towards the outside of the block and in a spiral at seam junctions.

S
Spool 4

Spring Beauty

* *

Pieces with curved edges are joined together to form a centre square. More curved-edge pieces are joined to form triangles that sit in the corners of this block. Match up any marks and seam lines, and use small stitches for curved edges.

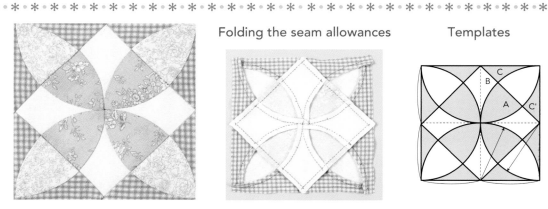

Folding the seam allowances

Templates

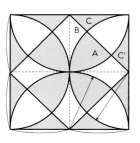

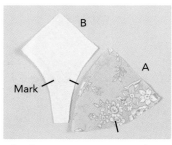

1 Prepare one piece A and one piece B. Mark seam lines and the curved edges as shown.

2 Bring pieces A and B right sides together as shown, then pin, keeping the pins close together.

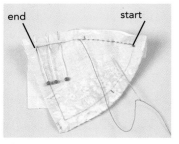

3 Sew along the seam line, making an extra stitch at the start and end. Fold the allowances towards piece A (block 1 complete).

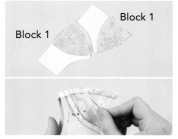

4 Make four blocks 1. Join them in pairs as in steps 2 and 3 (block 2 complete).

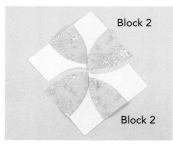

5 Make one more block 2. Fold the allowances towards pieces A.

6 Bring the two blocks 2, right sides together and pin without piercing the centre seam allowances.

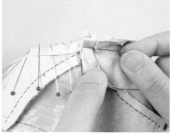

7 Sew along the seam line to the seam junction. Make an extra stitch without piercing the allowances. Sew to the end (block 3 complete).

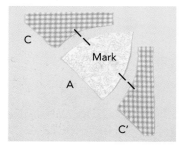

8 Prepare one piece A, one piece C and one piece C'.

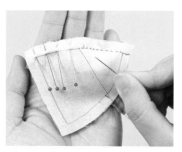

9 Pin the pieces A and C right sides together; sew. Fold the allowances towards piece A. Join on piece C' in the same way (block 4 complete). Make three more blocks 4.

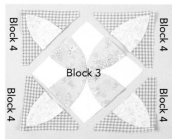

10 Prepare one block 3 and four blocks 4.

11 Pin blocks 3 and 4 right sides together. Sew, working stitch by stitch on overlapping allowances. Join on the other blocks 4 in the same way.

Stamp Basket

✳ ∘ ✳

This figurative block features four small baskets. The handles of the baskets are formed from bias strips of fabric, sewn onto pieces A. Use the handle template to draw its position onto the fabric, but not to cut out a handle shape. Use the same fabric for the background pieces.

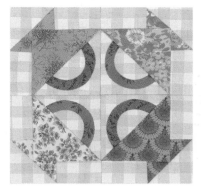

Folding the seam allowances

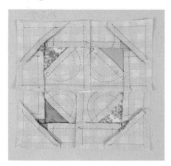

Templates

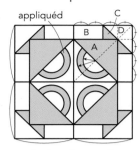

Use the handle template to mark its position

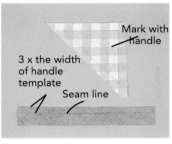

1 Prepare a piece A, drawing on the handle. Cut a bias strip of fabric that is about 1cm longer than the handle template and three times its width. Mark with a seam line.

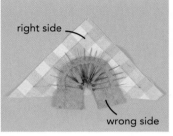

2 With the right sides of fabrics together, align the outer seam line on the bias strip with the inside edge of the handle curve on piece A; pin.

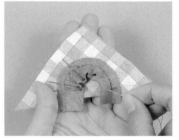

3 Sew along the outer seam line, using a thread colour similar to that of the bias strip.

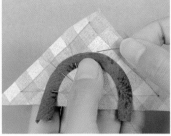

4 Fold the bias strip upwards so the right side is facing. Turn under the upper edge so it is aligned with the outside edge of the drawn handle. Pin and sew using slip stitches.

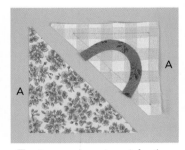

5 Prepare one piece A for the the basket and one piece A with a handle. Pin them right sides together along the long edges.

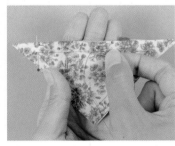

6 Sew, making an extra stitch at the start and end of the seam line. Trim the allowance to 6mm, then fold it towards the basket piece (block 1 complete).

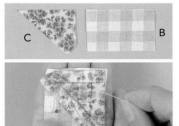

7 Pin one piece B and one piece C right sides together as shown and sew along the seam line. Fold the allowances towards piece C (block 2 complete).

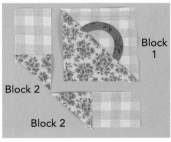

8 Make another symmetrical block 2. Assemble one block 1 and two blocks 2, folding the allowances towards block 1 (block 3 complete).

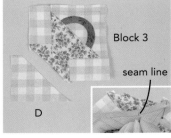

9 Pin a block 3 and a piece D right sides together, matching seam lines; sew. Fold the allowances towards block 3 (block 4 complete).

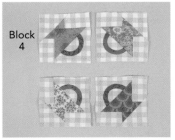

10 Make four blocks 4 and lay out flat to check positioning.

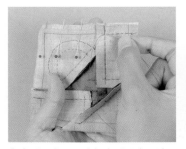

11 Pin the two blocks 4 right sides together in pairs; sew. Fold the allowances in the opposite direction for the two strips.

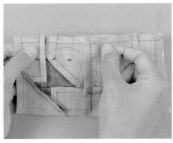

12 Pin the two strips right sides together, matching seam lines and junctions; sew.

Star Flower

* *

Assemble the centre section and then the outside pieces. Join pieces A and B with neat seams. Lay out your sections flat so you can check their position before assembling. Pieces B and D represent the petals and pieces A, the leaves, so chose your fabric colours accordingly.

Folding the seam allowances

Templates

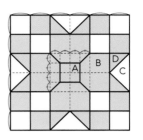

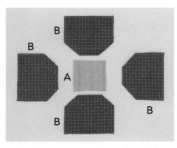

1 Prepare one piece A and four pieces B.

2 Pin the piece A and a piece B right sides together, as shown. Sew between the pins. Fold the seam allowance towards piece B.

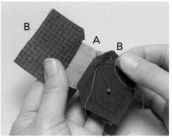

3 Join another piece B to the opposite edge of piece A. Pin the first edge of another piece B to piece A. Sew in place, finishing with an extra stitch. Do not cut the thread.

4 Pin the second edge in place, then continue sewing, making an extra stitch at the end. Sew along the third edge in the same way. Add the other piece B in the same way (block 1 complete).

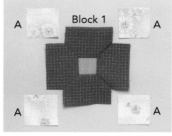

5 Block 1 is complete. Prepare four pieces A.

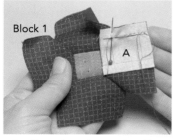

6 Pin a piece A to a piece B right sides together and along the first edge. Sew the seam, making an extra stitch at the end. Pin along the second edge and then sew to the end.

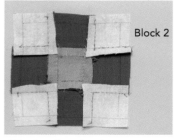

7 Join the other three pieces A to block 1 (block 2 complete). Trim the seam allowances to 6mm. Fold the allowances of pieces B towards the centre, and those of pieces A towards pieces B.

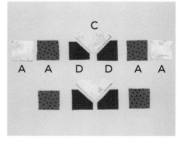

8 Prepare the pieces that go around the outside of the block. Join two pieces D on each side of a piece C, then join on two pieces A (block 3 complete).

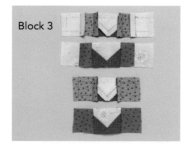

9 Fold the seam allowances of pieces C and A towards pieces D. Fold the allowances of pieces A towards the dark coloured pieces.

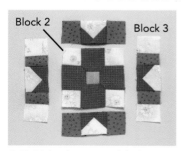

10 Make three more blocks 3. Join two more pieces A to either end of two blocks 3. Lay out the blocks flat to check their positioning.

11 Pin the shorter blocks 3 on either side of the block 2. Sew the seams, making extra stitches at the junction points. Join on the longer blocks 3.

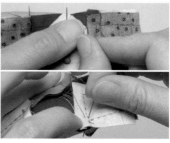

12 Work stitch by stitch through any overlapping seam allowances to avoid gapping.

S
Star Flower

Stick Diamond

* *

This block looks as if it is made up of squares set on top of long strips. In fact, the squares (pieces B) are joined to two trapezoids (pieces A) – using the same fabric for both trapezoids make them appear to be single strips. Pieces C, D and D′ give you pieces for the edges.

Folding the seam allowances

Templates

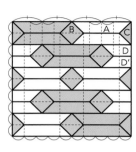

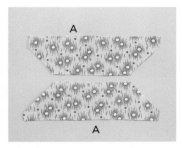

1 Prepare two pieces A.

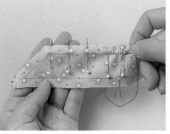

2 Pin the two pieces A right sides together as shown. Sew, making an extra stitch at the start and end of the seam line.

3 Trim the allowance to 6mm, then fold it to one side (block 1 complete).

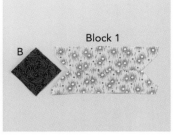

4 Prepare one piece B and one block 1.

5 Bring the block 1 and piece B right sides together and pin along the first edge; sew. Make an extra stitch at the end. Do not cut the thread.

6 Pin along the second edge.

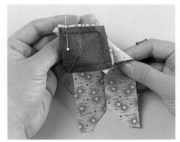

7 Sew, making an extra stitch at the start and end of the seam line. Fold the allowances towards block 1 (block 2 complete).

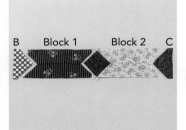

8 Prepare one block 1, one block 2 and two pieces C. Join them as in steps 5 to 7. Fold the allowances towards pieces A (block 3 complete).

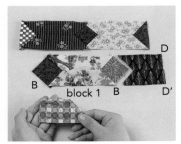

9 Join one piece D and one piece D′ (block 3). Join one block 1 to two pieces B, then join on block 3. Make another block 3 and join on this.

10 Prepare two more strips as in step 8 and one more strip as in step 9.

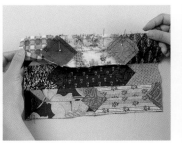

11 Pin two strips right sides together and sew, making an extra stitch at the start and end of the seam line and at seam junctions.

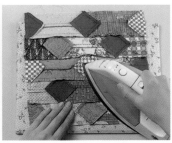

12 Join the strips in the order shown in step 10. Fold the allowances to one side.

S

Stick Diamond

Storm at Sea

* · *

Several blocks are combined to make a pattern reminiscent of waves. As this block is made up of many pieces, it is advisable to make it to a large size. All the pieces have straight edges. Make sure corners match up to get a smart finish.

Folding the seam allowances

Templates

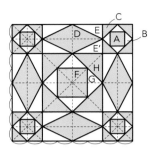

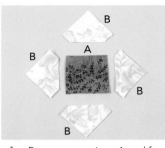

1 Prepare one piece A and four pieces B. Join the pieces B in the following order: left, right, top and bottom.

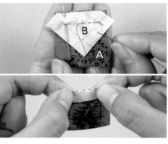

2 Pin the pieces A and a piece B right sides together. Sew along the seam as shown. Fold the seam allowances towards piece A. Join on the other pieces B to form block 1.

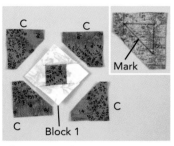

3 Prepare four pieces C to go round block 1. Mark the pieces C as shown.

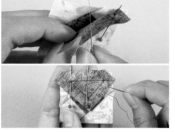

4 Pin block 1 and one piece C right sides together. Sew the seam. Fold the allowances towards piece C. Join on the other pieces C to form block 2.

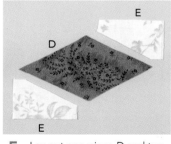

5 Lay out one piece D and two pieces E to check positioning. Sew the seams and fold them towards piece D.

6 Pin two pieces E' and the block from step 5 right sides together, then sew. Fold the allowances towards the darker fabric D (block 3 complete). Make three more blocks 3.

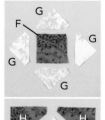

7 Prepare pieces F, G and H, then join them together as indicated, and as in steps 1 to 4. Mark the pieces H (block 4 complete).

8 Assemble two blocks 2 and one block 3. Pin the blocks, right sides together.

9 Sew along the seam, working stitch by stitch at the junctions. Fold the seam allowances towards the outer blocks (block 5 complete).

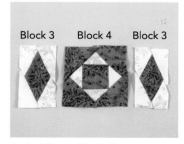

10 Join two blocks 3 and one block 4 as in step 9. Fold the seam allowances towards the upper block (block 6 complete).

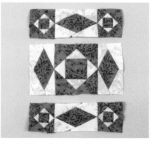

11 Two blocks 5 and one block 6 are made; join them as in step 9. Fold the allowances towards the block at the middle.

* Assembly idea

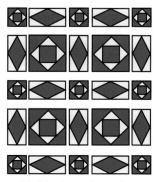

Assemble blocks as shown for a more intricate pattern.

Storm at Sea

Strawberry Basket

* *

Make up this block in two parts: assemble pieces A and B for the 'strawberries' part, then assemble pieces C, D and D' for the 'basket' part. Match up any marks and make an extra stitch at each junction point to avoid gapping. Alternate light and dark coloured fabrics for pieces A and B.

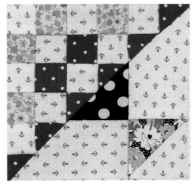

Folding the seam allowances

Templates

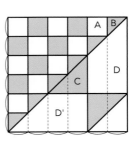

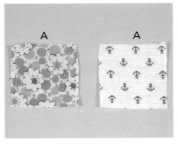

1 Prepare two pieces A.

2 Pin the two pieces A right sides together as shown. Sew along the seam line, making an extra stitch at the start and end.

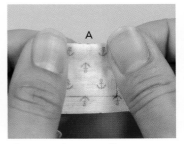

3 Trim the seam allowance to 6mm, then fold it towards the darker coloured piece.

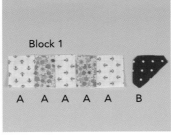

4 Join on another three pieces A, then add a piece B at the end to form block 1.

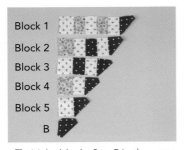

5 Make blocks 2 to 5 in the same way as block 1, with one fewer piece A each time. Prepare an additional piece B.

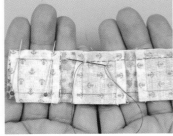

6 Pin blocks 1 and 2 right sides together, then sew along the seam, making an extra stitch at the junction points. Join on blocks 3, 4 and 5 and the extra piece B.

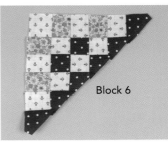

7 Blocks 1 to 5 are assembled to form block 6. Fold the seam allowances in alternate directions.

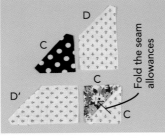

8 Prepare three pieces C, one piece D and one piece D'. Sew two pieces C together as shown (block 7 complete).

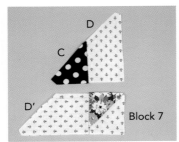

9 Join pieces C and D as shown, then join block 7 and piece D'. Fold the seam allowances towards the darker coloured piece.

10 Pin the two blocks from step 9 right sides together and sew along the seam. Fold the allowances upwards (block 8 complete).

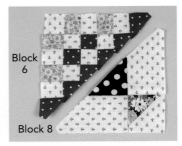

11 Blocks 6 and 8 are finished; lay them out to check their positioning.

12 Pin blocks 6 and 8 right sides together along the long edges. Sew along the seam, making an extra stitch at each junction point.

Strip Star

* • *

Choose two fabrics for the star at the centre of this block that will stand out from your other choices. The pieces are joined in a diagonal, across the block, before the other corner pieces are added. Keep corners matching and sew neat seams for a good finish.

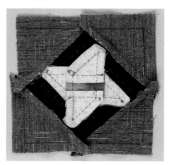

Folding the seam allowances

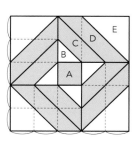

Templates

1 Prepare one piece A and two pieces B. Lay them out to check the positioning, paying attention to the direction of the pieces B.

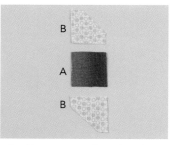

2 Pin a piece A and B right sides together as shown. Sew, making an extra stitch at the start and end of the seam line.

3 Trim the allowance to 6mm, then fold it towards piece A. Join on the other piece B (block 1 complete).

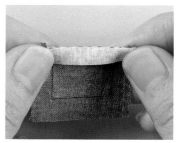

4 Prepare two pieces B and two pieces C. Lay them out to check the positioning, paying attention to the direction of the pieces.

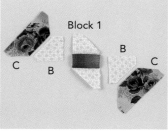

5 Pin a piece B and C right sides together as shown. Sew, making an extra stitch at the start and end of the seam line. Fold the allowances towards piece C (block 2 complete).

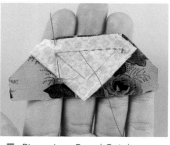

6 Prepare one block 1 and two blocks 2. Pin a block 1 and 2 right sides together. Sew, making an extra stitch at the start and end of the seam line. Join on the other block 2 (block 3 complete).

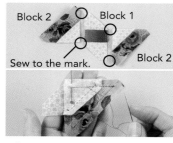

7 Join a piece D and E as shown. Fold the allowances towards the darker piece (block 4 complete). Make another block 4.

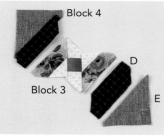

8 Pin blocks 3 and 4 right sides together as shown. Sew along the seam line without piercing the allowances. Fold the allowances towards the outside of the block.

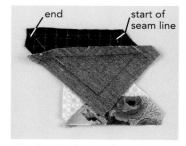

9 Join on the the other block 4 in the same way (block 5 complete). Join pieces C, D and E (block 6 complete). Make two blocks 6.

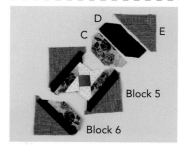

10 Bring blocks 5 and 6 right sides together and pin along the first edge; sew. Make an extra stitch at the end. Do not cut the thread.

11 Pin along the second edge, then sew along the seam line. Make an extra stitch at the end. Do not cut the thread.

12 Pin and sew the third edge the same way. Fold the allowances towards the outside of the block.

Sunburst

Level ★★★★☆

✱ · ✱

Chose a selection of strong and colourful fabrics for the outer ring of diamond shapes for this circular 'block'. The block is composed of diamonds and triangles, pieced together in eight groups and then joined. The disc at the centre is appliquéd in place.

Folding the seam allowances

Templates

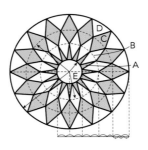

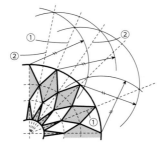

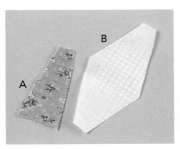

1 Prepare one piece A and one pieces B. Lay them out flat to check their positioning.

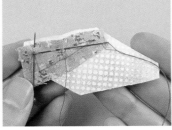

2 Pin pieces A and B right sides together as shown. Sew, making an extra stitch at the start and end of the seam.

3 Trim the allowance to 6mm, then fold it towards B (block 1 complete).

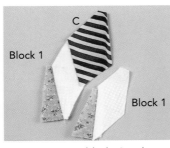

4 Prepare two blocks 1 and one piece C. Pin one block 1 and piece C right sides together, sewing along the seam line. Fold the allowances towards piece C.

5 Bring the block from step 4 and the block 1 right sides together and pin the first edge. Sew, making an extra stitch at the end. Do not cut the thread.

6 Pin the second edge without piercing the allowances. Sew the rest of the seam, making an extra stitch at the end. (block 2 complete).

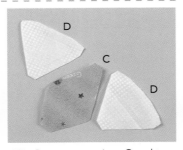

7 Prepare one piece C and two pieces D.

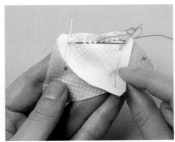

8 Pin the pieces C and D right sides together; sew (block 3 complete).

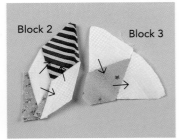

9 Fold the allowances in the direction of the arrows. Join a block 2 and 3 as described in steps 5 and 6.

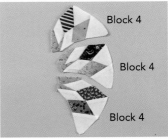

10 Fold the allowances towards block 3 (block 4 complete). Make eight blocks 4, then join them. Fold the allowances to one side.

11 Sew around the allowance of piece E. Put the template on the wrong side and pull the thread to turn under the allowance. Press and remove the template. Appliqué the piece to the centre of the block.

S

Sunburst

183

Sunflower 1

* • *

This figurative block represents a sunflower, with pieces A and B representing the petals. Chosing yellows for the petals and a brown fabric for the centre helps emphasise the sunflower effect. Match up points and curves for a neat finish.

Folding the seam allowances

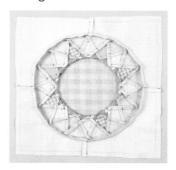

Templates

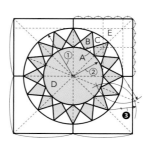

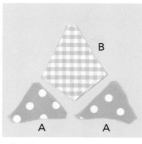

1 Prepare two pieces A and one piece B.

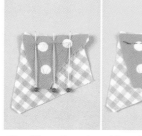

2 Pin a piece A and B right sides together as shown. Sew along the seam line. Join on the other piece A. Fold the allowances towards piece A (block 1 complete). Make eight blocks 1.

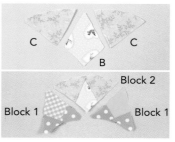

3 Prepare one piece B and two pieces C. Join them, folding the allowances towards piece B (block 2 complete).

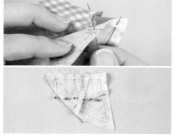

4 Bring a block 1 and 2 right sides together, then pin as shown, matching up the seams.

5 Sew, making an extra stitch at the seam junctions. Join on the other block 1. Fold the allowances towards block 1 (block 3 complete).

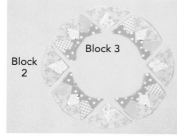

6 Prepare four blocks 2 and four blocks 3.

7 Pin a blocks and 3 right sides together, then sew as in steps 4 and 5. Fold the allowances towards the block 3. Repeat to join all the blocks 2 and 3.

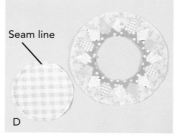

8 Prepare one pieces D and draw on the seam line.

9 Place piece D on the block, right sides together and pin along about a quarter of the edge; sew along the seam line. Continue to sew the piece D in place, a quarter of the edge at a time. Fold the allowances towards piece D.

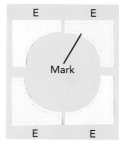

10 Prepare 4 pieces E and draw on the seam lines.

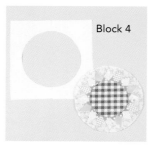

11 Join the pieces E to form a frame. Fold the allowances in one direction (block 4 complete).

12 Pin block 4 and the central block right sides together in the same way as in step 9, matching seam lines. Sew, then fold the allowances towards the central block.

S

Sunflower 1

Sunflower 2

Level ★★★★☆

This block represents a sunflower. Pieces A, C and F form a half-flower shape, while blocks G and J are the large leaves. The flower pieces are combined with the background to make the first block; the leaves for the second block. Choose shades of orange and brown for the flower parts.

Folding the seam allowances

Templates

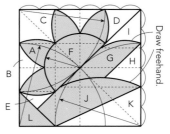

Drawing of the curve of piece A

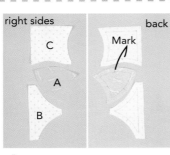

1 Prepare one piece A, one piece B and one piece C. Mark the seam lines and the centre points on curved edges.

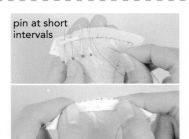

2 Pin the pieces A and B right sides together. Sew along the seam line. Fold the allowances towards piece A.

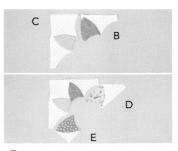

3 Join on piece C in the same way. Join one piece A and one piece B, one piece A and one piece D, and one piece A and one piece E. Join these blocks (block 1 complete).

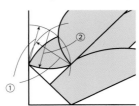
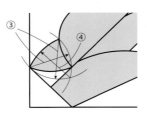

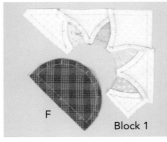

4 Prepare block 1 and one piece F. Mark the centre point of the curved edges on the block and piece F.

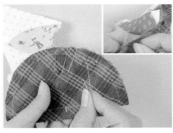

5 Pin block 1 and piece F right sides together up to the centre of the curved edges. Sew to this point, then pin and sew the other half of the curved edge (block 2 complete).

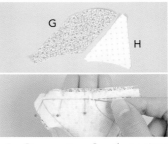

6 Pin one piece G and one piece H right sides together. Sew along the seam line, making an extra stitch at the start and end.

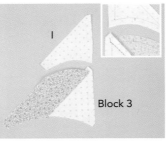

7 Sew block 3 and one piece I right sides together, along the seam line. Fold the allowances towards piece G (block 4 complete).

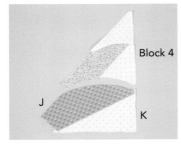

8 Join one piece J and one piece K (block 5 complete) Join blocks 4 and 5 as in step 2. Fold the allowances towards block 5 (block 6 complete).

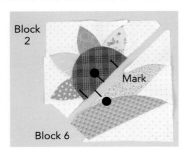

9 Lay out block 2 and block 6 flat to check their positioning. Make marks. Along the edges as shown.

10 Bring blocks 2 and 6 right sides together, then pin at the ends of the seam, at the marks and in between. Sew along the seam line (block 7 complete).

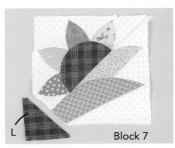

11 Join block 7 and one piece L right sides together. Fold the allowances towards piece L.

S

Sunflower 2

185

Sunrose

Level ★★★☆☆

* *

This block is made up of 'petals' with rounded edges and triangular 'leaves', all surrounding a central square. Choose suitably floral coloured fabrics for the 'petals' and shades of green for the 'leaves'. Match up seam lines and keep corners and curves neat to get a good finished block.

Folding the seam allowances

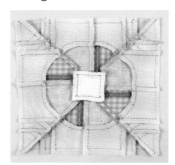

Templates

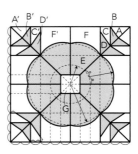

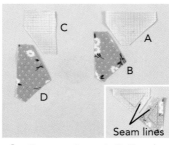

1 Prepare pieces A, B, C and D. Piece A joins to B; piece C joins to D. Mark the pieces with seam lines.

Fold the allowances in the direction of the arrows.

2 Pin the pieces A and B (then C and D) right sides together; sew. Fold the allowances towards the dark coloured piece. Join the two blocks obtained (block 1 complete).

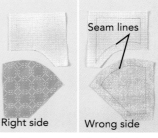

Seam lines

Right side   Wrong side

3 Prepare one piece E and one piece F and mark with seam lines.

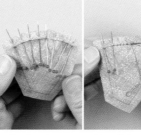

4 Pin the pieces E and F right sides together as shown. Sew, making an extra stitch at the start and end of the seam (block 2 complete).

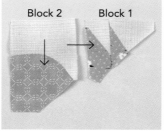

Block 2   Block 1

5 Prepare a block 1 and 2. Fold the allowances in the direction of the arrows shown above.

6 Pin blocks 1 and 2 right sides together. Sew, making an extra stitch at the start and end of the seam (block 3 complete).

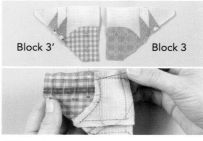

Block 3'   Block 3

7 Make another symmetrical block 3 (block 3' complete). Join the blocks 3 and 3' (block 4 complete). Make three more blocks 4.

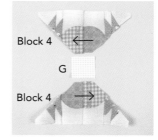

Block 4   Block 4   G

8 Fold the allowances in the direction of the arrows. Prepare one piece G.

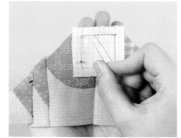

9 Pin block 4 and piece G right sides together. Sew, making an extra stitch at the start and end of the seam. Join on another block 4. Fold the allowances towards blocks 4 (block 5 complete).

10 Lay out the block 5 and the two other blocks 4 to check their positioning.

11 Pin the first edge of a block 4 to the block 5 and sew, without stitching in the allowances. Pin and sew the second and third edges in the same way. Join on the other block 4.

S
Sunrose

186

Tennessee Circle

✽ ✽

This block is reminiscent of a windmill so choose darker colours for the crossing motif at the centre. Start by forming a diagonal centre strip and then join smaller blocks to this. Match up seam lines and any marks, and make small stitches along curved edges.

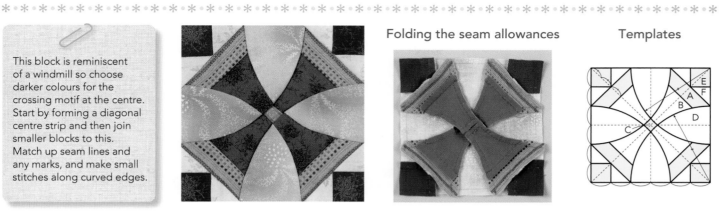

Folding the seam allowances

Templates

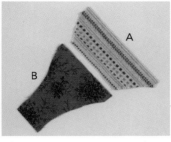

1 Prepare one piece A and one piece B.

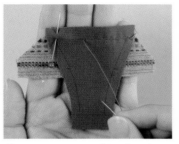

2 Pin pieces A and B right sides together as shown. Sew along the seam line, making an extra stitch at the start and end. Fold the allowances towards piece A (block 1 complete).

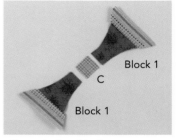

3 Make four blocks 1. Prepare two blocks 1 and one piece C.

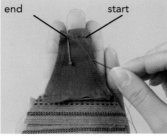

4 Pin a block 1 and piece C right sides together. Sew along the seam line, then fold the allowances towards piece C. Join the other block 1 in the same way (block 2 complete).

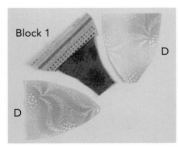

5 Prepare one block 1 and two pieces D. Mark with seam lines.

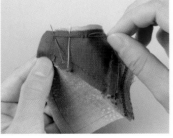

6 Pin block 1 and piece D right sides together and sew along the seam line. Fold the allowances towards piece D. Join on the other piece D (block 3 complete).

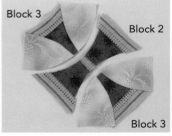

7 Prepare one block 2 and three blocks 3.

8 Pin blocks 2 and 3 right sides together. Sew along the first curved edge, following the seam line, making an extra stitch at the seam junctions.

9 Pin and sew along the rest of the edge, making extra stitches at the seam junctions. Join on the other block 3.

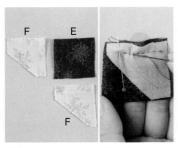

10 Join one piece E and two pieces F (block 4 complete).

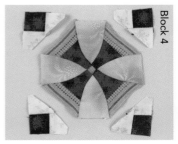

11 Prepare the central block and four blocks 4.

12 Join the blocks 4 to the corners of the central block then fold the allowances outwards.

Thirteen Squares

✳ ✳

Start by joining A and B pieces together to form diagonal strips, then combine these with C pieces to make four blocks. Use a strong colour for the A and B pieces and a light colour for the C pieces, so the design stands out.

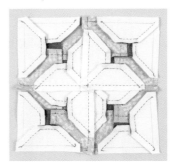

Folding the seam allowances

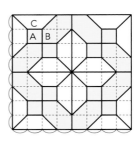

Templates

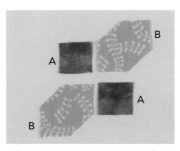

1 Prepare two pieces A and two piece B.

2 Pin a pieces A and B right sides together as shown and sew. Join the other pieces A and B.

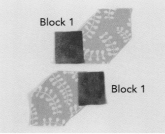

3 Fold the allowances towards pieces A (two blocks 1 complete). Lay out the two blocks 1 flat to check their positioning.

4 Pin the two blocks 1 right sides together as shown, matching the seam junction.

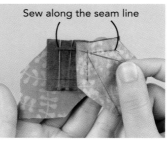

5 Sew along the seam line, making an extra stitch at the start and end. Trim the allowance to 6mm, then fold it to one side (block 2 complete).

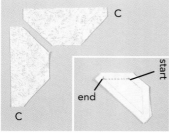

6 Prepare two pieces C. Pin right sides together and sew along the seam line. Fold the allowances to one side (block 3 complete).

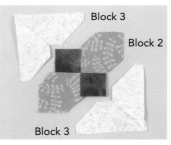

7 Prepare one block 2 and two blocks 3.

8 Pin the first edge of a block 3 to block 2 right sides together as shown; sew, making an extra stitch at the end. Do not cut the thread.

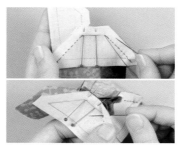

9 Pin and sew the remaining edges in the same way, one after the other, making sure not to sew through the allowances (block 4 complete).

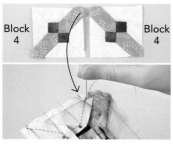

10 Make four blocks 4. Join them in pairs, sewing stitch by stitch on overlapping allowances, to form two strips.

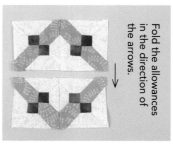

11 Fold back the allowances, alternating the direction for the two strips.

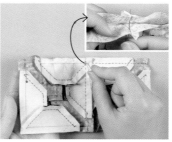

12 Pin the two strips right sides together as shown, matching up seam junctions. Sew, making extra stitches at the junction points.

Thousands Pyramids

✳ ✳

This block is composed of only isosceles triangles. Arranging triangles that alternate between dark and light colours will create a dramatic effect. Assemble the pieces into strips and then join these together. Make sure corners match up to get a neat finish.

Folding the seam allowances

Templates

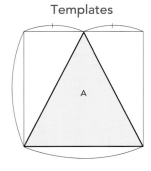

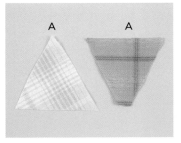

1   Prepare two pieces A.

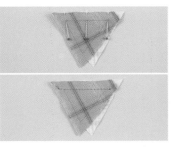

2   Pin two pieces A right sides together along a long edge. Sew, making an extra stitch at the start and end of the seam.

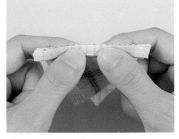

3   Trim the allowance to 6mm, then fold it towards the dark coloured piece.

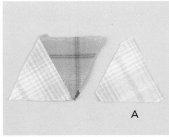

4   Prepare the adjacent piece A. Lay out flat the block from step 3 and the piece A to check their postioning.

5   Pin the block from step 3 and piece A right sides together as shown. Sew along the seam line.

6   Fold the allowances towards the dark colour piece.

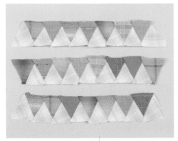

7   Add on other pieces A in the same way. Make three strips.

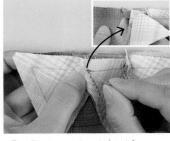

8   Pin two strips right sides together, matching up the seam junctions.

9   Sew along the seam lines.

10   Make extra stitches at the seam junctions but avoid sewing through the allowances.

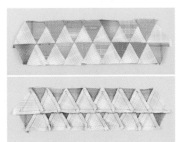

11   Fold the allowances to one side. Join on the third strip in the same way.

Three Stars

Level ★★★✿✿

* · *

Choose three different colours for the three stars of this block. Follow the steps below in the same order to ensure that you assemble the pieces in the correctly. Make any seam lines and marks match up and make extra stitches at the seam junctions.

Folding the seam allowances

Templates

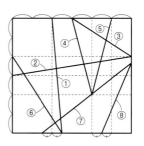

※ drawing order = ① to ⑮

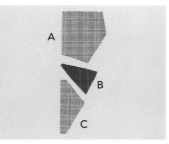

1 Prepare one piece A, one piece B and one piece C.

2 Pin the pieces A and B right sides together as shown. Sew along the seam line, making an extra stitch at the start and end. Join on piece C the same way.

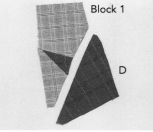

3 Trim the allowances and fold them towards piece B (block 1 complete). Prepare one piece D.

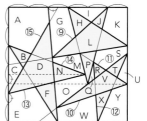

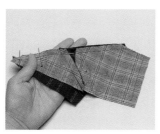

4 Pin block 1 and piece D right sides together as shown; sew along the seam line. Fold the allowances towards the darker piece (block 2 complete).

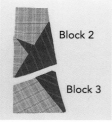

5 Join one piece E and one piece F (block 3 complete). Join the blocks 2 and 3. Fold the allowances towards piece D (block 4 complete).

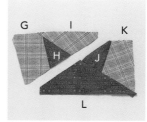

6 Join pieces G, H and I, and pieces J, K and L as shown. Then join the two blocks together to make block 5. Fold the allowances towards the dark coloured pieces.

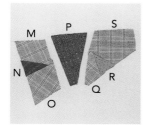

7 Join pieces M, N and O, and pieces Q, R and S as shown. Then join them towards piece P to make block 6. Fold the allowances towards the dark coloured pieces.

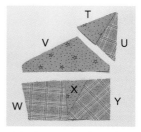

8 Join pieces T and U, and pieces W, X and Y as shown. Then join them towards piece V to make block 7.

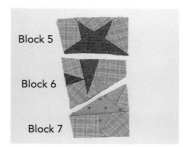

9 Lay the blocks 5 to 7 out flat to check their positioning.

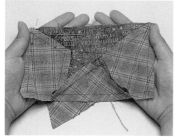

10 Pin blocks 5 and 6 right sides together, matching seam lines and junctions. Sew along the seam line. Join on block 7 in the same way.

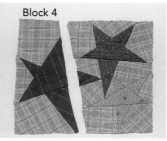

11 Fold the allowances towards the outer blocks. Lay out the block just made and the block 4 to check positioning.

12 Pin the two blocks right sides together, matching seam lines and junctions. Sew along the seam line.

T
Three Stars

Tile Puzzle

* *

This block is made up of nine smaller blocks: five of these feature an octagonal motif; four of them feature an upright cross. Choose two colours for the octagons and crosses and combine them as shown to get an interlocking pattern. Choose a contrast for the background.

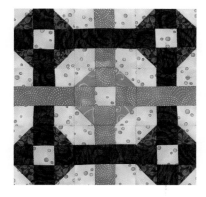

Folding the seam allowances

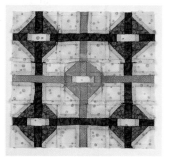

Templates

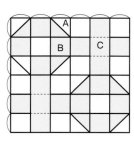

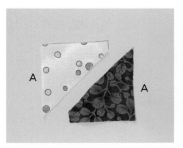

1 Prepare two pieces A.

2 Pin the two pieces A right sides together along the long edges. Sew along the seam line. Fold the allowances towards the dark coloured piece (block 1 complete).

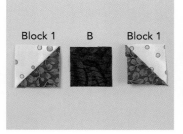

3 Prepare two blocks 1 and one piece C.

4 Pin and sew block 1 and the pieces B right sides together. Fold the allowances towards the dark piece B (block 2 complete).

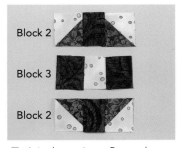

5 Join three pieces B together and fold the allowances towards the dark coloured pieces (block 3 complete). Prepare two blocks 2 and one block 3.

6 Pin the blocks 2 and 3 right sides together and sew along the seam lines, making extra stitches at seam junctions. Fold the allowances towards block 3 (block 4 complete).

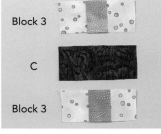

7 Prepare two blocks 3 and one piece C as shown. Join them, sewing along the seam line. Fold the allowances towards piece C (block 5 complete).

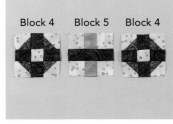

8 Prepare two blocks 4 and one block 5 as shown. Join, making a extra stitch on the junctions. Fold the allowances towards block 4 (block 6 complete).

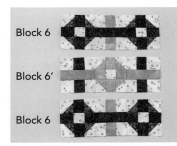

9 Make another block 6. Then join two blocks to a block 5, following the colour arrangement above, to form a block 6'.

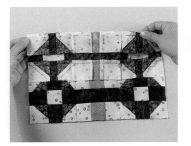

10 Join a block 6 and 6' right sides together, making an extra stitch at the seam junctions. Join on the other block 6. Fold the allowances in one direction.

* Assembling several blocks

Alternate the arrangement of blocks 4 and 5 to create a grid-like patttern.

* Tip

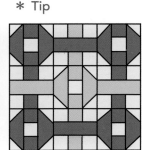

If pieces A and B are cut from only one fabric, it is possible to cut them as trapezoids.

Time and Energy

* *

Blocks are assembled and then these are joined to form the strips that make up the finished blocks. Match up seam lines on curved edges and use small stitches. Choose the same colour for the pieces A and for the background pieces B and C. Then choose a different pair of colours for the pin wheel block at the centre.

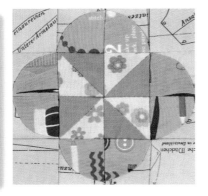

Folding the seam allowances

Templates

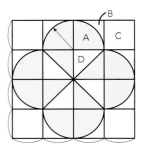

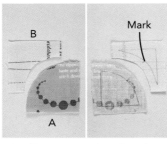

1   Prepare one piece A and one piece B. Mark the pieces with the seam lines.

2   Bring pieces A and B right sides together as shown and pin. Sew along the seam line.

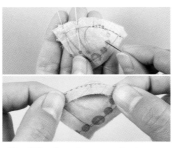

3   Trim the allowance to 6mm, then fold it towards piece A (block 1 complete).

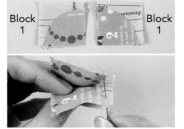

4   Make eight blocks 1. Bring two blocks 1 right sides together, then pin, using a pin to help you match up the seam junctions.

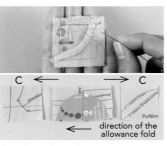

5   Sew along the seam line, working stitch by stitch at the overlapping allowances (block 2 complete). Join on two pieces C (block 3 complete).

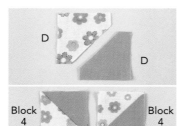

6   Join two pieces D (block 4 complete). Make four blocks 4. Fold the allowances towards the dark colour pieces.

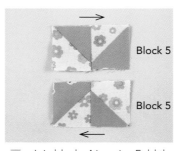

7   Join blocks 4 in pairs. Fold the allowances in the direction of the arrows (two blocks 5 complete).

8   Pin the two blocks 5 right sides together using a pin to help you match up the seam junctions.

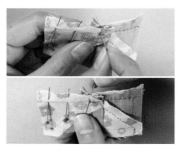

9   Sew along the seam line, working stitch by stitch at the overlapping allowances (block 6 complete).

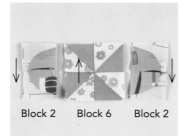

10   Join two blocks 2 and the block 6. Fold the allowances in the direction of the arrows (block 7 complete).

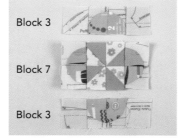

11   Prepare two blocks 3 and one block 7.

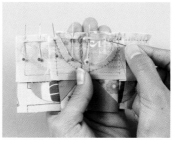

12   Pin a block 3 and 7 right sides together and sew along the seam line. Join on the other block 3. Fold the allowances outwards.

Tree

* ＊ * ＊

This figurative block represents a tree, set at a diagonal across the block. The pieces are joined together in slanting strips and then assembled into the design. Choose green fabrics for the main section of the tree and browns for the base; set them against a light background fabric.

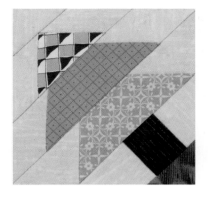

Folding the seam allowances

Templates

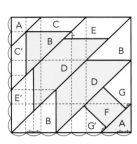

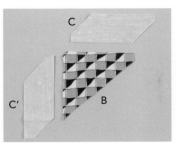

1 Prepare one piece B, one piece C and one piece C'.

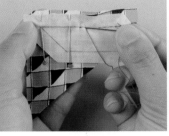

2 Pin pieces B and C right sides together as shown. Sew along the seam line, making an extra stitch at the start and end. Fold the allowances towards piece B.

3 Join on the piece C' in the same way. Fold the allowances towards the dark piece B (block 1 complete).

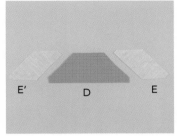

4 Prepare one piece D, one piece E and one piece E'.

5 Join the pieces D, E and E' as in steps 2 and 3. Fold the allowances towards the dark piece D (block 2 complete).

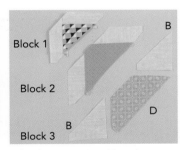

6 Join one piece D and two pieces B, then fold back the allowances towards piece D (block 3 complete).

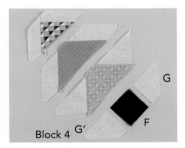

7 Join one piece F, one piece G and one piece G', then fold the allowances towards F (block 4 complete).

8 Lay out flat blocks 1 to 4 and two pieces A to check their positioning.

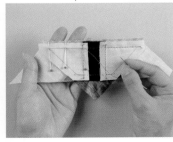

9 Pin the bottom piece A and block 4 right sides together. Sew along the seam line, making an extra stitch at the start and end. Join on blocks 3, 2 and 1 in that order.

10 To get a neat point at the top of the tree (block 1), mark the centre of the long edge of the top piece A. Bring the piece A and block 1 right sides together and use a pin to match that point up with the top of the tree. Pin along the seam.

11 Sew along the seam line, making an extra stitch at the start and end. Fold the allowances towards piece A.

T
Tree

Triangles and Squares

One of the simplest blocks to make, this is made up of only two different pieces, A and B. Choose two different colours for the A pieces and two different colours for the B pieces, to give the effect of small squares set against the background of larger squares.

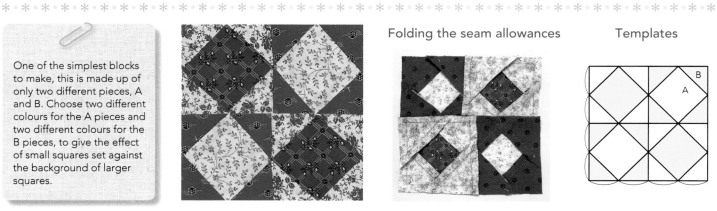

Folding the seam allowances

Templates

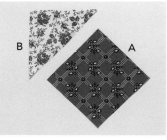

I   Prepare one piece A and one piece B

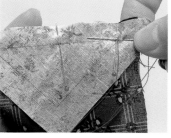

2   Pin the pieces A and B right sides together as shown. Sew, making an extra stitch at the start.

3   Sew along the seam line, making an extra stitch at the end.

4   Trim the allowance to 6mm, then fold them towards piece A.

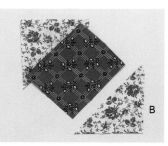

5   Prepare another piece B and lay it out with the block just assembled to check their positioning.

6   Pin the piece B to the opposite edge of the piece A, right sides together; sew. Fold the allowances towards piece A (block 1 complete).

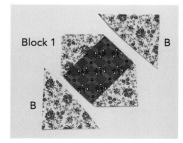

7   Prepare the two more pieces B. Trim off the excess allowances at the corners of the pieces B on block 1.

8   Pin block 1 and a piece B right sides together; sew. Join on the other piece B. Fold the allowances towards piece A (block 2 complete).

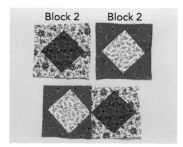

9   Make four blocks 2.

10   Pin two blocks 2 right sides together as shown. Sew, working stitch by stitch on the overlapping allowances. Join the other two blocks 2.

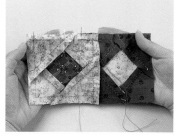

11   Fold back the allowances, alternating the direction for the two strips. Pin the two strips right sides together. Sew, making an extra stitch at the junctions.

12   Press on the wrong side to fold the allowances neatly.

T

Triangles and Squares

Tulip

* *

With only straight-edged pieces to sew, this is a simple block to make – though you should be careful not to stretch those diagonal edges that are cut on the bias. Use a green fabric for the large 'leaves' and a suitable colour for the 'flower' parts of the block.

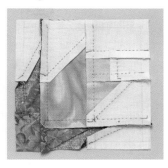

Folding the seam allowances

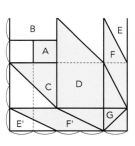

Templates

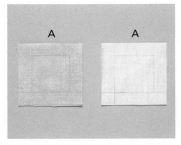

1 Prepare two pieces A. Here, the orange piece will form the heart of the tulip.

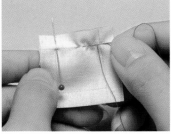

2 Pin the two pieces A right sides together along one edge. Sew along the seam line, making an extra stitch at the start and end.

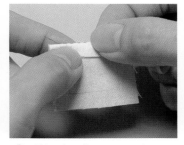

3 Trim the allowance to 6mm and fold it towards the dark coloured piece (block 1 complete).

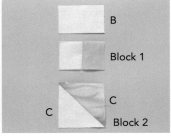

4 Join two pieces C along their long edges (block 2 complete). Prepare one block 1, one block 2 and one piece B and join together. Fold the allowances downwards (block 3 complete).

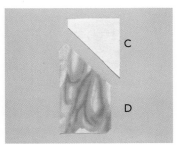

5 Prepare one piece C and one piece D. Pin them right sides together along the diagonal edges; sew. Fold the allowances towards piece D (block 4 complete).

6 Pin blocks 3 and 4 right sides together. Sew along the seam line, then fold the allowances towards block 4 (block 5 complete).

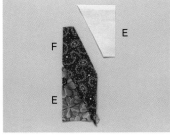

7 Join two pieces E and one piece F together as shown. Fold the allowances towards piece F. Join two pieces E' and one piece F' in the same way (blocks 6 and 6' complete).

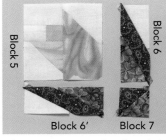

8 Pin two pieces G right sides together along the long diagonal edges; sew (block 7 complete). Lay the blocks out flat to check their positioning.

9 Pin blocks 6 and 7 right sides together. Sew along the seam line. Fold the allowances towards block 6.

10 Pin blocks 5 and 6' right sides together. Sew along the seam line, making an extra stitch at the seam junctions.

11 Pin the two remaining blocks right sides together. Sew along the seam line, making an extra stitch on the junctions. Fold the allowances towards the leaves.

T
Tulip

Tumbler

Level ✿✿✿✿✿

You can use a different fabric for each piece of this block (see below) but if you make every other piece the same fabric you can create a check-like pattern. The pieces are assembled in strips. Match up seam junctions and make extra stitches at seam junctions to avoid any gapping.

Folding the seam allowances

Templates

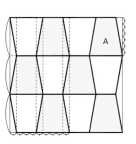

1 Lay out four pieces A flat to check the colour distribution and positioning.

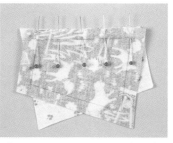

2 Bring two pieces A right sides together as shown, then pin along the seam.

3 Sew along the seam line, making an extra stitch at the start and end. Join on the other pieces A to form a strip.

4 Trim the allowance to 6mm, then fold it towards the dark coloured pieces.

5 Assemble the other pieces A into strips. Arrange the strips so the pieces of dark and light coloured fabric alternate.

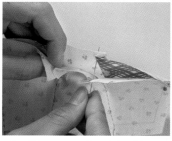

6 Bring two strips right sides together. Use a pin to help match up seam junctions.

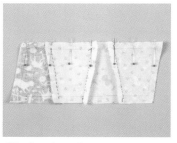

7 Pin along the seams, pinning through the seam junctions.

8 Sew along the seam line. Making an extra stitch at the start and end, and at the seam junctions.

* Using many different fabrics

Folding the seam allowances

When using different fabrics for every piece alternate the direction of the allowance folds for each strip.

T
Tumbler

196

Turkey Trucks

* *

This block is composed of several curved pieces. Assemble pieces A, B, C and C' to obtain small blocks then combine with pieces D and E. Choose strong colours for pieces A, B, B' and D that contrast with the fabric colours for C and E.

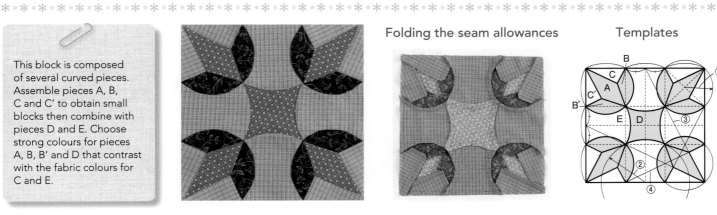

Folding the seam allowances

Templates

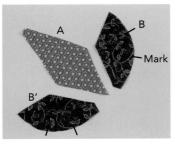

1 Prepare pieces A, B and B'. Make the marks as indicated.

2 Pin pieces A and B right sides together as shown. Sew along the seam line, making an extra stitch at the start and end.

3 Trim the seam allowance to 6mm, then fold it towards piece A. Join pieces A and B' in the same way, folding the allowance towards piece A (block 1 complete).

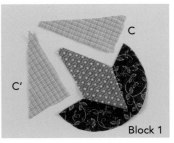

4 Prepare one block 1, one piece C and one piece C'. Lay them out flat to check their positioning.

5 Bring the pieces B and C right sides together, then pin the first edge. Sew, making an extra stitch at the end. Do not cut the thread.

6 Pin the piece A and the second edge of piece C right sides together. Sew from the corner to the end. Join on piece C' (block 2 complete).

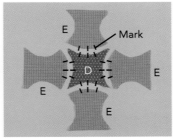

7 Prepare one piece D and four pieces E. Make the marks as indicated.

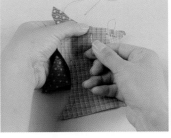

8 Bring a piece E and piece D right sides together, then pin. Sew between the marks. Join a piece E to the opposite side, then join on the other two pieces E.

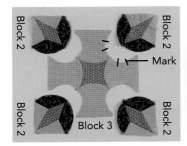

9 Fold the seam allowances towards the pieces E (block 3 complete). Prepare four blocks 2 and one block 3.

10 Bring a block 2 and block 3 right sides together and pin, matching up the seam junctions and without piercing the seam allowances.

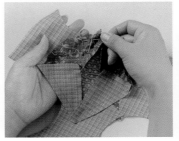

11 Sew along the curved edge of the first piece B, then make an extra stitch at the junction. Continue to sew to the end. Fold the seam allowances towards block 2.

* Tip

In step 11, do not sew down the seam allowances. Push your needle through them one by one.

Turkey Trucks

T

197

Twinkling Star

* *

This block represents two overlapping stars. Although the motif looks complex the pieces are similarly shaped. Ensure the edges of shapes match up before beginning to sew. Make extra stitches at the points where seams meet to make sure no gaps appear.

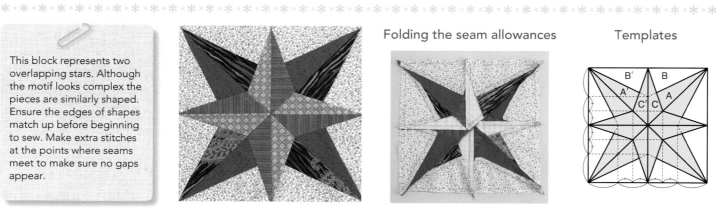

Folding the seam allowances

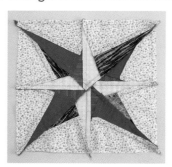

Templates

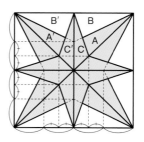

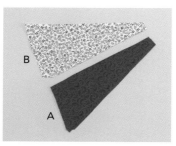

1 Prepare one piece A and one piece B. Lay them out flat to check their positioning.

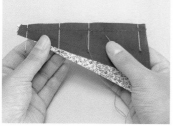

2 Pin the pieces A and B right sides together as shown and sew, making an extra stitch at the start and end of the seam.

3 Trim the seam allowance to 6mm, then fold it towards piece A (block 1 complete).

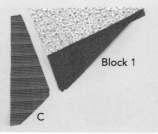

4 Prepare one block 1 and one piece C. Lay them out flat to check their positioning.

5 Pin block 1 and piece C right sides together as shown. Sew, then fold the seam allowance towards piece C (block 2 complete).

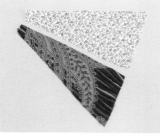

6 Prepare one piece A' and one piece B'. Assemble them as in step 2, folding the seam allowances towards piece A'.

7 Join the block from step 6 and one piece C' as shown in step 5. Fold the seam allowance towards piece C' (block 3 complete).

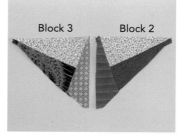

8 Prepare one block 2 and one block 3. Lay them out flat to check their positioning.

9 Pin blocks 2 and 3 right sides together as shown; sew. Make another block 2 and 3 and join (two blocks 4 complete). Fold the allowances in opposite directions

10 Bring two blocks 4 right sides together, then pin. Make extra stitches at the seam junctions. Sew stitch by stitch through the overlapping seam allowances (block 5 complete).

11 Make another block 5. Pin the two blocks 5 right sides together along the long edges, then sew.

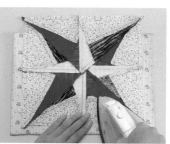

12 Iron the back of the finished block to flatten the seam allowances.

Twisted Log Cabin

* *

Although the pieces for this block are all square or triangular, they create a curve effect when joined together. Assemble the pieces in the order B, C, D and E around the piece A to form the square block. Take care with positioning as some of the pieces ae quite similar. Choose colours to accentuate the spiralling shape.

Folding the seam allowances

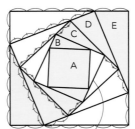

Templates

Divide one side of the square in 2:5.

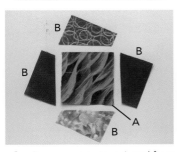

1 Prepare one piece A and four pieces B.

2 Bring the pieces A and a piece B right sides together as shown and pin.

3 Sew along the seam line, making an extra stitch at the start and end of the seam.

4 Trim the allowance to 6mm and fold it towards piece B.

5 Working clockwise, join the second piece B to the adjacent edge. Join on the other pieces B in the same way.

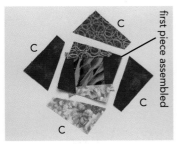

6 Join on the four pieces C in the same way, positioning them as shown.

7 Sew stitch by stitch through overlapping allowances.

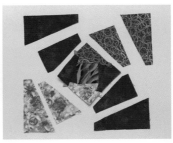

8 Join on the four pieces D and then the four pieces E in the same way.

* Assembling several blocks

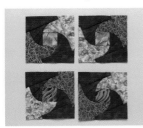

1 Prepare four blocks.

2 Pin two blocks right sides together. Sew along the seam line, working stitch by stitch on the overlapping allowances.

3 Join the other two blocks so you have two strips. Fold the allowances in opposite directions. Pin the two strips right sides together. Sew along the seam line.

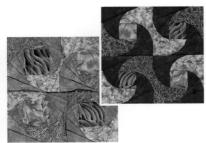

4 The four blocks are assembled. Fold the allowances to one side.

Twisting Spool

Level ★ ★ ☆ ☆ ☆

* ＊

Pieces are combined to make two roughly triangular blocks that are then joined together to form this design. A clever arrangement of tirangles and strips suggest the twist at the centre. Choose two different fabric for the piecse A and B and combine them as shown here.

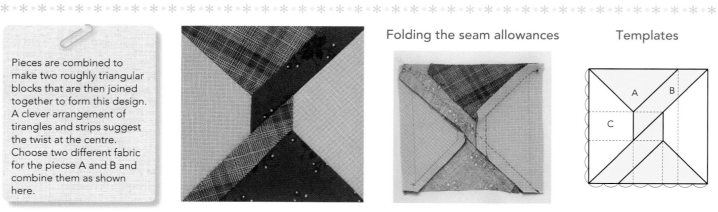

Folding the seam allowances

Templates

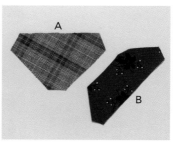

1 Prepare one piece A and one piece B and mark with the seam lines.

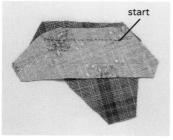

2 Pin pieces A and B right sides together as shown. Sew along the seam line, making an extra stitch at the start and end.

3 Trim the allowance to 6mm, then fold it towards B (block 1 complete).

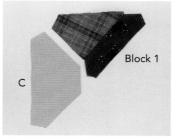

4 Prepare one block 1 and one piece C.

5 Bring block 1 and piece C right sides together and pin along the first edge. Sew along the seam line.

6 Make an extra stitch at the corner; do not cut the thread.

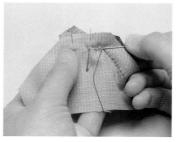

7 Pin the second edge without piercing the allowances. Sew along the seam line, making an extra stitch at the end (block 2 complete).

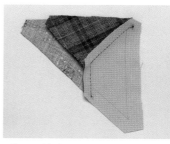

8 Fold the allowance towards block 1.

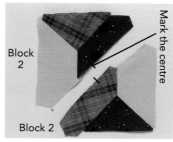

9 Make another block 2, inverting the fabrics for the A and B pieces. Mark the centre of the long edges, as shown.

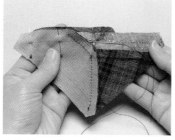

10 Bring the two blocks 2 right sides together and pin. Sew along the seam line making one extra stitch at the start and end of the seam.

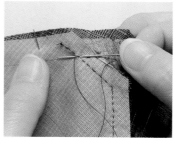

11 Make an extra stitch at the seam junctions.

12 Trim the allowances, then fold them to one side.

T

Twisting Spool

200

Walking Triangles

✱·✱

First join two pieces A and two pieces B. Make four small blocks, then assemble them by making the corners of these blocks match up. With all the seams being sewn in a straight line, this block is a good one for beginners.

Folding the seam allowances

Templates

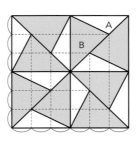

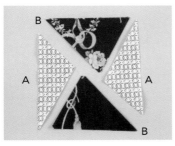

1 Prepare two pieces A and two pieces B.

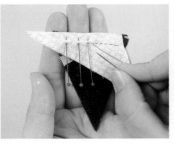

2 Pin pieces A and B right sides together as shown. Sew along the seam line, making an extra stitch at the start and end.

3 Trim the seam allowance to 6mm, then fold it towards piece A (block 1 complete).

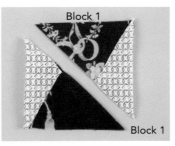

4 Join the other pieces A and B to make a second block 1 and lay them out as shown.

5 Pin the long edges of the two blocks 1 right sides together. Sew along the seam. Fold the allowance to one side (block 2 complete).

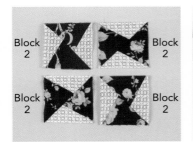

6 Prepare three more blocks 2.

7 Pin two blocks 2 right sides together. Sew along the seam, working stitch by stitch through the overlapping allowances.

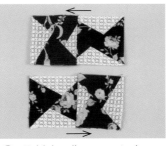

8 Fold the allowances in the direction indicated by the arrows above.

9 Bring the two strips right sides together, then pin along the seam as shown.

10 Sew along the seam, working stitch by stitch through the overlapping allowances and making an extra stitch at the junction points.

Wheat

* · *

This block represents an ear of wheat. With sharply pointed triangles creating the motif, It is important to get neat angles, so match up corners carefully and fold down the allowances at each stage. Making extra stitches at seam junctions can help prevent gaps at these points.

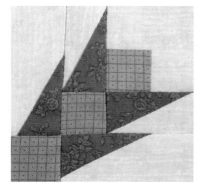

Folding the seam allowances

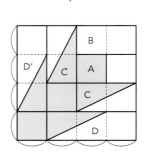

Templates

		B
D'	C	A
	C	
		D

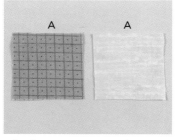

1 Prepare two pieces A in a light and dark fabric.

2 Pin the two pieces A right sides together as shown. Sew along the seam line, making an extra stitch at the start and end.

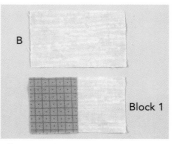

3 Trim the allowance to 6mm, then fold it towards the dark coloured piece (block 1 complete). Prepare one piece B.

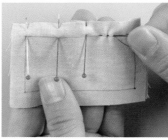

4 Pin the piece B and block 1 right sides together as shown. Sew along the seam line, making an extra stitch at the start and end.

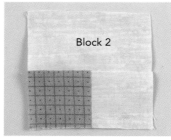

5 Fold the allowances towards block 1 (block 2 complete).

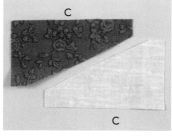

6 Prepare two pieces C in light and dark fabric. Pin right sides together, then sew. Fold the allowances towards the dark coloured piece (block 3 complete).

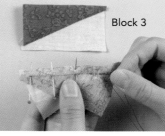

7 Join two pieces C' in the same way. Fold the allowances towards the dark coloured piece (block 3' complete).

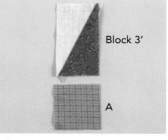

8 Pin one block 3' and a piece A right sides together. Sew along the seam line. Fold the allowances towards piece A (block 4 complete).

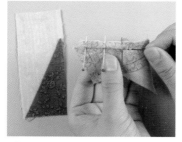

9 Join one piece C and one piece D. Fold the allowances towards the dark coloured piece (block 5 complete). Join the pieces C' and D in the same way (block 5' complete).

10 Join one piece A and the block 5. Fold the allowances towards piece A (block 6 complete).

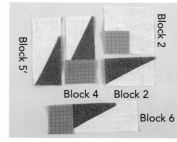

11 Lay out the blocks flat to check their positioning.

12 Pin two adjacent blocks right sides together; sew, making an extra stitch at the seam junctions. Join the remaining blocks as shown in step 11.

Whirling Triangles

* *

Small triangles and trapezoid shapes are combined to form a hexagonal block. If you choose two markedly different fabrics for the A and B pieces, the B pieces will contrast against the A pieces and appear to be one shape, with whirling arms.

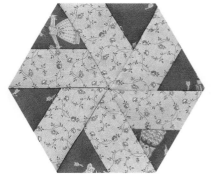

Folding the seam allowances

Templates

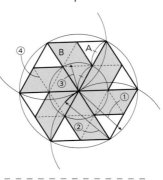

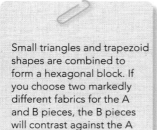

1 Prepare one piece A and one piece B. Mark the centre point of the long edge of piece B.

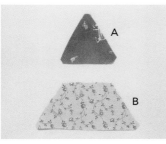

2 Pin pieces A and B right sides together as shown. Sew along the seam line, making an extra stitch at the start and end.

3 Trim the allowance to 6mm, then fold it towards piece B (block 1 complete).

4 Make six blocks 1. Lay them out flat in threes to check their positioning.

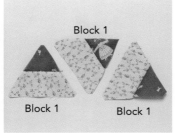

5 Join two blocks 1 right sides together, positioned as in step 4, matching the seam junction on one to the mark on the long edge of the other.

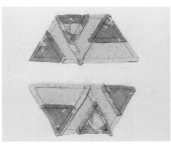

6 Join on the other block 1 in the same way). Fold the allowances towards piece B (block 2 complete). Join the other three blocks 1 in the same way.

7 Bring the two blocks 2 right sides together, then pin without piercing the allowances. Sew along the seam line, making an extra stitch at the start and end.

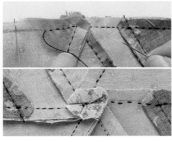

8 Fold down the allowances at centre of the block in a spiral.

---

* Assembling several blocks

1 Join finished blocks into strips, matching up seam junctions.

2 Bring two strips right sides together and pin the first edge. Sew up to the first corner, making an extra stitch at the end: do not cut the thread.

3 Pin the next edge, then sew to the next corner.

4 Continue to sew edge by edge in the same way. Fold down the allowances in a spiral.

W

Walking Triangles

Wild Goose Chase

* *

Pieces A and B are combined into strips that cross with piece C. Pieces D form the triangles between the arms of the cross. Use a striking fabric for the centre piece C and contrasting colours for the pieces A and B for the arms of the cross.

Folding the seam allowances

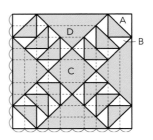

Templates

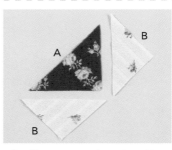

1 Prepare one piece A and two pieces B.

2 Pin pieces A and B right sides together as shown. Sew along the seam line, making an extra stitch at the start and end. Fold the allowances towards piece A.

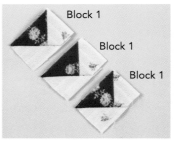

3 Join on the other piece B in the same way (block 1 complete). Make three blocks 1.

4 Pin two blocks 1 right sides together. Sew along the seam line. Join the other block 1 in the same way. Fold the allowances towards piece A (block 2 complete).

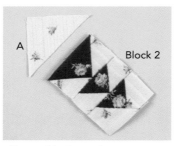

5 Pin block 2 and one piece A right sides together. Sew along the seam line.

6 Fold the allowances towards block 2 (block 3 complete). Make four blocks 3.

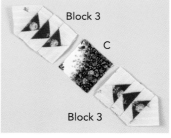

7 Prepare two blocks 3 and one piece C.

8 Pin block 3 and piece C right sides together. Sew along the seam line. Fold the allowances towards piece C. Join on the other block 3 (block 4 complete).

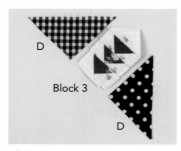

9 Prepare one block 3 and two pieces D.

10 Pin block 3 and piece D right sides together. Sew along the seam line. Fold back the allowances towards piece D. Join the other piece D (block 5 complete).

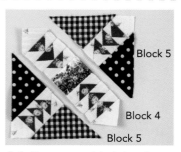

11 Prepare one block 4 and two blocks 5.

12 Pin a block 4 and 5 right sides together. Sew along the seam line. Join on the other block 5.

Wild Wave

* *

This block represents waves so choose fabrics in shades of blue with white. Pieces A, B and C are joined to obtain four horizontal strips that are joined together to finish this block. This block is easy to make but you need to pay attention to the direction of the pieces.

Folding the seam allowances

Templates

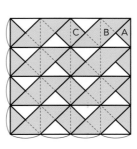

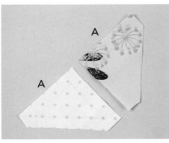

1 Prepare two pieces A.

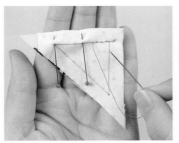

2 Pin the two pieces A right sides together as shown. Sew along the seam line, making an extra stitch at the start and end.

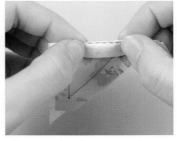

3 Trim the allowance to 6mm, then fold it towards the dark coloured piece (block 1 complete).

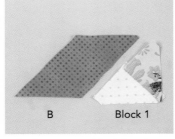

4 Prepare one block 1 and one piece B.

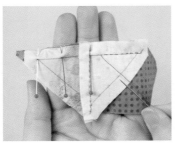

5 Pin block 1 and piece B right sides together. Sew along the seam line. Fold the allowances towards piece B (block 2 complete). Make two blocks 2.

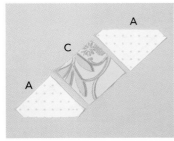

6 Prepare two pieces A and one piece C.

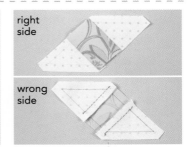

7 Join the pieces A and C along the seam lines. Fold the allowances towards piece C (block 3 complete).

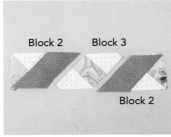

8 Prepare two blocks 2 and one block 3.

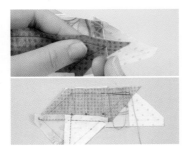

9 Pin blocks 2 and 3 right sides together as shown. Sew along the seam line, then fold the allowances towards piece B. Join on the other block 2 in the same way.

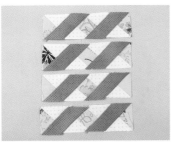

10 Repeat steps 8 and 9 to make three more strips.

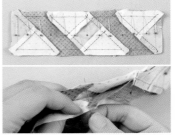

11 Pin two strips right sides together.

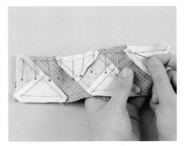

12 Sew along the seam line, making an extra stitch at the seam junctions. Sew stitch by stitch on overlapping allowances.

W

Wild Wave

Windblown Square

* *

The central square is formed by joining pieces A, B and C. Smaller triangular blocks made up of two pieces D are joined around this central square. Match up seam lines to get neat corners. Use two contrasting colours of fabric to get a strong design.

Folding the seam allowances

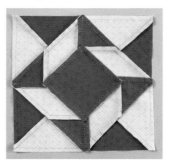

Templates

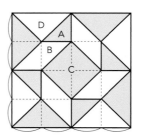

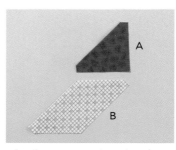

1 Prepare one piece A and one piece B. Lay them out flat to check their positioning.

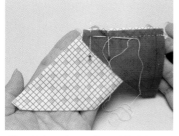

2 Bring pieces A and B right sides together, as shown, then pin. Sew along the seam.

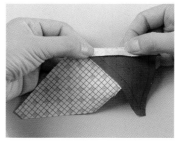

3 Trim the seam allowance to 6mm, then fold it towards piece A (block 1 complete).

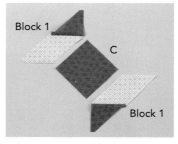

4 Prepare two blocks 1 and one piece C.

5 Pin one block 1 and piece C right sides together. Sew along the seam line of the piece B. Fold the seam allowance towards block 1. Join on the other block 1 (block 2 complete).

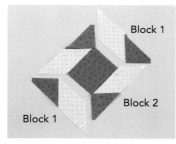

6 Prepare two blocks 1 and one block 2. Lay them out flat to check their positioning.

7 Pin the first edge of blocks 1 and 2 right sides together. Do not pin through the seam allowances of piece C. Sew along the seam, making an extra stitch at the end.

8 Do not cut the thread. Pin the along the second edge.

9 Bring the out the needle at the corner without piercing the seam allowances. Pull the thread through firmly, then sew to the next corner. Pin the third edge, then sew to the end.

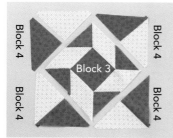

10 Join the other block 1 and block 2 in the same way. Fold the seam allowances outwards (block 3 complete). Join two pieces D in pairs to make four blocks 4.

11 Pin block 3 and a block 4 right sides together as shown. Sew, making an extra stitch at the seam junction. Join another block 4 to the opposite edge.

12 Join the two other blocks 4 to block 3. Fold the seam allowances outward.

Winding Ways

* *

Although there are only three pieces for this block they have curved edges and narrow points, so take care to match up any marks and use plenty of pins to help stop gapping. Assemble the block in two parts, the upper and lower blocks, then join them by matching their centre points.

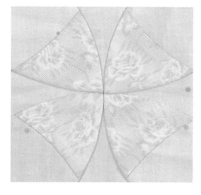

Folding the seam allowances

Templates

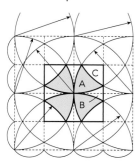

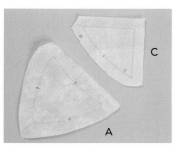

1 Prepare one piece A and one piece C. Mark the centre points of the curved edges.

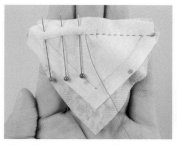

2 Pin pieces A and C right sides together, matching centre points. Sew along the seam line, making an extra stitch at the start and end.

3 Trim the allowance, then snip into the allowance of piece A. Fold the allowances towards piece A (block 1 complete).

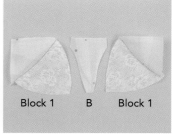

Block 1   B   Block 1

4 Prepare two blocks 1 and one piece B. Mark the centre points of the curved edges.

5 Pin block 1 and piece B right sides together, matching the centre points. Sew along the seam line, making an extra stitch at the start and end. Fold the allowances towards block 1.

6 Join on the other block 1 in the same way (block 3 complete).

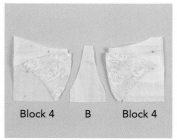

Block 4   B   Block 4

7 Join a piece A and C (as in step 2) then join on one piece B (block 4 complete). Make two blocks 4 and prepare one piece B. Mark the centre points of the curved edges.

8 Join block 4 and piece B right sides together, matching the centre points. Fold the allowances towards block 4. Join on the other block 4 in the same way (block 5 complete).

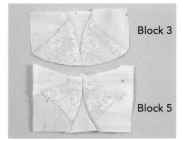

Block 3

Block 5

9 Lay out the blocks 3 and 5 flat to check their positioning.

10 Bring blocks 3 and 5 right sides together and pin to the centre. Sew up to the centre, working stitch by stitch on overlapping allowances.

11 Pin the other half of the seam, then continue sewing to the end. Fold the allowances towards the upward curve.

* Assembling several blocks

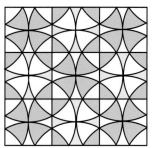

Make several blocks and alternate the colour ways as you join them.

Window Fan

✳ ✳

This block is made up of four pieces the same shape. Match up any marks to help assemble the curved edges. Do not sew through the allowances at the centre. Alternate dark and light coloured fabrics. If you join several Window Fans you can create pinwheel and flower patterns.

Folding the seam allowances

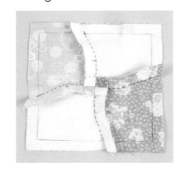

Templates

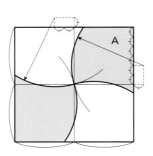

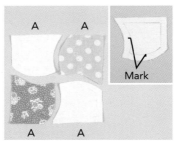

1 Prepare four pieces A. Make a mark in the centre of the curved edges as shown.

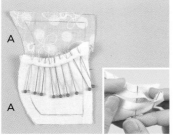

2 Bring two pieces A right sides together and pin, making sure you match up the marks.

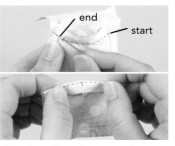

3 Sew along the seam, then fold the allowance to one side (block 1 complete).

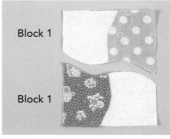

4 Join the two other pieces A in the same way to make a second block 1.

5 Pin the two blocks 1 right sides together.

6 Sew along the seam, making an extra stitch at the junction points. Do not pierce the overlapping seams. Fold the allowances in the same direction (block 2 complete).

✳ Assembling several blocks

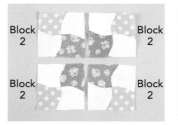

1 Prepare four blocks 2. Lay them out to check the positioning and the arrangement of colours.

2 Pin two blocks 2 right sides together and sew along the seam, making an extra stitch at the beginning and end (block 3 completed).

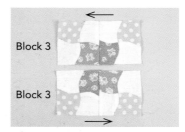

3 Assemble another block 3. Fold the seam allowances on both blocks 3 in the direction of the arrows shown above.

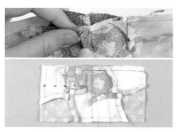

4 Pin the two blocks 3 right sides together. Sew along the seam, making an extra stitch at the junction points.

5 Fold the seam allowances to one side. The four blocks 2 have been assembled.

✳ Variation

Divide up the square in a different way to obtain a pinwheel block.

Winter Dahlia

Level ★ ★ ★ ☆ ☆

* *

After assembling the outer section of this block, its inner edge is gathered before appliquéing on the central disc. This gives the floral motif an unusual effect. Use the same fabric for the inner petals (pieces B) to highlight them. Take care matching curved edges and seam junctions.

Folding the seam allowances

Templates

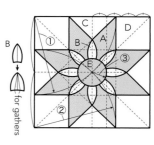

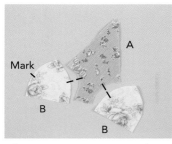

1 Prepare one piece A and two pieces B. Mark the curved edges as shown.

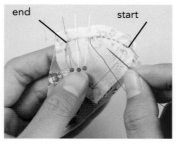

2 Pin pieces A and B right sides together, matching the marks. Sew along the seam line, making an extra stitch at the start and end. Join on the other piece B (block 1 complete).

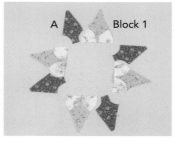

3 Fold the allowances towards pieces B. Then assemble block 1 and one dark piece A.

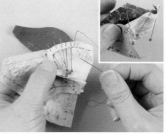

4 Pin block 1 and the dark piece A right sides together, matching the marks. Sew from the end to the mark (block 2 complete). Make four blocks 2.

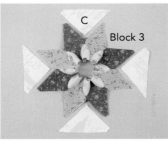

5 Join the four blocks 2 in a ring (block 3 complete). Prepare four pieces C.

6 Pin the block 3 and one piece C right sides together along the first edge. Sew along the seam line, making an extra stitch at the start and end without stitching in the allowances.

7 Pin the second edge, then continue sewing to the end. Join the other three blocks C in the same way (block 4 complete).

8 Join the block 4 and four pieces D as in steps 6 and 7.

9 Make even stitches around the seam allowance at the centre of the block. Pull on the thread to gather gently. Do not fasten off.

10 Make even stitches around the allowance of piece E. Put the template on the wrong side and pull the thread to turn under the allowance. Press and remove the template. Make eight evenly spaced marks around the edge.

11 Pin piece E to the centre of the block, matching the marks to the centre of pieces A and adjusting the gathers if necessary.

12 Sew the piece E in place with slip stitches.

W

Winter Dahlia

209

Yacht

* • *

This figurative block represents a sailing yacht. Because the pieces are joined along straight edges, this is an easy block to assemble. Don't stretch any edges cut on the diagonal or the pattern will be distorted. Choose a fabric with some blue in it for the piece D.

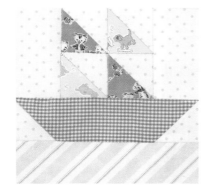

Folding the seam allowances

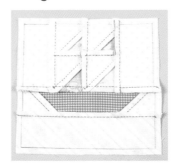

Templates

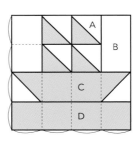

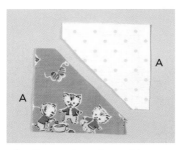

1 Prepare two pieces A in different colours.

2 Pin the two pieces A right sides together as shown. Sew along the seam line, making an extra stitch at the start and end.

3 Trim the allowance to 6mm, then fold it towards the dark coloured piece (block 1 complete).

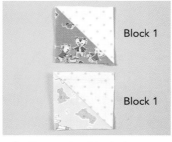

4 Prepare two blocks 1.

5 Pin the two blocks 1 right sides together. Sew along the seam line (block 2 complete).

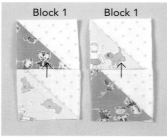

6 Prepare two blocks 2. Fold the allowances in the direction of the arrows.

7 Bring the two blocks 2 right sides together, then pin at the ends, the junctions and in between. Sew along the seam line (block 3 complete).

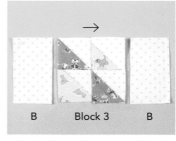

8 Fold the allowances of block 3 in the direction of the arrows. Prepare one block 3 and two pieces B.

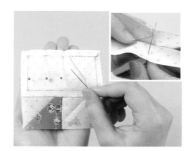

9 Pin a block 3 and piece B right sides together. Sew along the seam line. Make an extra stitch at the start, end and seam junctions. Join on the other piece B (block 4 complete).

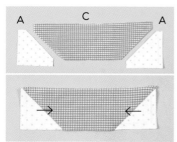

10 Join two pieces A and one piece C as in step 2 and 3. Fold the allowances in the direction of the arrows (block 5 complete).

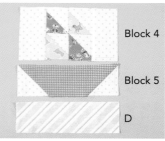

11 Prepare a block 4, a block 5 and a piece D.

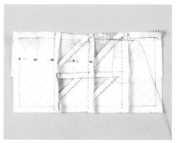

12 Pin the two blocks right sides together. Sew along the seam line. Join on the piece D in the same way. Fold the allowances towards block 5.

COLOUR VARIATIONS

Here are some examples of colour variations for 24 of the blocks in this book.

Octagon

Pale and pastel colours

Fabrics with indistinct patterns have been used for the larger pieces. The dark colour of small triangular pieces makes for an interesting contrast.

Harmony and elegance

Cut the large pieces in two different floral fabrics. Choose one highly patterned fabric and one that's more open for a pleasing dynamic.

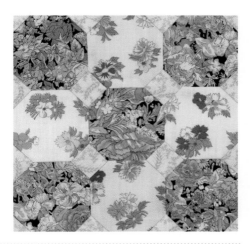

Dutch Windmill

Unity of colour and rhythm

By choosing brown fabrics ranging from light to dark, the contrast between the pieces is accentuated. The diversity of the patterns enhances this effect.

Graduated soft colours

Choose brown and beige fabrics in several shades between light and dark. The darkest colours should be used preferably for small pieces.

Card Trick

Bright and modern

Boldly patterned fabrics featuring blue, black and green stand out well from a background cut from white fabrics with black patterns of varying light intensity.

Natural colours and classic patterns

By choosing two light floral fabrics and two darker checked fabrics, the four cards are well defined. The polka-dot fabric used for the background reinforces the style of the whole.

Guiding Star

Depth and intensity

Two red fabrics of different intensity are used to make the main motif with a plain fabric chosen for the background. The strong reds bring a richness and depth to this block.

Large patterns with impact

This variation shows that it is possible to use two fabrics with large patterns – here flowery – while maintaining balance and elegance, as long as there is a strong contrast.

Windblown Square

Graphic patterns

Combining a diamond-patterned fabric and a pop-art print results in a thoroughly modern block. Limiting the colours allows the patterns to stand out well.

Dark and bright colours

To add contrast without dampening down the brightness of the other fabrics, pieces in shades of brown are chosen.

Thirteen Squares

Checks and stripes

By choosing fabrics in similar colours, a harmony is created. Give the motif a bit more dynamism by using strips and checks for some of the pieces. This brings rhythm to the block while maintaining unity.

Clear and fresh

For the small square pieces, choose soft but pastel colours which blend well with the pale green of the square frame. The beige background combines perfectly with the light colours of the motif.

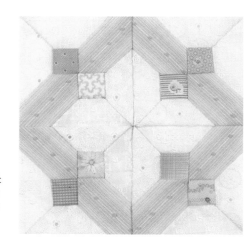

Scarp Windmill

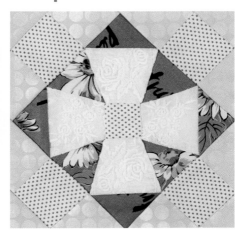

Material effects

Juxtaposing different materials creates a rich and interesting effect. Here a lace fabric, a shiny printed one and a printed cotton are combine. The light blue fabric with flowers enhances the white of the lace.

Chic tones and contrasts

The dark brown pieces throw the contrasting light fabric chosen for the trapezoid pieces into sharp relief. Stripes on the cross pieces run outwards to highlight its form.

Charming Puzzle

Enchancing colours

To enhance the brown floral fabric, blue was chosen as a colour for the other printed fabrics since it picks out some of the elements in the brown fabric. The clear fabric of the background unites the whole design

Highlighting pieces

To enhance the printed fabric at the centre, other bright blue and red fabrics were chosen. Simple patterns like small checks and dots work almost like plain fabrics.

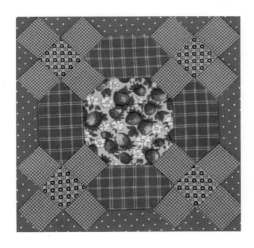

Rose Dream

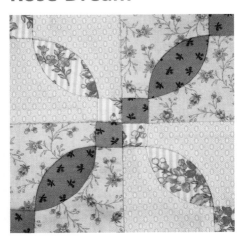

Chain effects

Choosing two distinct colours for the small central squares creates a chain effect with the pieces layered diagonally. Striped or dotted fabrics reinforce this interesting variation.

Multicoloured but balanced

Even if several colours are used, as shown here, by harmonising the brightness of each one, a balance is achieved. The white tone of the background unifies the many colours.

Double Sawtooth

Using a large pattern

A fabric with a distinct and large pattern is chosen for the centre piece. Picking out some of the colours in the pattern for the surrounding triangles unifies the design.

Monochrome

To accompany a fabric with a large black and white pattern, use different black and white fabrics for the other pieces. Varying the size of the patterns will be enough to bring rhythm into this monochrome block.

Pete's Paintbox

Tone on tone

Choosing similar tones of one colour makes for a design where no one piece stands out. Introducing a strong pattern with another colour – as in the border here – adds emphasis.

Romantic allure

This block is made in shades of pink. Use a fabric with a distinctive pattern for the border pieces. These will be highlighted by bright plain fabrics in between.

Honey Bee

Highlighting the theme

To emphasise the idea of bees foraging among flowers, floral fabrics were chosen for the pieces of the central nine-patch block. The light floral fabric used for the background further accentuates the spring-like atmosphere of this block.

Softness and simplicity

Choose light colours for a soft look. Here, mauve, blue and pink hues give a soft and harmonious look to the whole.

Mosaic

Shade intensity

Fabrics in tones of light and dark pink are chosen here. The lighter fabrics are used for larger pieces and the darker fabrics for smaller ones, creating a soft harmony.

Combine checked fabrics

Three different checks are chosen for the central motif but they are unified by common colours. Opt for the darker fabric for the small pieces to highlight the larger ones.

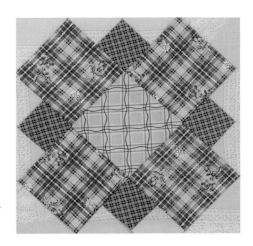

Rock Garden

Contrasting patterns

By choosing fabrics with contrasting patterns, the shape of each piece is accentuated. Two fabrics in different patterns are chosen for each star.

Muted shades

Pieces cut from in blue and bluish gray fabrics are combined here to create a subtle blend of colours. An off-white fabric highlights the central star.

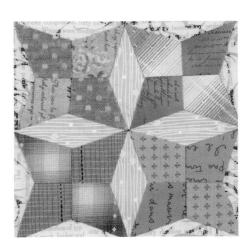

Wild Goose Chase

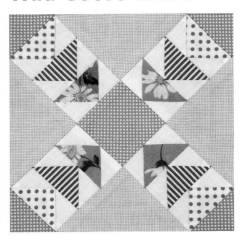

Colour unity

By placing darker blues towards the centre and lighter blues towards the outside, a gradient of colours is created. A white lace fabric enhances the light blue colour of the background. Choose polka dot and striped fabrics to bring rhythm to the composition.

Contrast for impact

The triangles and the central square are deliberately made with dark fabrics so that the bright and monochrome background fabrics highlight the cross.

Figurative Blocks

Peony

The diamond petals are strong shapes and so a combination of fabrics with patterns of the same intensity create a nuance that makes them stand out. Choose a background fabric with subtle patterns to enhance the flower.

Here, fabrics in pink tones are chosen for the petals. By selecting fabrics of different luminosity, each petal is subtly deliniated. Keeping the background fabric in the same tone perfects the harmony of the block.

Dahlia

The template is slightly different from one on page 53.

Yellow and green combine perfectly to represent this charming flower. Play with prints with both floral and geometric patterns; for example, set checks at an angle to bring energy to the whole design.

Cut the petal pieces in shades of dark red and brown to get a chic-looking block. Using fabrics in shades of blue for the other pieces skillfully counterbalances the warm tones of this block.

Painted Daisy

Using two patterns with both large and small motifs but in the same shades of pink creates a block with a strong impact. Light and dark shades emphasise the contrast.

Combining two boldly patterned fabrics will only work if they are not too similar. Here, one with an open pattern and light background is teamed with one with a tight pattern on a dark ground. The black piece with green dots adds a complementary colour that lights up the whole.

English Ivy

To represent the ivy which gave its name to this block, the colours green and brown seem ideal. Choosing of two different greens brightens up the design. Using a gently patterened background fabric lightens the final result.

When a fabric with complex and colourful patterns is chosen, it is best to match fabrics to the main shades of the print to avoid overloading the block with multiple colours. The combination of greenish gray and orange creates a certain modernity here.

Coffee Cup

For an elegant effect the colours of the printed fabrics for this block are limited – here to turquoise, white and black. Opt for a light background to highlight the cup motif so it remains clearly visible.

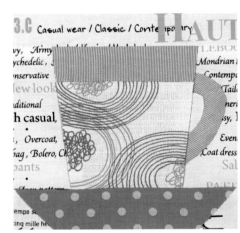

Combining a lightly patterned background with densely patterned pieces for the cup is particularly successful here, giving a very dynamic block. The polka-dot saucer completes the design, bringing an ideal touch of freshness.

Stamp Basket

Using fabrics in similar tones with a variety of patterns for the baskets helps to avoid monotony. Light and similarly patterned background pieces help unify the design.

To get a bright and fresh look, choose clear and bright colours – here orange, green, yellow and pink – that really pop out of the block. Keep fabric patterns running in straight lines or at angles for to bring rhythm to the design.

Assembling Blocks and Continuous Patterns

Bethlehem Star

Selecting fabrics in different strengths of colour for the diamonds makes it possible to create cube shapes between the stars.

Fanfare

The long 'petals' are accentuated with bright fabric pieces. Choosing a darker fabric for the central squares and triangles gives an interesting kaleidoscope effect.

Twisted Log Cabin

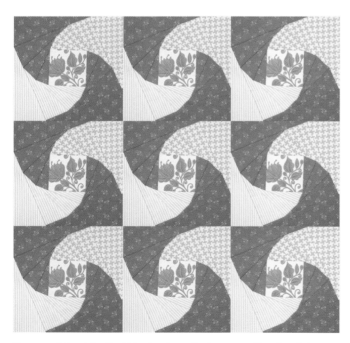

By assembling identical blocks always in the same direction, it is easy to create this wave effect.

By alternating the direction of the same blocks during assembly, flower patterns in different prints appear.

You may also like...

ISBN 978-6059192781

SIZE 20 x 27 cm / 7.8 x 10.6"

PAGE COUNT 80pp + Pattern Sheet

PRODUCT CODE 6710

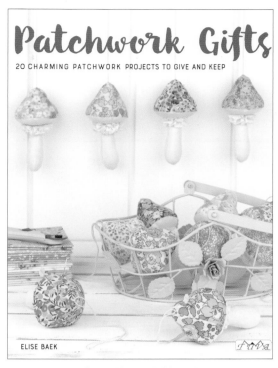

ISBN 978-605-9192-60-6

SIZE 21.6 x 28 cm / 8.5 x 11"

PAGE COUNT 144pp

PRODUCT CODE 6710

ISBN 978-605-9192-16-3

SIZE 21.6 x 28 cm / 8.5 x 11"

PAGE COUNT 144pp

PRODUCT CODE 6450

ISBN 978-605-9192-47-7

SIZE 21.6 x 28 cm

PAGE COUNT 104pp

PRODUCT CODE 6460

Tuva Publishing
www.tuvapublishing.com

Address Merkez Mah. Cavusbasi Cad. No:71
Cekmekoy - Istanbul 34782 / Turkey
Tel: +9 0216 642 62 62

210 Traditional Quilt Blocks

First Print 2021 / February

All Global Copyrights Belong To
Tuva Tekstil ve Yayıncılık Ltd.

Content Quilting

Editor in Chief Ayhan DEMİRPEHLİVAN
Project Editor Kader DEMİRPEHLİVAN
Technical Editors Rachel VOWLES, Leyla ARAS, Büşra ESER
Graphic Designers Ömer ALP, Abdullah BAYRAKÇI, Tarık TOKGÖZ
Photography Toshitsugu Ayabe, Nobuyuki Suzuki, Kazumasa Yamamoto
Layout Miyuki Yamanaka, Yoko Maki
Text Naomi Sekiguchi, Yukari Kamiya, Nozomu Kunitani, Yurika Kurosawa

ISBN 978-605-7834-23-2

Lady Boutique Series No.4208
Kaiteiban Patchwork no Pattern Lesson 210
Copyright © Boutique-sha, Inc. 2016
Original Japanese edition published in Japan by Boutique-sha, Inc.
English translation rights arranged with Boutique-sha, Inc.

 TuvaYayincilik TuvaPublishing
 TuvaYayincilik TuvaPublishing